Rationality for Mortals

EVOLUTION AND COGNITION

General Editor: Stephen Stich, Rutgers University

Rationality for Mortals

How People Cope with Uncertainty

Gerd Gigerenzer

OXFORD
UNIVERSITY PRESS

OXFORD

UNIVERSITY PRESS

Oxford University Press, Inc., publishes works that further
Oxford University's objective of excellence
in research, scholarship, and education.

Oxford   New York
Auckland   Cape Town   Dar es Salaam   Hong Kong   Karachi
Kuala Lumpur   Madrid   Melbourne   Mexico City   Nairobi
New Delhi   Shanghai   Taipei   Toronto

With offices in
Argentina   Austria   Brazil   Chile   Czech Republic   France   Greece
Guatemala   Hungary   Italy   Japan   Poland   Portugal   Singapore
South Korea   Switzerland   Thailand   Turkey   Ukraine   Vietnam

Published by Oxford University Press, Inc.
198 Madison Avenue, New York, New York 10016

www.oup.com

First issued as an Oxford University Press paperback, 2010

Oxford is a registered trademark of Oxford University Press

Library of Congress Cataloging-in-Publication Data
Gigerenzer, Gerd.
Rationality for mortals : how people cope with uncertainty / Gerd Gigerenzer.
    p.   cm. — (Evolution and cognition)
Includes bibliographical references and index.
ISBN 978-0-19-974709-2
1. Reasoning (Psychology)   2. Thought and thinking.   I. Title.
BF442.G54 2008
153.4'3—dc22   2007029644

Printed in the United States of America
on acid-free paper

PREFACE

This book is a collection of essays on rationality, risk, and rules of thumb and is a sequel to an earlier volume, *Adaptive Thinking: Rationality in the Real World* (Oxford University Press, 2000). The essays, which have been edited and updated with new material, focus on heuristic and statistical thinking. These are complementary mental tools, not mutually exclusive strategies; our minds need both. This interplay between these two modes of thinking will become evident in the course of the book. Beforehand I would like to point out some principles of the research philosophy underlying this collection of papers.

1. *Topic-oriented rather than discipline-oriented research.* There are two ways to do social science: One is to be curious about a topic (such as the rationality of rules of thumb) and to assemble a group of researchers who approach it from different disciplines, methodologies, and theories. The second is to identify with a discipline or subdiscipline (such as social psychology) and to research topics only within its confines. I would say that most of psychology practices the discipline-oriented version of science; in many departments the cognitive wing rarely speaks with the developmental wing, the personality unit sees little merit in the evolutionary psychologists, and vice versa. Such territorial behavior is a huge obstacle to progress in the field. In this tradition, there is little curiosity or even awareness as to what other disciplines know about the same topic, and, at worst, one looks down at everyone else as either inferior or at best irrelevant. When Peter M. Todd and I founded the Center for Adaptive Behavior and Cognition (ABC) in 1995, we followed a deliberately topic-oriented research program. Not only psychologists from different subdisciplines talk, work, and publish together at the center, but also economists, computer scientists, mathematicians, engineers, behavioral biologists, political scientists, philosophers, and anyone else who is curious about our common topic: How do people make decisions when time and information is limited, and the future uncertain? The papers on which this volume is based were published in

psychological, economic, educational, medical, and philosophical journals or books and are herewith made more easily accessible. Important topics do not respect the historically grown disciplinary borders,and if we strive for exciting knowledge rather than a comfortable career, we need to be in love with the topic, not with our professional in-group.

2. *Multiple methodologies.* Science has not one method, but many. These include observation in the natural world, experimentation in the laboratory, mathematical proof, computer simulation with real data, analysis of surveys and demographical statistics, and thought experiments for the great geniuses, such as Galileo and Einstein. In the social sciences, a climate of anxious identification with a subdiscipline goes hand in hand with methodological rituals. Sociologists tend to rely on multiple regression analyses of survey and demographic data and show little interest in other methods; experimental psychologists have largely reduced their methodological imagination to running laboratory experiments and checking significance levels; educational researchers tend to compute structural equation models whether their assumptions hold or not; and economists excel in mathematical proofs, scorning those mathematical innumerates who have no skills apart from running experiments. Methodological uniformity and discipline-oriented research are two sides of the same coin. In contrast, topic-oriented research can free us from the straightjacket of methodological rituals, allowing us to consider and choose proper methodologies for the problem at hand and to verify a result obtained with one method by using other methods.

3. *Mix of real-world and laboratory studies.* Science does not only take place in the laboratory. To determine what laboratory research tells us about the world, we need to check with the outside world, and to determine whether our observations in the world are correct, we need to test them in the laboratory. A good mix is indispensable. Otherwise, we run the danger of growing so obsessed with the zillionth variation on a toy problem that we can no longer say how it relates to the world outside the lab.

Each of these three principles creates heterogeneity. Together, they can provide a momentum for research that is creative, innovative, and enjoyable. Many believe that interdisciplinary research is unrewarding and exhaustingly time consuming because one needs to learn a common language and deal with naive questions, only for everyone to soon return to the safe haven of their home disciplines. Fortunately, none of that has been my experience.

The single most important success factor is setting up the right environment. In my research department, we meet for an afternoon coffee break every day. There is no obligation to attend, therefore everyone comes. In an informal atmosphere, chatting and ingesting caffeine, one learns about what the others know. Having all offices located on the same floor is another essential enabler for collaboration. When members of a department work on different floors, collaboration decreases by some 50 percent. Our minds are adapted to the past, and many of us behave as if we still lived in the savanna, where contact takes place on a flat plane, not in the trees or below ground. These and other principles, such as an open-door policy, create an environment that overcomes the anxiety of exposing one's ignorance and satisfies human curiosity to learn more about the world. An enjoyable bonus is that one can learn something new every day.

The research underlying this book would not have been possible without the generous funding of the Max Planck Society, which allows truly inter-disciplinary research. Four of the thirteen papers on which the chapters are based were coauthored, and I would like to express my pleasure of having collaborated with Eva van den Broek, Adrian Edwards, Barbara Fasolo, Ralph Hertwig, John Hutchinson, Kontantinos Katsikopoulos, and Liqi Zhu. My special thanks go to Rona Unrau, who has assisted me in editing the entire volume. Thanks are also extended to Leslie Watkins for her meticulous copyediting. Many dear colleagues and friends have contributed to and commented on the research underlying these collected papers: I would like to thank Jerome R. Busemeyer, Valerie M. Chase, Anja Dieckmann, Barbara Fasolo, Thalia Gigerenzer, William Goldstein, Nigel Harvey, Ralph Hertwig, Ulrich Hoffrage, Oswald Huber, Derek Koehler, Craig McKenzie, Ben R. Newell, Torsten Reimer, Jörg Rieskamp, Lael Schooler, and Peter Todd.

CONTENTS

Rationality for Mortals

Chapter 1

Bounded and Rational

At first glance, *Homo sapiens* is an unlikely contestant for taking over the world. "Man the wise" would not likely win an Olympic medal against animals in wrestling, weightlifting, jumping, swimming, or running. The fossil record suggests that *Homo sapiens* is perhaps 400,000 years old and is currently the only existing species of the genus *Homo*. Unlike our ancestor, *Homo erectus,* we are not named after our bipedal stance, nor are we named after our abilities to laugh, weep, and joke. Our family name refers to our wisdom and rationality. Yet what is the nature of that wisdom? Are we natural philosophers equipped with logic in search of truth? Or are we intuitive economists who maximize our expected utilities? Or perhaps moral utilitarians, optimizing happiness for everyone?

Why should we care about this question? There is little choice, I believe. The nature of *sapiens* is a no-escape issue. As with moral values, it can be ignored yet will nonetheless be acted upon. When psychologists maintain that people are unreasonably overconfident and fall prey to the base rate fallacy or to a litany of other reasoning errors, each of these claims is based on an assumption about the nature of *sapiens*—as are entire theories of mind. For instance, virtually everything that Jean Piaget examined, the development of perception, memory, and thinking, is depicted as a change in logical structure (Gruber & Vonèche, 1977). Piaget's ideal image of *sapiens* was logic. It is not mine.

Disputes about the nature of human rationality are as old as the concept of rationality itself, which emerged during the Enlightenment (Daston, 1988). These controversies are about norms, that is, the evaluation of moral, social, and intellectual judgment (e.g., Cohen, 1981; Lopes, 1991). The most recent debate involves four sets of scholars, who think that one can understand the nature of *sapiens* by (a) constructing *as-if theories of unbounded rationality,*

This chapter is a revised version of G. Gigerenzer, "Bounded and Rational," in *Contemporary Debates in Cognitive Science*, ed. R. J. Stainton (Oxford, UK: Blackwell, 2006), 115–133.

by (b) constructing *as-if theories of optimization under constraints,* by (c) demonstrating *irrational cognitive illusions,* or by (d) studying *ecological rationality.* I have placed my bets on the last of these. Being engaged in the controversy, I am far from dispassionate but will be as impartial as I can.

Four Positions on Human Rationality

The heavenly ideal of perfect knowledge, impossible on earth, provides the gold standard for many ideals of rationality. From antiquity to the Enlightenment, knowledge—as opposed to opinion—was thought to require certainty. Such certainty was promised by Christianity but began to be eroded by events surrounding the Reformation and Counter-Reformation. The French astronomer and physicist Pierre-Simon Laplace (1749–1827), who made seminal contributions to probability theory and was one of the most influential scientists ever, created a fictional being known as Laplace's superintelligence or demon. The demon, a secularized version of God, knows everything about the past and present and can deduce the future with certitude. This ideal underlies the first three of the four positions on rationality, even though they seem to be directly opposed to one another. The first two picture human behavior as an approximation to the demon, while the third blames humans for failing to reach this ideal.

I will use the term *omniscience* to refer to this ideal of perfect knowledge (of past and present, not future). The mental ability to deduce the future from perfect knowledge requires *omnipotence,* or *unlimited computational power.* To be able to deduce the future with certainty implies that the structure of the world is *deterministic.* Omniscience, omnipotence, and determinism are ideals that have shaped many theories of rationality. Laplace's demon is fascinating precisely because he is so unlike us. Yet as the Bible tells us, God created humans in his own image. In my opinion, social science took this story too literally and, in many a theory, re-created us in proximity to that image.

Unbounded Rationality

The demon's nearest relative is a being with "unbounded rationality" or "full rationality." For an unboundedly rational person, the world is no longer fully predictable, that is, the experienced world is not deterministic. Unlike the demon, unboundedly rational beings make errors. Yet it is assumed that they can find the *optimal* (best) strategy, that is, the one that maximizes some criterion (such as correct predictions, monetary gains, or happiness) and minimizes error. The seventeenth-century French mathematicians Blaise Pascal and Pierre Fermat have been credited with this more modest view of rationality, defined as the maximization of the expected value, later changed by Daniel Bernoulli to the maximization of expected utility (chap. 10). In unbounded rationality, the three O's reign: *optimization* (such as maximization) replaces determinism, whereas the assumptions of omniscience and omnipotence are maintained. I will use the term *optimization* in the following way:

> *Optimization* refers to a *strategy* for solving a problem, not to an *outcome*. An optimal strategy is the *best* for a given class of problems (but not necessarily a perfect one, for it can lead to errors). To refer to a strategy as optimal, one must be able to prove that there is no better strategy (although there can be equally good ones).

Because of their lack of psychological realism, theories that assume unbounded rationality are often called as-if theories. They do not aim at *describing* the actual cognitive processes, but are concerned only with *predicting* behavior. In this program of research, the question is: if people were omniscient and had all the necessary time and computational power to optimize, how would they behave? The preference for unbounded rationality is widespread. This is illustrated by those consequentionalist theories of moral action, which assume that people consider (or should consider) the consequences of all possible actions for all other people before choosing the action with the best consequences for the largest number of people (Gigerenzer, 2008). It underlies theories of cognitive consistency, which assume that our minds check each new belief for consistency with all previous beliefs encountered and perfectly memorized; theories of optimal foraging, which assume that animals have perfect knowledge of the distribution of food and of competitors; and economic theories that assume that actors or firms know all relevant options, consequences, benefits, costs, and probabilities.

Optimization under Constraints

Unbounded rationality ignores the constraints imposed on human beings. A *constraint* refers to a limited mental or environmental resource. Limited memory span is a constraint of the mind, and information cost is a constraint on the environment. The term *optimization under constraints* refers to a class of theories that model one or several constraints.

Lack of omniscience—together with its consequence, the need to search for information—is the key issue in optimization under constraints, whereas the absence of models of search is a defining feature of theories of unbounded rationality. Models of search specify a searching direction (where to look for information) and a stopping rule (when to stop search). The prototype is Wald's (1947) sequential decision theory. In Stigler's (1961) classical example, a customer wants to buy a used car. He continues to visit used car dealers until the expected costs of further search exceed its expected benefits. Here, search takes place in the environment. Similarly, in Anderson's (1990) rational theory of memory, search for an item in memory continues until the expected costs of further search exceed the expected benefits. Here, search occurs inside the mind. In each case, omniscience is dropped but optimization is retained: The stopping point is the optimal cost-benefit trade-off.

Optimization and realism can inhibit one another, with a paradoxical consequence. Each new realistic constraint makes optimization calculations more difficult, and eventually impossible. The ideal of optimization, in turn, can undermine the attempt to make a theory more realistic by demanding new unrealistic assumptions—such as the knowledge concerning cost and benefits of search necessary for estimating the optimal stopping point. As a consequence, models of optimization under constraints tend to be more complex than models of unbounded rationality, depicting people in the image of econometricians (Sargent, 1993). This unresolved paradox is one reason why constraints are often ignored and theories of unbounded rationality preferred. Since many economists and biologists (wrongly) tend to equate optimization under constraints with *bounded rationality,* the latter is often dismissed as an unpromisingly complicated enterprise and ultimately nothing but full rationality in disguise (Arrow, 2004). Theories of optimization under constraints tend to be presented as as-if theories, with the goal of predicting behavior but not the mental process—just as models of unbounded rationality do. Many sophisticated Bayesian models in cognitive science are of this kind, sacrificing the goal of modeling cognitive processes for that of applying an optimization model.

Cognitive Illusions: Logical Irrationality

Unbounded rationality and optimization under constraints conceive of humans as essentially rational. This is sometimes justified by the regulating forces of the market, by natural selection, or by legal institutions that eliminate irrational behavior. The "heuristics and biases" or "cognitive illusions" program (Kahneman & Tversky, 1996; Gilovich, Griffin, & Kahneman, 2002) opposes theories assuming that humans are basically rational. It has two goals. The main goal is to understand the cognitive processes that produce both valid and invalid judgments. Its second goal (or method to achieve the first one) is to demonstrate errors of judgment, that is, systematic deviations from rationality also known as cognitive illusions. The cognitive processes underlying these errors are called heuristics, and the major three proposed are representativeness, availability, and anchoring and adjustment, with some new additions, including "affect." The program has produced a long list of biases. It has shaped many fields, such as social psychology and behavioral decision making, and helped to create new fields, such as behavioral economics and behavioral law and economics.

Although the heuristics-and-biases program disagrees with rational theories on whether or not people follow some norm of rationality, it does not question the norms themselves. Rather, it retains the norms and interprets deviations from these norms as cognitive illusions: "The presence of an error of judgment is demonstrated by comparing people's responses either with an established fact... or with an accepted rule of arithmetic, logic, or statistics" (Kahneman & Tversky, 1982: 493). For instance, when Wason and Johnson-Laird (1972) criticized Piaget's logical theory of thinking as descriptively incorrect, they nevertheless retained the same logical standards as normatively correct for the behavior studied. When Tversky and Kahneman (1983) reported that people's reasoning violated a law of logic (the "conjunction rule"), they nevertheless retained logic as the norm for rational judgment.

The heuristics-and-biases program correctly argues that people's judgments do in fact systematically deviate from the laws of logic or optimization. But it has hesitated to take two necessary further steps: to rethink the norms, and to provide testable theories of heuristics. The laws of logic and probability are neither necessary nor sufficient for rational behavior in the real world (see below), and mere verbal labels for heuristics can be used post hoc to "explain" almost everything.

The term *bounded rationality* has been used both by proponents of optimization under constraints, emphasizing rationality, and by the heuristics-and-biases program, emphasizing irrationality. Even more confusing is the fact that the term was coined by Herbert A. Simon, who was not referring to optimization or irrationality but to an ecological view of rationality (see next section), which was revolutionary in thinking about norms, not just behavior.

The Science of Heuristics: Ecological Rationality

The starting point for the study of heuristics is the relation between mind and environment rather than between mind and logic (Gigerenzer, Todd, & the ABC Research Group, 1999; Gigerenzer & Selten, 2001a). Humans have evolved in natural environments, both social and physical. To survive and reproduce, the task is to adapt to these environments or else to change them. Piaget called these two fundamental processes *assimilation* and *accommodation,* but he continued to focus on logic. The structure of natural environments, however, is ecological rather than logical. In Simon's words: "Human rational behavior is shaped by a scissors whose two blades are the structure of task environments and the computational capabilities of the actor" (Simon, 1990: 7). Just as one cannot understand how scissors cut by looking only at one blade, one will not understand human behavior by studying either cognition or the environment alone.

The two key concepts are *adaptive toolbox* and *ecological rationality.* The analysis of the adaptive toolbox is descriptive, whereas that of ecological rationality is normative. The adaptive toolbox contains the *building blocks* for *fast and frugal heuristics.* A heuristic is fast if it can solve a problem in little time and frugal if it can solve it with little information. Unlike as-if optimization models, heuristics can find good solutions independent of whether an optimal solution exists. As a consequence, using heuristics rather than optimization models, one does not need to "edit" a real-world problem in order to make it accessible to the optimization calculus (e.g., by limiting the number of competitors and choice alternatives, by providing quantitative probabilities and utilities, or by ignoring constraints). Heuristics work in real-world environments of natural complexity, where an optimal strategy is often unknown or *computationally intractable*.

A problem is computationally intractable if no mind or machine can find the optimal solution in reasonable time, such as a lifetime or a millennium. The game of chess is one example, where no computer or mind can determine the best sequence of moves. In order to be able to compute the optimal strategy, one could trim down the 8×8 board to a 4×4 one and reduce the number of pieces accordingly. Whether this result tells us much about the real game, however, is questionable.

The study of ecological rationality answers the question: In what environments will a given heuristic work? Where will it fail? Note that this normative question can only be answered if there is a process model of the heuristic in the first place, and the results are gained by proof or simulation. As mentioned beforehand, the ecological rationality of a verbal label such as "representativeness" cannot be determined. At most one can say that representativeness is sometimes good and sometimes bad—without being able to explicate the "sometimes."

The science of heuristics has three goals, the first descriptive, the second normative, and the third of design.

> *The adaptive toolbox.* The goal is to analyze the adaptive toolbox, that is, the heuristics, their building blocks, and the evolved capacities exploited by the building blocks. Heuristics should be specified in the form of computational models. This analysis includes the phylogenetic and ontogenetic development of the toolbox as well as cultural and individual differences.
>
> *Ecological rationality.* The goal is to determine the environmental structures in which a given heuristic is successful, that is, the match between mind and environment (physical and social). This analysis includes the coevolution between heuristics and environments.
>
> *Design.* The goal is to use the results of the study of the adaptive toolbox and ecological rationality to design heuristics and/or environments for improving decision making in applied fields such as health care, law, and management.

To see how this program differs from the cognitive illusions program, consider four general beliefs about heuristics that are assumed to be true in the cognitive illusions program but that turn out to be misconceptions from the point of view of the ecological rationality program (table 1.1). First, heuristics are seen as second-best approximations to the "correct" strategy defined by an optimization model; second and third, their use is attributed either to our cognitive limitations or to the fact that the problem at hand is not important; and finally, it is assumed that more information and more computation is always better if they are free of charge. I use an asset-allocation problem to demonstrate that, as a general truth, each of these beliefs is mistaken. Rather, one has to measure heuristics and optimization models with the same yardstick—neither is better per se in the real world.

Table 1.1: Four common but erroneous beliefs about heuristics

Misconception	Clarification
1. Heuristics produce second-best results; optimization is always better.	Optimization is not always the better solution, for instance, when it is computationally intractable or lacks robustness due to estimation errors.
2. Our minds rely on heuristics only because of our cognitive limitations.	We rely on heuristics for reasons that have to do with the structure of the problem, including computational intractability, robustness, and speed of action.
3. People rely or should rely on heuristics only in routine decisions of little importance.	People rely on heuristics for decisions of low and high importance, and this it not necessarily an error.
4. More information and computation is always better.	Good decision making in a partly uncertain world requires ignoring part of the available information and, as a consequence, performing less complex estimations because of the robustness problem. See investment example.

Investment Behavior

In 1990, Harry Markowitz received the Nobel Prize in Economics for his theoretical work on optimal asset allocation. He addressed a vital investment problem that everyone faces in some form or other, be it saving for retirement or earning money on the stock market: how best to invest your money in N assets. Markowitz proved that there is an optimal portfolio that maximizes the return and minimizes the risk. One might assume that when he made his own retirement investments he relied on his award-winning optimization strategy. But he did not. Instead he relied on a simple heuristic, the $1/N$ rule:

Allocate your money equally to each of N funds.

There is considerable empirical evidence for this heuristic: About 50 percent of people studied rely on it, and most consider only about 3 or 4 funds to invest in. Researchers in behavioral finance have criticized this behavior as naïve. But how much better is optimizing than $1/N$? A recent study compared twelve optimal asset-allocation policies (including that of Markowitz) with the $1/N$ rule in seven allocation problems, such as allocating one's money to ten American industry portfolios. The twelve policies included Bayesian and non-Bayesian models of optimal choice. Despite their complexity, none could consistently beat the heuristic on various financial measures (DeMiguel, Garlappi, & Uppal, 2006).

How can a heuristic strategy be better than an optimizing one? At issue is not computational intractability, but robustness. The optimization models performed better than the simple heuristic in data fitting (adjusting their parameters to the data of the past ten years) but worse in predicting the future. Similar to the results that will be reported in the following chapters (figures 2.6 and 3.1), they thus overfitted the past data. The $1/N$ heuristic, in contrast, does not estimate any parameter and consequently cannot overfit.

Note that $1/N$ is not always superior to optimization. The important question of when in fact it predicts better can be answered by studying the rule's *ecological rationality*. Three relevant environmental features for the performance of $1/N$ and the optimizing models are:

(i) the predictive uncertainty of the problem,
(ii) the number N of assets, and
(iii) the size of the learning sample.

Typically, the larger the uncertainty and the number of assets and the smaller the learning sample, the greater the advantage of the heuristic. Since the uncertainty of funds is large and cannot be changed, we focus on the learning sample, which comprised 10 years of data in the above study. When would the optimization models begin to outperform the heuristic? The authors report that with 50 assets to allocate one's wealth to, the optimization policies would need a window of 500 years before it eventually outperformed the $1/N$ rule.

Note that $1/N$ is not only an investment heuristic. Its range is broader. For instance, $1/N$ is employed to achieve fairness in sharing among children and adults (dividing a cake equally), where it is known as the equality rule; it is the voting rule in democracies, where each citizen's vote has the same weight; it represents the modal offer in the ultimatum game; and it is a sibling of the tallying rules that will be introduced in chapter 2, where each reason is given the same weight. $1/N$ can achieve quite different goals, from making money to creating a sense of fairness and trust.

Markowitz's use of $1/N$ illustrates how each of the four general beliefs in table 1.1 can be wrong. First, the $1/N$ heuristic was better than the optimization models. Second, Markowitz relied on the heuristic not because of his cognitive limitations. Rather, as we have seen, his choice can be justified because of the structure of the problem. Third, asset allocations, such as retirement investments, are some of the most consequential financial decisions in one's life. Finally, the optimization models relied on more information and more computation than $1/N$, but that did not lead to better decisions.

The Problem with Content-Blind Norms

In the heuristics-and-biases program, a norm is typically a law (axiom, rule) of logic or probability rather than a full optimization model. A law of logic or probability is used as a *content-blind norm* for a problem if the "rational" solution is determined independent of its content. For instance, the truth table of the material conditional *if P then Q* is defined independent of the content of the Ps and Qs. The definition is in terms of a specific syntax. By content, I mean the semantics (what are the Ps and Qs?) and the pragmatics (what is the goal?) of the problem. The program of studying whether people's judgments deviate from content-blind norms proceeds in four steps:

Syntax first. Start with a law of logic or probability.
Add semantics and pragmatics. Replace the logical terms (e.g., material conditional, mathematical probability) by English terms (e.g., if...then; probable), add content, and define the problem to be solved.
Content-blind norm. Use the syntax to define the "rational" answer to the problem. Ignore semantics and pragmatics.
Cognitive illusion. If people's judgments deviate from the "rational" answer, call the discrepancy a cognitive illusion. Attribute it to some deficit in the human mind (not to your norms).

Content-blind norms derive from an internalist conception of rationality. Examples are the use of the material conditional as a norm for reasoning about any content and the set-inclusion or "conjunction rule" (chap. 4). Proponents of content-blind norms do not use this term but instead speak of "universal principles of logic, arithmetic, and probability calculus" that tell us how we should think (Piatelli-Palmarini, 1994:158). Consider the material conditional.

In 1966, the British psychologist Peter Wason invented the *selection task,* also known as the *four-card problem,* to study reasoning about conditional statements. This was to become one of the most frequently studied tasks in the psychology of reasoning. Wason's starting point was the material conditional $P \rightarrow Q$, as defined by the truth table in elementary logic. In the second step, the Ps and Qs are substituted by some content, such as "numbers" (odd/even) and "letters" (consonants/vowels). The material conditional "$\rightarrow$" is replaced by the English terms "if...then," and a rule is introduced:

If there is an even number on one side of the card, there is a consonant on the other.

Four cards are placed on the table, showing an even number, an odd number, a consonant, and a vowel on the surface side. People are asked which cards need to be turned around in order to see whether the rule has been violated. In the third step, the "correct" answer is defined by the truth table: to turn around the P and the not-Q card, and nothing else, because the material conditional is false if and only if P∩not-Q. However, in a series of experiments, most people picked other combinations of cards, which was evaluated as a reasoning error due to some cognitive illusion. In subsequent experiments, it was found that the cards picked depended on the content of the Ps and Qs, and this was labeled the "content effect." Taken together, these results were interpreted as a demonstration of human irrationality and a refutation of Piaget's theory of operational thinking. Ironically, as mentioned before, Wason and Johnson-Laird (1972) and their followers held up truth-table logic as normative even after they criticized it as descriptively false.

Are content-blind norms reasonable norms? Should one's reasoning always follow truth-table logic, the conjunction rule, Bayes's rule, the law of large numbers, or some other syntactic law, irrespective of the content of the problem? My answer is no and for several reasons. A most elementary point is that English terms such as "if…then" are not identical to logical terms such as the material conditional "→". This confusion is sufficient to reject logic as a content-blind norm. More interesting, adaptive behavior has other goals than logical truth or consistency, such as dealing intelligently with other people. For instance, according to Trivers's (2002) theory of reciprocal altruism, each human possesses altruistic and cheating tendencies. Therefore, one goal in a social contract is to search for information revealing whether one has been cheated by the other party (Cosmides, 1989). Note that the perspective is essential: You want to find out whether you were cheated by the other party, not whether you cheated the other. Logic, in contrast, is without perspective. Consider a four-card task whose content is a social contract between an employer and an employee (Gigerenzer & Hug, 1992):

> If a previous employee gets a pension from the firm, then that person must have worked for the firm for at least 10 years.

The four cards read: got a pension, worked 10 years for the firm, did not get a pension, worked 8 years for the firm. One group of participants was cued into the role of the employer and asked to check those cards (representing files of previous employees) that could reveal whether the rule was violated. The far majority picked "got a pension" and "worked for 8 years." Note that this choice is consistent with both the laws of the truth table and the goal of cheater detection. Proponents of content-blind norms interpreted this and similar results as indicating that social contracts somehow facilitated logical reasoning. But when we cued the participants into the role of an employee, the far majority picked "did not get a pension" and "worked for 10 years." (In contrast, in the employer's group, no participant had checked this information.) Now the result was inconsistent with the truth table, but from the employee's perspective, again consistent with the goal of not being cheated. Search for information was Machiavellian: to avoid being cheated oneself, not to avoid cheating others.

The perspective experiment clearly demonstrates that logical thinking is not central to human reasoning about these problems as well as that truth-table logic is an inappropriate norm here. Yet several decades and hundreds of thousands of dollars of grant money have been wasted trying to show that human thinking violates the laws of logic. We have learned next to nothing about the nature of thinking from these studies. The same holds for research on other content-blind norms (Gigerenzer, 2001). Inappropriate norms tend to suggest wrong questions, and the answers to these generate more confusion than insight into the nature of human judgment. My point is not new. Wilhelm Wundt (1912/1973), known as the father of experimental psychology, concluded that logical norms have little to do with thought processes and that attempts to apply them to learn about psychological processes have been absolutely fruitless. But psychologists do learn. For instance, Lance Rips, who had argued that deductive logic might play a central rule in cognitive architecture (Rips, 1994), declared that he would not defend this "imperialist" theory anymore (Rips, 2002).

Rethinking Cognitive Biases

The above selection task illustrates the limits of logical norms for understanding good thinking. That is not to say that logic is never an appropriate norm, but rather that, like other analytical and heuristic tools, its domain is restricted. Violations of logical reasoning were previously interpreted as cognitive fallacies, yet what appears to be a fallacy can often also be seen as adaptive behavior, if one is willing to rethink the norms. More recently, a reevaluation of so-called cognitive biases that takes into account the structure of the environment and the goals of the decision maker has finally taken place. Table 1.2 illustrates a dozen cognitive illusions that are under debate. What unites these examples is the fact that as soon as researchers began to study the structure of information in the environment, an apparently dull cognitive illusion often took on the form of a sharp pair of scissors.

Consider the first item in the list, overconfidence bias, as an illustration. In a series of experiments, participants answered general-knowledge questions, such as:

Which city is farther north—New York or Rome?

How confident are you that your answer is correct?

50 percent / 60 percent / 70 percent / 80 percent / 90 percent / 100 percent

The typical finding was that when participants were 100 percent confident of giving a correct answer, the average proportion correct was lower, such as 80 percent; when they said they were 90 percent confident, the average proportion correct was 75 percent, and so on. This "miscalibration" phenomenon was labeled *overconfidence bias* and interpreted as a cognitive illusion. The explanation was sought in the minds of people who participated in the experiments, not in the environment. It was attributed to a confirmation bias in memory search: People first choose an answer, then search for confirming evidence only and grow overly confident. Yet Koriat, Lichtenstein, and Fischhoff's (1980) experiments showed only small or nonsignificant effects that disappeared in a replication (Fischhoff & MacGregor, 1982). Others proposed that people are victims of insufficient cognitive processing or suffer from self-serving motivational biases or from fear of invalidity. No explanation could be verified. In a social psychology textbook, the student was told: "Overconfidence is an accepted fact of psychology. The issue is what produces it. Why does experience not lead us to a more realistic self-appraisal?" (Myers, 1993: 50). Overconfidence bias was taken as the explanation for various kinds of personal and economic disasters, such as the large proportion of start-ups that quickly go out of business. As Griffin and Tversky (1992: 432) explained, "The significance of overconfidence to the conduct of human affairs can hardly be overstated." Finally, in a Nobel laureate's words, "some basic tendency toward overconfidence appears to be a robust human character trait" (Shiller, 2000: 142).

Eventually several researchers realized independent of each other that this phenomenon is a direct reflection of the *unsystematic* variability in the environment (Erev, Wallsten, & Budescu, 1994; Pfeiffer, 1994; Juslin, Winman, & Olsson, 2000). The large unsystematic variability of confidence judgments leads, *in the absence of any overconfidence bias,* to regression toward the mean, that is, the average number correct is always lower than a high confidence level. When one plots the data the other way round, the same unsystematic variability produces a pattern that looks like *underconfidence:* When participants answered 100 percent correctly, their mean confidence was lower, such as 80 percent, and so on (Dawes & Mulford, 1996). The phenomenon seems less a result of systematic cognitive bias and more a consequence of task environments with unsystematic error. Every unbiased mind and machine exhibits it.

To return to the initial question, which city is in fact farther north, New York or Rome? Temperature is a very good cue for latitude, but not a certain one. The correct answer is Rome. When researchers predominantly select

Table 1.2: Twelve examples of phenomena that were first interpreted as cognitive illusions (left) but later revalued as reasonable judgments given the environmental structure (right)

Is a phenomenon due to a "cognitive illusion"...	...or to an environmental structure plus an unbiased mind?
Overconfidence bias (defined as miscalibration)	"Miscalibration" can be deduced from an unbiased mind in an environment with unsystematic error, causing regression toward the mean (Dawes & Mulford, 1996; Erev et al., 1994).
Overconfidence bias (defined as mean confidence minus proportion correct)	"Overconfidence bias" can be deduced from an unbiased mind in an environment with unrepresentative sampling of questions; disappears largely with random sampling (Gigerenzer et al., 1991; Juslin et al., 2000).
Hard-easy effect	"Hard-easy effect" can be deduced from an unbiased mind in an environment with unsystematic error, causing regression toward the mean (Juslin et al., 2000).

Table 1.2 (continued)

Overestimation of low risks and underestimation of high risks	This classical phenomenon can be deduced from an unbiased mind in an environment with unsystematic error, causing regression toward the mean (Hertwig, Pachur, & Kurzenhäuser, 2005).
Contingency illusion	"Contingency illusion" can be deduced from an unbiased mind performing significance tests on samples with unequal sizes, such as minorities and majorities (Fiedler, Walther, & Nickel, 1999).
Most drivers say they drive more safely than average	The distribution of the actual number of accidents is highly skewed, which results in the fact that most drivers (80% in one U.S. study) have fewer than the average number of accidents (Lopes, 1992; Gigerenzer, 2002a).
Availability bias (letter "R" study)	"Availability bias" largely disappears when the stimuli (letters) are representatively sampled rather than selected (Sedlmeier, Hertwig, & Gigerenzer, 1998).
Preference reversals	Consistent social values (e.g., don't take the largest slice; don't be the first to cross a picket line) can create what look like preference reversals (Sen, 2002).
Probability matching	Probability matching is suboptimal for an individual studied in isolation but not necessarily for individuals in an environment of social competition (Gallistel, 1990).
Conjunction fallacy	"Conjunction fallacy" can be deduced from the human capacity for semantic inference in social situations (Hertwig & Gigerenzer, 1999).
False consensus effect	This "egocentric bias" can be deduced from Bayes's rule for situations where a person has no knowledge about prior probabilities (Dawes & Mulford, 1996).
Violations of logical reasoning	A number of apparent "logical fallacies" can be deduced from Bayesian statistics for environments where the empirical distribution of the events (e.g., P, Q, and their negations) is highly skewed (McKenzie & Amin, 2002; Oaksford & Chater, 1994) and from the logic of social contracts (Cosmides & Tooby, 1992).

The general argument is that an unbiased (not omniscient) mind plus a specific environmental structure (such as unsystematic error, unequal sample sizes, skewed distributions) is *sufficient* to produce the phenomenon. Note that other factors can also contribute to these phenomena. The moral is not that people would never err but that in order to understand good and bad judgments, one needs to analyze the structure of the problem or of the natural environment.

questions where a reliable cue fails (but do not inform experiment partici-pants), the mean proportion correct will be lower than the mean confidence. This difference has also been called overconfidence, the second item in table 1.2, and attributed to people's mental flaws rather than to researchers' unrepresentative sampling. When researchers began to sample questions randomly from the real world (e.g., comparing all metropolises on latitude), this alleged cognitive illusion largely disappeared (see chap. 7).

Cognitive Luck

Matheson (2006) discusses the study of ecological rationality as a way to overcome the epistemic internalism of the Enlightenment tradition. But he raises a concern: "If cognitive virtue is located outside the mind in the way that the Post-Enlightenment Picture suggests, then it turns out to be something bestowed on us by features of the world not under our control: It involves an intolerable degree of something analogous to what theoretical ethicists call 'moral luck' (cf. Williams, 1981, Nagel, 1993)—'cognitive luck,' we might say." His worry is based on the assumption that internal ways to improve cognition are under our control, whereas the external ones are not.

This assumption, however, is not always correct and reveals a limit of an internalist view of cognitive virtue. I conjecture that changing environments can in fact be easier than changing minds. Consider a fundamental problem in our health systems, namely that a large number of physicians are innu-merate (Gigerenzer, 2002a), as illustrated by screening for breast cancer. A woman with a positive mammogram asks the physician what the prob-ability is that she actually has cancer. What do physicians tell that worried woman? In 2007, I asked 160 experienced gynecologists this question. To help them out, I gave them the relevant information, in the form of *condi-tional probabilities* (expressed as percentages).

> Assume that you screen women in a particular region for breast cancer with mammography. You know the following about women in this region:
>
>> The probability that a woman has breast cancer is 1 percent (prevalence).
>>
>> If a woman has breast cancer, the probability is 90 percent that she will have a positive mammogram (sensitivity).
>>
>> If a woman does not have breast cancer, the probability is 9 percent that she will still have a positive mammogram (false positive rate).
>
> A woman who tested positive asks if she really has breast cancer or what the probability is that she actually has breast cancer. What is the best answer?
>
>> (1) "It is not certain that you have breast cancer, yet the prob-ability is about 81 percent." [14]

(2) "Out of 10 women who test positive as you did, about 9 have breast cancer." [47]

(3) "Out of 10 women who test positive as you did, only about 1 has breast cancer." [20]

(4) "The chance that you have breast cancer is about 1 percent." [19]

Note that the gynecologists' answers ranged between 1 percent and 9 out of 10 (90 percent)! The best answer is 1 out of 10, which only 20 percent of them gave. (The numbers in brackets give the percentage of gynecologists [out of 160] who chose each answer.) The most frequent answer was 9 out of 10. Consider for a moment the undue anxiety and panic women with positive mammograms have been caused by such physicians who do not understand the medical evidence.

In an earlier study with 48 physicians from various specialized fields (Hoffrage & Gigerenzer, 1998), we asked for numerical estimates (rather than multiple-choice selection), with similar results. Once again, the estimates ranged between 1 percent and 90 percent. One-third of the physicians thought the answer was 90 percent, one-third gave estimates between 50 percent and 80 percent, and one-third between 1 percent and 10 percent. Physicians' intuitions could hardly vary more—a worrying state of affairs.

This result illustrates a larger problem: When physicians try to draw a conclusion from conditional probabilities, their minds tend to cloud over (chap. 9). What can be done to correct this? From an internalist perspective, one might recommend training physicians how to insert the probabilities into Bayes's rule. Yet this proposal is doomed to failure. When we taught students statistics in this way, their performance dropped by 50 percent just one week after they successfully passed the exam and continued to fade away week by week (Sedlmeier & Gigerenzer, 2001). Moreover, the chance of convincing physicians to take a statistics course in the first place is almost nil; most have no time, little motivation, or believe they are incurably innumerate. Are innumerate physicians then inevitable? No. In the ecological view, thinking does not happen simply in the mind, but in interaction between the mind and its environment. This opens up a second and more efficient way to solve the problem: to change the environment. The relevant part of the environment is the representation of the information, because the representation does part of the Bayesian computation. Natural (nonnormalized) frequencies are such an efficient representation; they mimic the way information was encountered before the advent of writing and statistics, throughout most of human evolution. Here is the same information as above, now in *natural frequencies:*

10 out of every 1,000 women have breast cancer.

Of these 10 women, we expect that 9 will have a positive mammogram.

Of the remaining 990 women without breast cancer, some 89 will still have a positive mammogram.

Imagine a sample of women who have positive mammograms. How many of these women actually have cancer? _____ out of _____ .

When I presented the numerical information in natural frequencies, the confusion in most physicians' minds disappeared; 87 percent of the gynecologists chose "1 out of 10." Most realized that out of some 98 [89+9] women who test positive, only 9 are likely to have cancer. Thus, the chances of having breast cancer based on a positive screening mammogram are less than 10 percent, or about 1 in 10. Proper representation of information, such as natural frequencies, helps physicians to understand the outcomes of medical tests and treatments (see also Elmore & Gigerenzer, 2005) and prevents needless shocks to wrongly informed patients. In 2006, this program of teaching transparent risk communication became part of continuing education for gynecologists in Germany; I myself have trained some one thousand physicians in using representations that turn innumeracy into insight (see chap. 9).

Similarly, by changing the environment, we can make many so-called cognitive illusions largely disappear, enable fifth and sixth graders to solve Bayesian problems before they even heard of probabilities (chap. 12), and help judges and law students understand DNA evidence (Hoffrage, Lindsey et al., 2000). Thus, an ecological view actually extends the possibilities to improve judgment, whereas an internalist view limits the chances. To summarize, worrying about "cognitive luck" is bound to an internalist view, where enablers outside the mind are considered suspicious. From an ecological view, environmental structures, not luck, naturally and inevitably influence the mind and can be designed to enable insight. Cognitive virtue is, in my view, a relation between a mind and its environment, very much like the notion of ecological rationality.

What Is the Rationality of *Homo sapiens?*

What makes us so smart? I have discussed four answers. The first is that we are smart because we behave as if we were omniscient and had unlimited computational power to find the optimal strategy for each problem. This is the beautiful fiction of unbounded rationality. The second is a modification of the first that diminishes omniscience by introducing the need for searching for information and the resulting costs but insists on the ideal of optimization. These two programs define the theories in much of economics, biology, philosophy, and even the cognitive sciences. Both have an antipsychological bias: They try to define rational behavior without cognitive psychology, promoting as-if theories, which illustrates that "black box" behaviorism is still alive. In the image of Laplace's demon, *Homo economicus* has defined *Homo sapiens:* We are basically rational beings, and the nature of our rationality can be understood through the fictions of omniscience, omnipotence, and optimization. The heuristics-and-biases program has attacked that position but only on the descriptive level, using content-blind norms as the yardstick to diagnose human irrationality. The conclusion has been that we are mostly or sometimes irrational, committing systematic errors of reasoning.

There is now a literature that tries to determine which of these positions is correct. Are we rational or irrational? Or perhaps 80 percent rational and 20 percent irrational? Some blessed peacemakers propose that the truth lies in the middle and that we are a little of both, so there is no real disagreement. For instance, the debate between Kahneman and Tversky (1996) and myself (Gigerenzer, 1996) has been sometimes misunderstood as concerning the question of *how much* rationality or irrationality people have. In this view, rationality is like a glass of water, and Kahneman and Tversky see the glass as half-empty, whereas I see it as half-full. For instance, Samuels, Stich, and Bishop (2004: 264) conclude their call for "ending the rationality war" with the assertion that the two parties "do not have any deep disagreement over the extent of human rationality" (but see Bishop, 2000). However, the issue is not quantity, but quality: *what* exactly rationality and irrationality are in the first place. We can easily agree how often experiment participants have or have not violated the truth-table logic or some other logical law in an experimental task. But proponents of the heuristics-and-biases program count the first as human irrationality and the second as rationality. I do not. I believe that we need a better understanding of human rationality than that relative to content-blind norms. These were of little relevance for *Homo sapiens,* who had to adapt to a social and physical world, not to systems with artificial syntax, such as the laws of logic.

The concept of ecological rationality is my answer to the question of the nature of *Homo sapiens.* It defines the rationality of heuristics independently of optimization and content-blind norms, by the degree to which they are adapted to environments. The study of ecological rationality facilitates understanding a variety of counterintuitive phenomena, including when one reason is better than many, when less is more, and when partial ignorance pays. *Homo sapiens* has been characterized as a tool-user. There is some deeper wisdom in that phrase. The tools that make us smart are not bones and stones, but the heuristics in the adaptive toolbox.

Chapter 2

Fast and Frugal Heuristics

If you open a book on judgment and decision making, chances are that you will stumble over the following moral: Good reasoning must adhere to the laws of logic, the calculus of probability, or the maximization of expected utility; if not, there must be a cognitive or motivational flaw. Don't be taken in by this fable. Logic and probability are mathematically beautiful and elegant systems. But they do not always describe how actual people—including the authors of books on decision making—solve problems, as the subsequent story highlights. A decision theorist from Columbia University was struggling whether to accept an offer from a rival university or to stay. His colleague took him aside and said, "Just maximize your expected utility—you always write about doing this." Exasperated, the decision theorist responded, "Come on, this is serious."

The study of heuristics investigates how people actually make judgments and decisions in everyday life, generally without calculating probabilities and utilities. The term *heuristic* is of Greek origin and means "serving to find out or discover." In the title of his Nobel Prize–winning paper of 1905, Albert Einstein used the term *heuristic* to indicate an idea that he considered incomplete, due to the limits of our knowledge, but useful (Holton, 1988). For the Stanford mathematician George Polya (1954), heuristic thinking was as indispensable as analytical thinking for problems that cannot be solved by the calculus or probability theory—for instance, how to find a mathematical proof. The advent of computer programming gave heuristics a new prominence. It became clear that most problems of any importance are computationally intractable; that is, we know neither the optimal solution nor a method to find it. This holds even for well-defined problems, such as chess, the classic computer game Tetris, and the traveling salesman problem (Michalewicz &

This chapter is a revised version of G. Gigerenzer, "Fast and Frugal Heuristics: The Tools of Bounded Rationality," in *Blackwell Handbook of Judgment and Decision Making*, ed. D. J. Koehler and N. Harvey (Oxford, UK: Blackwell, 2004), 62–88.

Fogel, 2000). It also holds for less well-structured problems, such as which job offer to accept, what stocks to invest in, and whom to marry. When optimal solutions are out of reach, we are not paralyzed to inaction or doomed to failure. We can use heuristics to discover good solutions.

What Is a Heuristic?

How does a baseball outfielder catch a fly ball? He might compute the trajectory of the ball and run to the point where it is supposed to land. How else could he do it? In Richard Dawkins's words (1976/1989: 96):

> When a man throws a ball high in the air and catches it again, he behaves as if he had solved a set of differential equations in predicting the trajectory of the ball. He may neither know nor care what a differential equation is, but this does not affect his skill with the ball. At some subconscious level, something functionally equivalent to the mathematical calculations is going on.

Note that Dawkins carefully inserts the qualifier "as if." To compute the trajectory is no simple feat; no computer program or robot to date can compute it in real time. What about an experienced player? First, we might assume that the player intuitively knows the family of parabolas, because, in theory, balls have parabolic trajectories. In order to select the right parabola, the player needs to be equipped with sensory organs that can measure the ball's initial distance, initial velocity, and projection angle. Yet in the real world, influenced by air resistance, wind, and spin, balls do not fly in parabolas. Thus, the player would further need to be capable of estimating the speed and direction of the wind at each point of the ball's flight, in order to compute the resulting path and the point where the ball will land, and to then run there. All this would have to be completed within a few seconds—the time a ball is in the air. This explanation is based on the ideals of *omniscience* and *omnipotence*: To solve a complex problem, a person constructs a complete representation of its environment and relies on the most sophisticated computational machinery.

An alternative vision exists, which does not aim at complete representation and information. It poses the question: Is there a smart heuristic that can solve the problem? One way to discover heuristics is to study experienced players. Experimental studies have shown that players actually use several heuristics (e.g., McLeod & Dienes, 1996). The simplest one is the *gaze heuristic*, which works if the ball is already high up in the air:

> *Gaze heuristic:* Fixate your gaze on the ball, start running, and adjust the speed so that the angle of gaze remains constant.

The angle of gaze is the angle between the eye and the ball, relative to the ground (figure 2.1). A player who uses this heuristic does not need to estimate wind, air resistance, spin, or the other causal variables. He can get away

Figure 2.1: How to catch a fly ball? Players rely on unconscious rules of thumb. When a ball comes in high, a player fixates his gaze on the ball, starts running, and adjusts the speed so that the angle of gaze remains constant.

with ignoring every piece of causal information. All the relevant information is contained in one variable: the angle of gaze. Note that a player using the gaze heuristic is not able to compute the point at which the ball will land. But the player will be there where the ball lands.

The gaze heuristic is a fast and frugal heuristic. It is fast because it can solve the problem within a few seconds, and it is frugal because it requires little information, just the angle of gaze. The heuristic consists of three building blocks: fixate your gaze on the ball, start running, and adjust your running speed. These building blocks can be part of other heuristics, too.

> *Definition:* A fast and frugal heuristic is a strategy, conscious or unconscious, that searches for minimal information and consists of building blocks that exploit evolved capacities and environmental structures.

Heuristics can be highly effective because they are anchored in the evolved brain and in the external environment. Let me explain.

Heuristics exploit evolved capacities. A heuristic is *simple* because it can take advantage of the evolved or learned capacities of an organism. For example, it is easy for humans to track a moving object against a noisy background; three-month-old babies can already hold their gaze on moving targets (Rosander & von Hofsten, 2002). Tracking objects, however, is difficult for a robot; a computer program as capable as a human mind of solving this problem does not yet exist. Similarly, in contrast to robots, humans are able to run. Thus, the gaze heuristic is simple for humans but not for robots. Simplicity is not only a characteristic of beauty; it also enables *fast, frugal, transparent,* and *robust* judgments. The gaze heuristic, like all heuristics, is transparent in the sense that it can be easily understood and taught to a novice, and the term *robust* refers to the ability of heuristics to generalize to new situations (see below). To summarize, a heuristic exploits hard-wired or learned cognitive and motor processes, and these features make it simple.

Heuristics exploit structures of environments. The rationality of heuristics is not logical, but ecological. Ecological rationality implies that a heuristic is not good or bad, rational or irrational per se, only relative to an environment. It can exploit particular environmental structures or change an environment. For instance, the gaze heuristic transforms the complex trajectory of the ball in the environment into a straight line. All heuristics are to some degree domain-specific; they are designed to solve specific classes of problems. The gaze heuristic can solve problems that involve the interception of moving objects. If you learn to fly an airplane, you will be taught a version of it: When another plane is approaching, and you fear a collision, then look at a scratch in your windshield and observe whether the other plane moves relative to that scratch. If it does not, dive away quickly. For the pilot, the goal is to avoid a collision, whereas for the outfielder, the goal is to produce a collision. The nature of the heuristic is the same. To summarize, evolved capacities can make a heuristic simple, while the structure of the environment can make it smart.

Heuristics are distinct from as-if optimization models. The idea of calculating the ball's trajectory by solving differential equations is a form of optimization. When optimization is proposed to explain human behavior (as opposed to building artificial systems), this is called *as-if optimization.* As-if optimization models are silent about the actual process, although it is sometimes suggested that the measurements and calculations might happen unconsciously. The gaze heuristic, however, illustrates that the logic of a heuristic, conscious or unconscious, can be strikingly distinct from as-if optimization. This yields an advantage. With a good model of a heuristic, one can deduce predictions that cannot be obtained from an as-if optimization model. The gaze heuristic, for instance predicts that players catch the ball while running, which follows from the fact that the player must move to keep the angle of gaze constant. Similarly, when the ball is thrown to the side of the player, one can predict that the player will run a slight arc, as can be observed in baseball outfielders and in dogs who catch Frisbees (e.g., Shaffer & McBeath, 2002). In summary, a model of a heuristic is a rule whose purpose is to describe the actual process—not merely the outcome—of problem solving.

Models of Heuristics

A model of a heuristic specifies (i) a process rule, (ii) the capacities that the rule exploits to be simple, and (iii) the kinds of problems the heuristic can solve, that is, the structures of environments in which it is successful.

Models of heuristics need to be distinguished from mere labels. For instance, terms such as *representativeness* and *availability* are common-sense labels without specification of a process and the conditions under which a heuristic succeeds and fails. These need to be developed into test-able models; otherwise they can account for almost everything post hoc.

There already exist a number of testable models for heuristics, such as satisficing (Selten, 2001; Simon, 1982), elimination-by-aspects (Tversky, 1972), and various heuristics for multiattribute choice discussed in Payne, Bettman, & Johnson 1993. Much of this earlier work addressed heuristics for preferences, not for inferences, that is, for problems where no single external criterion of success exists. Criteria for the accuracy of heuristics were typically internal, such as whether they used all of the information or how closely they mimicked the gold standard of a weighted additive model. Because there were no external criteria for accuracy, the true power of heu-ristics could not be fully demonstrated.

I focus on heuristics for inferences—such as comparative judgments, classification, and estimation. From the seminal work on heuristics with simple unit weights (+1 and −1; see Dawes, 1979), we know that the predic-tive accuracy of simple heuristics can be as high as or higher than that of the gold standard of weighing and adding. For instance, unit weights matched multiple regression in predicting the academic performance of students (Dawes & Corrigan, 1974), and the take-the-best heuristic was as successful as Bayes's rule at predicting the outcomes of basketball games in the 1996 NBA season, but it did so faster and with less information (Todorov, 2002). Models of heuristics for classification, estimation, comparative judgments, and choice are discussed in Gigerenzer, Todd, and the ABC Research Group 1999, and Gigerenzer and Selten 2001b. In what follows, I will select a few heuristics and discuss their ecological rationality and the empirical evidence.

Recognition Heuristic

Imagine you are a contestant in a TV game show and face the $1 million question: "Which city has more inhabitants, Detroit or Milwaukee?"

What is your answer? If you are American, then your chances of finding the right answer, Detroit, are not bad. Some 60 percent of undergraduates at the University of Chicago did (Goldstein & Gigerenzer, 1999). If, how-ever, you are German, your prospects look dismal because most Germans know little about Detroit, and many have not even heard of Milwaukee. How many correct inferences did the less knowledgeable German group that we tested make? Despite a considerable lack of knowledge, virtually all of the Germans answered the question correctly. How can people who know less about a subject nevertheless make more correct inferences? The answer is that the Germans used a fast and frugal heuristic, the recognition heuristic: If you recognize the name of one city but not the other, then infer that the recognized city has the larger population. The Americans could not use the heuristic, because they had heard of both cities. They knew too much.

The recognition heuristic is useful when there is a strong correlation—in either direction—between recognition and criterion. For simplicity, let us assume that the correlation is positive. For two-alternative choice tasks, the heuristic can be stated as follows:

> *Recognition heuristic:* If one of two objects is recognized and the other is not, then infer that the recognized object has the higher value with respect to the criterion.

The recognition heuristic builds on an evolved capacity for recognition—such as face, voice, and name recognition. No computer program yet exists that can perform face recognition as well as a human child. Note that the capacity for recognition is different from that for recall. For instance, one may recognize a face but not recall anything about who that person is. If people use the recognition heuristic in an adaptive way, they will rely on it in situations where it is ecologically rational.

> *Ecological Rationality:* The recognition heuristic is successful when ignorance is systematic rather than random, that is, when recognition is strongly correlated with the criterion.

The direction of the correlation between recognition and the criterion can be learned from experience, or it can be genetically coded. Substantial correlations exist in competitive situations, such as between name recognition and the excellence of colleges, the value of companies' products, and the quality of sports teams. One way to measure the degree of ecological rationality of the recognition heuristic (the correlation between recognition and criterion) is the *recognition validity* α, which is the proportion of times a recognized object has a higher criterion value than an unrecognized object in a reference class, such as cities, companies, or sports teams:

$$\alpha = R/(R+W), \qquad (2.1)$$

where R is the number of correct (right) inferences the recognition heuristic would achieve, computed across all pairs in which one object is recognized and the other is not, and W is the number of incorrect (wrong) inferences, computed under the same circumstances.

The research summarized in Table 2.1 suggests that people use the recognition heuristic in a relatively adaptive way, that is, it is followed most consistently when the recognition validity is high. For instance, Pohl (2006, Exp. 1) used the 20 largest Swiss cities and asked one group of participants to judge which of two cities has the larger population and another group to judge which of the two cities was located farther from the Swiss city Interlaken. Recognition is valid for inferring population ($\alpha = .86$) but not for inferring distance ($\alpha = .51$). Participants were not informed about validity. Nevertheless, they intuitively followed the recognition heuristic for

Table 2.1: People tend to rely on the recognition heuristic in situations where the recognition validity is substantially above chance (.5).

Task	Reference	Recognition validity α	Consistent with recognition heuristic
Career point total of NHL hockey players	Snook & Cullen 2006	.87	96%
Winner of 2003 Wimbledon tennis matches	Serwe & Frings 2006	.73 (amateurs) .67 (laypeople)	93% 88%
Winner of 2005 Wimbledon tennis matches	Scheibehenne & Bröder 2007	.71 (amateurs) .69 (laypeople)	89% 79%
Winner of 2004 European Soccer Championship matches	Pachur & Biele 2007	.71	91%
Population of German cities	Goldstein & Gigerenzer 2002	.80	90%
Population of Swiss cities	Pohl 2006, Exp. 1 and 2	.86 (Exp. 1) .72 (Exp. 2)	89% 75%
Distance of Swiss cities from Interlaken	Pohl 2006, Exp. 1	.51	54%
Population of European cities	Pohl 2006, Exp. 3	.89 (Italian) .82 (Belgian)	88% 89%
Largest mountains, rivers, and islands	Pohl 2006, Exp. 4	.49 (mountains) .74 (rivers) .85 (islands)	89% 94% 81%
Population of European cities	Volz et al. 2006	.63	84%
Prevalence of infectious diseases	Pachur & Hertwig 2006	.62 (Study 1) .62 (Study 2)	62% 69%

For instance, when judging which of two NHL hockey players has the higher career point total ($\alpha = .87$), participants followed the recognition heuristic in 96% of the cases. All studies tested inferences from memory (not from givens) with recognition that is ecologically valid (rather than defined as objects presented in a previous experimental session, as in many memory tasks).

inferring population in 89 percent of all cases, compared to in only 54 percent for inferring distance, which is almost at chance level. The correlation between recognition validity and proportion of judgments consistent with the recognition heuristic in Table 2.1 is $r = .55$.

The adaptive toolbox perspective implies two processes that precede the use of the recognition heuristic: recognition and evaluation. To be able to use the heuristic, one alternative must be recognized and the other not. To decide whether to use the heuristic (as opposed to another strategy) in a given situation, an evaluation process is enacted. Consistent with this hypothesis, a neuroimaging study (Volz et al., 2006) showed that different brain regions were activated for mere recognition judgments ("Which of the two cities do you recognize?") compared to tasks that allow the recognition heuristic to be used ("Which city has the larger population?"). Specifically, a deactivation was observed within the anterior frontomedian cortex (aFMC) when people did not follow the recognition heuristic. Since the aFMC has been previously associated with self-referential judgments, this result indicates that the recognition heuristic is the default, but that contradicting source knowledge can inhibit its use.

Knowledge that seems to inhibit the use of the recognition heuristic includes (i) low recognition validity (see above); (ii) recognizing individual objects for reasons that have nothing do to with the criterion, such as recognizing Chernobyl because of its nuclear power accident (Oppenheimer, 2003); and (iii) direct criterion knowledge for the recognized object, such as when comparing the population of the town around the corner with a known small population to that of an unknown city. Reliance on the recognition heuristic seems to be largely maintained even in the presence of contradicting cue information. For instance, the median participant in Richter and Späth (2006, Exp. 3) judged a recognized city as larger than an unrecognized one in 100 percent of the cases when they were told that the recognized city had an international airport, 97 percent when they were given no information, and 97 percent when they were told that the recognized city had no such airport. Contradicting cue information has an effect on some participants, but the majority in this experiment abided by the default: "go with what you know."

The recognition heuristic should not be confused with *availability* (Tversky & Kahneman, 1974). Availability refers to ease of recall, not recognition. The recognition heuristic implies several counterintuitive phenomena that cannot be deduced from any other theory I am aware of. As mentioned before, recognition information tends to dominate contradictory clues, in rats as well as in people, even if there is conflicting evidence (Pachur, Bröder, & Marewski, in press). Next, I will deduce a counterintuitive phenomenon, the *less-is-more effect,* and the conditions under which it occurs.

The Less-Is-More Effect

Equation 2.2 specifies the proportion of correct answers c on an exhaustive test of all pairs of N objects (such as cities, soccer teams) for a person who recognizes n of these objects.

$$c = \frac{2n(N-n)}{N(N-1)}\alpha + \frac{(N-n)(N-n-1)}{N(N-1)}\frac{1}{2} + \frac{n(n-1)}{N(N-1)}\beta \qquad (2.2)$$

The three terms on the right side of the equation correspond to the three possibilities: A person recognizes one of the two objects, none, or both. The first term accounts for the correct inferences made by the recognition heuristic, the second term for guessing, and the third term equals the proportion of

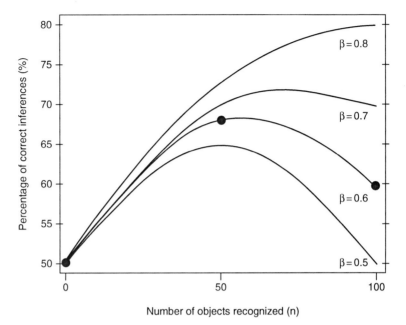

Figure 2.2: The less-is-more effect is a consequence of the recognition heuristic. It occurs when the recognition validity α is larger than the knowledge validity β (and α and β are constant). The curves shown are for $\alpha = .8$. A less-is-more effect can occur between people with the same β, as shown by the middle and right-hand point. It can also occur between people with different knowledge validities. For instance, a person who recognizes only half of the objects ($n = 50$) and has no useful knowledge ($\beta = .5$) will nevertheless make more correct inferences than a person who recognizes all objects ($n = 100$) and has useful knowledge ($\beta = .6$).

correct inferences made when knowledge beyond recognition is used. The *knowledge validity* β is the relative frequency of getting a correct answer when both objects are recognized, which is computed like the recognition validity. All parameters in equation 2.2 can be independently measured.

When one plots equation 2.2, a counterintuitive implication can be seen (figure 2.2). Consider first the curve for $\beta = .5$, that is, for people who have no predictive knowledge beyond recognition. A person who has heard of none of the objects will perform at chance level (50 percent, left side). A person who has heard of all objects will also perform at chance level (50 percent, right side). Only a person who has heard of some but not all objects can use the recognition heuristic, and their accuracy will first increase with n but then decrease again. The reason is that the recognition heuristic can be used most often when about half of the objects are recognized, in comparison to when all or none are recognized. When half of the objects are recognized, a person can use the recognition heuristic about half of the time, which results in some 65 percent (40 percent for $\alpha = .8$ plus 25 percent for guessing) correct inferences, as can be calculated from equation 2.2. The next curve with three dots shows a less-is-more effect in the presence of knowledge beyond mere recognition, for $\beta = .6$. The left dot represents a person who has not heard of any objects, while the dot on the right represents someone who has heard of all objects and has recall knowledge that does better than chance. The middle dot represents a person who recognizes less objects but gets more correct inferences. In general, assuming that α and β are constant, the following result can be proven (Goldstein & Gigerenzer, 2002):

> *Less-is-more effect:* The recognition heuristic will yield a less-is-more effect if $\alpha > \beta$.

A less-is-more effect can emerge in at least three different situations. First, it can occur between two groups of people, when a more knowledgeable group makes worse inferences than a less knowledgeable group in a given domain. An example is the performance of the American and German students on the question of whether Detroit or Milwaukee is larger. Second, a less-is-more effect can occur between domains, that is, when the same group of people achieve higher accuracy in a domain in which they know little than in a domain in which they know a lot. For instance, when American students were tested on the 22 largest American cities (such as New York versus Chicago) and on the 22 largest German cities (such as Cologne versus Frankfurt), they scored a median 71 percent (mean 71.1 percent) correct on their own cities but slightly higher on the less familiar German cities, with a median of 73 percent correct (mean 71.4 percent). This effect was obtained despite a handicap: Many Americans already knew the three largest U.S. cities in order and did not have to make any inferences. A similar less-is-more effect was demonstrated with Austrian students, whose scores for correct answers were slightly higher for the 75 largest American cities than for the 75 largest German cities (Hoffrage, 1995; see also Gigerenzer, 1993a). Third, a less-is-more effect can occur during knowledge acquisition, that is, when an individual's performance curve first increases but then decreases again.

Less-Is-More in Groups

Consider now group decision making. Three people sit in front of a computer screen on which such questions as "Which city has more inhabitants: Milan or Modena?" are displayed. The task of the group is to find the correct answer through discussion, and they are free to use whatever means. In this task, the correct solution is difficult to "prove" by an individual group member; thus, one might expect that the majority determine the group decision (the *majority rule*; see Gigone & Hastie, 1997). Consider now the following conflict. Two group members have heard of both cities, and each concluded independently that city A is larger. But the third group member has not heard of A, only of B, and concludes that B is larger (relying on the recognition heuristic). After the three members finished their negotiation, what will their consensus be? Given that two members have at least some knowledge of both cities, one might expect that the consensus is always *A*, which is also what the majority rule predicts. In fact, in more than half of all cases (59 percent), the group voted for *B* (Reimer & Katsikopoulos, 2004). This number rose to 76 percent when two members relied on mere recognition.

That group members let their knowledge be dominated by others' lack of recognition may seem odd. But in fact this apparently irrational decision increased the overall accuracy of the group. This result can be analytically deduced and intuitively seen from figure 2.2. When the recognition heuristic is used in group decisions, a less-is-more effect results if $\alpha > \beta$, just as in figure 2.2, but more strongly. Consistent with the theory, Reimer and Katsikopoulos (2004) observed that when two groups had the same average α and β, the group that recognized *fewer* cities (smaller *n*) typically had *more* correct answers. For instance, the members of one group recognized on average only 60 percent of the cities, and those in a second group 80 percent; but the first group got 83 percent answers correct in a series of more than one hundred questions, whereas the second got only 75 percent. Thus, group members seem to intuitively trust the recognition heuristic, which can improve accuracy and lead to the counterintuitive less-is-more effect between groups.

Heuristics Based on Reasons and Imitation

When recognition is not valid, or people know too much, heuristics can involve the search for reasons or cues. A few years after his voyage on the *Beagle*, the 29-year-old Charles Darwin divided a scrap of paper (titled "This Is the Question") into two columns with the headings "Marry" and "Not Marry" and listed supporting reasons for each of the two possible courses of action, such as "nice soft wife on a sofa with good fire" opposed to "conversation of clever men at clubs." Darwin concluded that he should marry, writing "Marry—Marry—Marry Q. E. D." decisively beneath the first column (Darwin, 1887/1969: 232–233). The following year, Darwin married his cousin, Emma Wedgwood, with whom he eventually had 10 children. How did Darwin decide to marry, based on the possible consequences he envisioned—children, loss of time, a constant companion? He did not tell us. But we can use his "Question" as a thought experiment to illustrate various visions of decision making.

Darwin searched his memory for reasons. There are two visions of search: optimizing search and heuristic search. Following Wald's (1947) optimizing models of sequential analysis, several psychological theorists postulated versions of sequential search and stopping rules (e.g., Busemeyer & Townsend, 1993). In the case of a binary hypothesis (such as to marry or not marry), the basic idea of most sequential models is the following: A threshold is calculated for accepting one of the two hypotheses, based on the costs of the two possible errors, such as wrongly deciding that to marry is the better option. Each reason or observation is then weighted, and the evidence is accumulated until the threshold for one hypothesis is met, at which point the search is stopped and the hypothesis is accepted. If Darwin had followed this procedure, he would have had to estimate, consciously or unconsciously, how many conversations with clever friends are equivalent to having one child and how many hours in a smoky abode can be traded against a lifetime of soft moments on the sofa. Weighting and adding is a mathematically convenient assumption, but it assumes that there is a common currency for all beliefs and desires in terms of quantitative probabilities and utilities. These models are often presented as *as-if* models, the task of which is to predict the outcome rather than the process of decision making, or it is assumed that the calculations might be performed unconsciously using the common currency of neural activation.

The second vision of search is that people use heuristics—either social heuristics or reason-based heuristics—that exploit some evolved capacities. Social heuristics exploit the capacity of humans for social learning and imitation (imitation need not result in learning), which is unmatched among the animal species. For instance, the following heuristic generates social facilitation:

Imitate the majority: If you see the majority of your peers display a behavior, engage in the same behavior.

Studies have reported behavior copying in animals and humans. Dugatkin (1992) argued that female guppies choose between males by copying the mate preferences of other females. In modern human societies, teenagers admire a movie star because everyone else in their peer group adulates that person. Advertisement exploits this heuristic by portraying a product surrounded by many admirers (not just one). People may display disgust for members of a minority because they notice that most of their peers do the same. For the marriage problem, this heuristic makes a man start thinking of marriage at a time when most other men in his social group do, say, around age 30. Copying the behavior of one's peers is a most frugal heuristic, for it virtually guarantees the peer group's approbation and is sometimes even a condition for peer acceptance, and one does not need to consider the pros and cons of one's behavior.

Imitate the majority tends to be ecologically rational in situations where

  (i) the observer and the demonstrators of the behavior are exposed to similar environments, such as social systems;
 (ii) the environment is stable rather than changing quickly; and
(iii) the environment is noisy and consequences are not immediate, that is, it is hard or time-consuming to figure out whether a choice is good or bad, such as which political or moral action is preferable (Goldstein et al., 2001).

In environments where these conditions do not hold, copying the behavior of the majority can lead to disaster. For instance, copying the production and distribution systems of other firms can be detrimental when an economy changes from local to global.

Darwin, however, seems to have based his decision on reasons. I will describe two classes of heuristics that search for reasons. Unlike optimizing models, they do not both weight and add cues. One class of heuristics dispenses with adding and searches cues in order (a simple form of weighing). I will refer to this class as *one-reason decision making*. The second class dispenses with weighing and adds up cues until a threshold is met. I will refer to the second class as *tallying* heuristics. Each of the heuristics consists of three building blocks: a rule for search, stopping, and decision making. I will specify some of the conditions under which each class of heuristics will be successful, and in order to do this, I will turn to inference rather than preference.

Take-the-Best and Tallying

Consider the task of predicting which alternative, *a* or *b*, has the higher value on a criterion, where *a* and *b* are elements of a set of *N* alternatives (which can be actions, objects, events). The prediction can be based on *M* binary cues $(1, 2, \ldots, i, \ldots, M)$, where the cue values *1* and *0* indicate higher and lower criterion values, respectively. For instance, take an experiment by Newell, Weston, and Shanks (2003). The participants were presented with a series of choices between the shares of two fictional companies. In each trial, two companies were presented on a computer screen, and the participants were asked to infer which share would prove to be more profitable. To help find the more profitable share, participants could acquire information concerning six cues, such as: "Does the company invest in new projects?" and "Does the company have financial reserves?" The cost of information about each cue was 1 p (pence). After participants had bought as many cues as they desired, they made their choice, and feedback was given whether the answer was correct. When the answer was correct, the participants received 7 p minus the amount they had spent searching for information. How do people make an inference when they have to search for information?

One hypothesis about how people make inferences is the *take-the-best* heuristic (Gigerenzer & Goldstein, 1999), which is a form of one-reason decision making. It consists of three building blocks: a search rule, a stopping rule, and a decision rule.

Take-the-Best

1. Search by validity: Search through cues in order of their validity. Look up the cue values of the cue with the highest validity first.
2. One-reason stopping rule: If one object has a positive cue value (*1*) and the other does not (*0* or unknown), then stop search and proceed to Step 3. Otherwise exclude this cue and return to Step 1. If no more cues are found, guess.
3. One-reason decision making: Predict that the object with the positive cue value (1) has the higher value on the criterion.

The validity of a cue *i* is defined as

$$v_i = R_i / P_i, \tag{2.3}$$

where R_i = number of correct predictions by cue i and P_i = number of pairs where the values of cue i differ between objects. If the cue orders are learned by feedback in an experiment, individual orderings may differ from the theoretical value, depending on the size of the learning sample, among others. In the Newell, Weston, and Shanks (2003) task, for example, the participant would start by looking up the most valid cue for predicting profitability and see if the two companies differed with respect to that cue. If they did, the participant would stop search and choose accordingly; if not, the participant would look up the next most valid cue and repeat the process until a choice was made. By using this stopping rule, participants can draw inferences without having to look up all of the available cue values. Note that v_i does not result in the best order of cues but in a good-enough one: The problem of determining the optimal order is NP-hard, that is, computationally intractable (Martignon & Hoffrage, 2002). An important feature of the search rule is that the validities are *unconditional* (unlike the beta-weights in multiple regression or the conditional probabilities in Bayes's rule); that is, the validity of the second cue is not computed conditional on the first cue, and so on. This form of simplicity generates robustness (see below).

Now consider an example for a tallying heuristic, which relies on adding but not on weighing (or order):

Tallying

1. Search rule: Search through cues in random order. Look up the cue values.
2. Stopping rule: After m $(1 < m \leq M)$ cues, stop search and determine which object has more positive cue values (1) and proceed to Step 3. If the number is equal, return to Step 1 and search for another cue. If no more cues are found, guess.
3. Decision rule: Predict that the object with the higher number of positive cue values (1) has the higher value on the criterion.

Versions of tallying have been discussed in the literature, such as unit-weight models in which all cues ($m = M$; also known as Dawes' rule), or the m significant cues are looked up (Dawes, 1979). Unlike as-if models, which predict outcomes only, these models of heuristics predict process and outcome and can be subjected to a stronger test. In Newell, Weston and Shank's study (2003), each of the three building blocks was tested independently.

Search rule   In theory, participants can search through cues in many different ways. If they looked up all six cues (which is unlikely, given the payoff function), there would be 6! = 720 different orders. The search rule of the tallying heuristic does not predict a specific order, but the search rule from the take-the-best heuristic makes a strong prediction. People will search by one of these orders, the one defined by v_i. In order to learn the validities, Newell, Weston, and Shanks (2003) exposed each participant to 120 learning trials, with feedback (correct/incorrect) given after each response. The six cues varied in their validity. The learning phase was followed by a test phase with 60 trials. During the test phase, 75 percent of the participants followed the search rule of take-the-best. When there were only two cues, this number increased to 92 percent. Thus, the great majority of participants did not search randomly, but in order of validity.

Stopping rule   The logical possibilities for stopping search are fewer than those for search. There are six possibilities, after the first, second,..., sixth cue (not counting the possibility that people would not search but simply guess). Tallying postulates that participants add up more than one cue, but it leaves open how many (i.e., the number m must be independently estimated). In contrast, take-the-best postulates that search is stopped immediately after the first discriminating cue is found, not beforehand and not later. Note that each stopping rule can be valid independent of the results for the search rule. For instance, people can search in 1 of the 719 orders not consistent with v_i but stop after the first discriminating cue is found, or search can follow validity but is stopped only after all cues have been looked up. Thus, the empirical result for the search rule does not constrain the stopping behavior. Newell, Weston, and Shanks (2003) reported that in 80 percent of all cases (where participants bought any information at all), participants followed the stopping rule, and this number increased to 89 percent when there were only two cues. This means that the great majority stopped search immediately after they found the first cue that made a difference.

Decision rule   In theory, participants can use infinite ways to combine the information concerning six cues. This includes linear models, weighted or unweighted. If a person follows the one-reason stopping rule, this constrains the ways to arrive at a decision (whereas, as mentioned before, the search rules impose no constraints on the stopping and decision rules). If only one piece of discriminating information is obtained, it seems that the only reasonable decision rules left are forms of one-reason decision making. The multiple-reason stopping rule, in contrast, would not constrain possible decision rules. Newell, Weston, and Shanks (2003) report that the decision rule of take-the-best was followed by their participants in 89 percent of trials, both for six and two cues.

That people often rely on *noncompensatory* heuristics has been long known. Take-the-best is a noncompensatory strategy because it is lexicographic: It relies on the first cue that allows for a decision and ignores all the rest—thus, these other cues cannot compensate. Consider a classic review of 45 studies in which the process of decision making was investigated by means of mouselab, eye movement, and other process-tracking techniques. The choice set varied between studies, including apartments, microwaves, and birth control methods:

> The results firmly demonstrate that noncompensatory strategies were the dominant mode used by decision makers. Compensatory strategies

were typically used only when the number of alternatives and dimensions were small or after a number of alternatives have been eliminated from consideration. (Ford et al., 1989: 75)

Those were the days, however, when many psychologists quickly dismissed intuitive judgments as "cognitive fallacies." If participants in experiments ignored part of the available information or did not properly weigh and add all pieces of information, their behavior was often called irrational or more politely excused as the unavoidable consequence of people's limited cognitive capacities. Consider what Keeney and Raiffa, two eminent decision theorists, have to say about lexicographic heuristics. They warn us that such a heuristic

"is more widely adopted in practice than it deserves to be,"
"is naively simple," and
"will rarely pass a test of 'reasonableness'" (Keeney & Raiffa, 1993: 77–78).

Yet those who dismissed people's judgments as fallacies never tested whether it was actually true that lexicographic heuristics lead to less accurate judgments than do weighting and adding all information. It simply appeared self-evident. In 1996, Daniel Goldstein and I put this question to test for the first time and showed that take-the-best can be more accurate than multiple regression, precisely *because* it ignores information. This finding led to the study of the ecological rationality of heuristics, that is, the situations in which given heuristics succeed. The reasonableness of a heuristic is an empirical question, not one of a priori beliefs.

There are now a substantial number of experiments that have analyzed under what conditions people use take-the-best (e.g., Bröder, 2000, 2003; Newell & Shanks, 2003; Rieskamp & Otto, 2006) and where take-the-best was compared with other heuristics or optimizing models in the same task (Bröder, 2000, 2002; Bröder & Schiffer, 2003a, 2003b; Lee & Cummins, 2004; Newell et al, 2004; Rieskamp & Hoffrage, 1999; Todorov, 2002). For instance, Bergert and Nosofsky (2007) tested the reaction time predictions of take-the-best against those of a weighted additive model and concluded that the vast majority of participants were consistent with the heuristic's process predictions. Nosofsky and Bergert (2007) tested take-the-best against exemplar models and concluded that the reaction time data again favors a version of take-the-best. One-reason decision making has also been observed in high-stake decisions. British magistrates seem to make bail decisions on the basis of one good reason only (Dhami, 2003; Dhami & Ayton, 2001), and so do British general practitioners when they prescribe lipid-lowering drugs (Dhami & Harries, 2001). Many parents rely on one reason to decide which doctor to drive to in the night when their child becomes seriously ill (Scott, 2002). In contrast, comparatively little experimental work has examined tallying (Bröder, 2000; Rieskamp & Hoffrage, 1999).

Take-the-best and tallying have been proposed and tested as components of a number of judgmental processes, such as in probabilistic mental models

Question:

Which has more cholesterol: cake or pie?			
Cues	Original	Feedback	Recall
Saturated fat (80%)	cake? pie	"cake"	cake > pie
Calories (70%)	cake > pie		[stop search]
Protein (60%)	[stop search]		
Choice	cake		cake
Confidence	70%		80%

Figure 2.3: A process model of hindsight bias (Hoffrage, Hertwig, & Gigerenzer, 2000). Participants learn cues (saturated fat, calories, protein) and their validities (in parentheses) in order to judge which of two supermarket food items has more cholesterol. There are three points in time: original judgment, feedback, and recall of the original judgment. The original judgment is generated by take-the-best, which implies that cues are looked up in memory in the order of validity. In the example given, the first cue, saturated fat, does not stop search because the participant is ignorant of whether cake or pie has a higher value (indicated by "?"). The second cue stops search because the participant learns that cake has more calories than pie (indicated by ">"). The answer is *cake,* and the confidence is 70 percent, that is, the validity of the cue. At the second point in time, feedback is given that *cake* was correct. Feedback is automatically used to update missing information in memory about cues (question marks). Thus, at the time of the recall, the "?" for saturated fat is likely to have changed into ">," following the direction of feedback. Recall of the original judgment again follows take-the-best, but now the first cue stops search and the recalled answer is *cake* as before, whereas the recalled confidence is 80 percent, which is incorrect and known as hindsight bias. By manipulating what participants know and don't know, one can predict for each question whether hindsight bias will or will not occur.

theory (Gigerenzer, Hoffrage, & Kleinbölting, 1991; Slegers, Brake, & Doherty, 2000) and RAFT, the first process model for the hindsight bias (Hoffrage, Hertwig, & Gigerenzer, 2000). We know from many studies that hindsight bias sometimes occursand sometimes not, but why this happens remained unexplained. The process model can predict for each participant and question whether it will or will not occur (figure 2.3). The bias itself seems to be a by-product of an adaptive memory updating process.

Ecological Rationality

What structures of environments can each of the two heuristics exploit? Consider a situation with five binary cues, as in figure 2.4 (left), where the weights correspond to the order of cues in take-the-best. In an environment where the weights (e.g., beta-weights) decrease exponentially, such as 1/2, 1/4, 1/8, and so on, no linear model, including multiple regression, can outperform the faster and more frugal take-the-best. One can see this result intuitively because the sum of all cue weights to the right of a cue can never be larger than this cue's weight—they cannot compensate for the cues with higher weights. In formal terms, assume M binary cues ordered according to their weights W_j, with $1 \leq j \leq M$. A set of cue weights is noncompensatory if for each weight:

$$W_j > \sum_{k>j} W_k \qquad (2.4)$$

I refer to this environmental structure as *noncompensatory information*, illustrated in figure 2.4 (left). Here, take-the-best makes the same inferences as a linear strategy (with the same order of cue weights). Thus, we get the following result, where the term *outperform* refers to goodness of fit (Martignon & Hoffrage, 2002):

> *In an environment with noncompensatory information, no linear strategy can outperform the faster and more frugal take-the-best heuristic.*

Now we understand one environmental structure in which relying on only one cue is rational. Noncompensatory information is a special case of large *variability* in cue weights, which also favors take-the-best relative to linear models and is discussed in Hogarth and Karelaia 2005 and 2006. Another structure in which take-the-best performs better, on average, than Dawes' rule is *scarce information* (Martignon & Hoffrage, 2002):

$$M < \log_2 N, \qquad (2.5)$$

where M and N are the number of cues and objects, respectively. An example of scarce information is a sample with eight objects but only two cues. Here, relying on one good reason and ignoring the rest leads, on average, to more accurate judgments than does tallying all reasons.

These results are for conditions under which take-the-best is as accurate as weighting and adding, but do not explain the further finding that it is often more accurate in prediction (as opposed to data fitting) than multiple regression (Czerlinski et al., 1999), neural networks, classification and regression trees, and exemplar models (Brighton, 2006; Nosofsky & Bergert, 2007; see also chap. 3). The reasons for the latter have not yet been identified. One hypothesis is that in tasks with limited predictability, it pays to ignore dependencies between cues, as take-the-best does, whereas virtually all "rational" strategies try to capture these dependencies. This hypothesis is supported by the observation that if take-the-best orders cues conditionally to other cues, its predictive accuracy decreases to the level of the "rational" strategies (Brighton & Gigerenzer, 2008; Martignon & Hoffrage, 2002).

Tallying will not do well with noncompensatory information. It can instead exploit environments where the cue weights do not differ much.

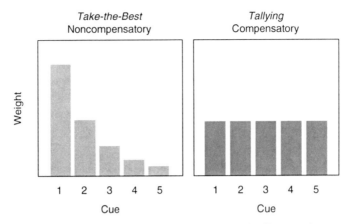

Figure 2.4: Ecological rationality of take-the-best and tallying. The environment on the left side has perfectly noncompensatory information (the weights of five binary cues decrease exponentially); the one on the right side has perfectly compensatory information (all weights are equal). Take-the-best (but not tallying) can exploit noncompensatory information, and tallying (but not take-the-best) can exploit compensatory information (Martignon & Hoffrage, 1999).

When all cues have the same weights, as the extreme case in figure 2.4 (right) shows, a tallying heuristic that tallies all cues $(m=M)$ will lead to the same accuracy as any linear model. In this environment, take-the-best does not perform as well as tallying.

How Do People Know Which Heuristic to Use?

Research suggests that people hardly ever make conscious decisions about which heuristic to use but that they quickly and unconsciously tend to adapt heuristics to changing environments, provided there is feedback. This adaptive process is illustrated by an experiment by Rieskamp and Otto (2006). Participants took on the role of bank consultants with the task of evaluating which of two companies applying for a loan was more creditworthy on the basis of six cues, such as qualification of employees and profitability (similar to the experiment by Newell, Weston, & Shanks, 2003, except that there were no costs for looking up cue values). For the first 24 pairs of companies, no feedback was provided as to the correctness of the participant's inferences. Participants followed take-the-best in only about 30 percent of the cases, which is not unusual for situations where information is free. In the following trials, feedback was given. For one group of participants, the environment was noncompensatory (see figure 2.4); that is, the more creditworthy company was determined by the cue with the highest validity (on which the two companies differed) in about 90 percent of the cases.

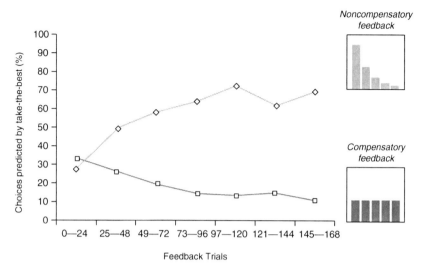

Figure 2.5: How people adapt their heuristics to the structure of environment (based on Rieskamp & Otto, 2006).

For the second group, the environment was compensatory; that is, feedback was determined by the weighted additive rule in about 90 percent of the cases. Did people intuitively adapt their heuristics to the structures of the environments? As can be seen in figure 2.5, feedback about the structure of the environment changed the frequency of using take-the-best. People learned without instruction that different heuristics are successful in different environments. Bröder (2003) reported that people with higher IQs are better at detecting the structure of the environment and consequently at knowing which heuristic to use. While individual correlates of strategy use are difficult to find, individual correlates of strategy adaptation seem to be easier to demonstrate.

This experiment illustrates individual learning of heuristics by feedback. Rieskamp and Otto's (2006) strategy-selection theory provides a computational model for how people select heuristics from the adaptive toolbox. Which heuristic to use for which problem can also be learned by evolutionary and cultural learning. For instance, the work by Dugatkin (1996) suggests the possibility that a female guppy comes already equipped with a heuristic for mate choice that resembles take-the-best. When she has to decide between two potential mates, the most important cue seems to be the extent of orange color. If one male is noticeably more orange than the other, this cue is sufficient to stop search and decide in favor of him. Evolutionary learning is slower than individual learning, while social learning is the fastest way to learn what heuristic to use and when. A novice baseball outfielder, pilot, or sailor can be taught the gaze heuristic in a few minutes.

Robustness

A good heuristic needs to be robust. *Robustness* is the ability to make predictions about the future or unknown events, whereas *fitting* refers to the ability to fit the past or already known data. An excellent fit can mean little more than *overfitting* (Mitchell, 1997), which is essentially a problem of estimation error. To define overfitting, we need to distinguish between a learning sample from which a model estimated its parameters and the test sample on which it is tested. Both samples are randomly drawn from the same population.

> *Definition:* A model *O* overfits the learning sample if there exists an alternative model *R* such that *O* has a smaller error than *R* in the learning sample but a larger error in the test sample. In this case, *R* is called the more *robust* model.

Consider figure 2.6, which shows the accuracy of three heuristics compared to multiple regression, averaged across 20 real-world problems (Czerlinski, Gigerenzer, & Goldstein, 1999). In each problem, the task was to predict which of two objects scores higher on a criterion. For instance, one problem was to predict which Chicago public high school has the higher dropout rate. The cues included the attendance rates of the students, the socioeconomic and ethnic compositions of the student bodies, the sizes of the classes, and the scores of the students on various standardized tests. Other problems involved the prediction of people's attractiveness judgments, of homelessness rates, of professors' salaries, and of adolescents' obesity at age 18. The three heuristics were take-the-best, minimalist (which is like take-the-best but searches cues in random order), and a tallying heuristic that looks up all cues ($m = M$), that is, a unit weight linear rule. Take-the-best and minimalist were most frugal; they looked up, on average, only 2.4 and 2.2 cues before they stopped search. Tallying and multiple regression looked up all cue information (exhaustive search), which amounted to an average of 7.7 cues. How accurate were the heuristics?

The important point is to distinguish between data fitting and prediction. In data fitting, the test sample is the same as the learning sample, and here it is a mathematical truism that models with more adjustable parameters generally fit better. Consequently, multiple regression had the best fit. However, the true test of a model concerns its predictive accuracy, which was tested by cross-validation; that is, the four models learned their parameters on half of the data and were tested on the other half. The predictive accuracy of take-the-best and tallying was, on average, higher than that of multiple regression. This result may sound paradoxical because multiple regression processed all the information, more than each of the heuristics did.

The intersecting lines in figure 2.6 show that multiple regression overfitted the data relative to both take-the-best and tallying. An intuitive way to understand overfitting is the following: A set of observations consists of information that generalizes to the other samples and of information that

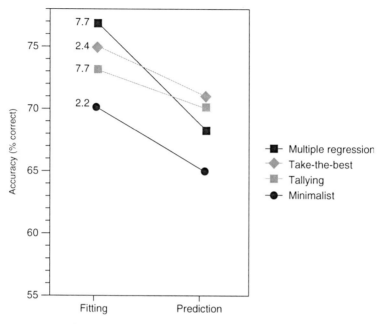

Figure 2.6: Simplicity can lead to higher predictive accuracy. The predictive power of three heuristics is compared to that of multiple regression in 20 problems. Two of the heuristics (take-the-best and minimalist) are from the one-reason decision-making family; the third (unit weight linear rule) is from the tallying family. The 20 prediction problems include psychological, economic, environmental, biological, and health problems. Most were taken from statistical textbooks, where they served as good examples for the application of multiple regression. The number of cues varied between 3 and 19, and these were binary or dichotomized at the median. For each of the 20 problems and each of the four strategies, the 95 percent confidence intervals were ≤ 0.4 percentage points. Although multiple regression has the best fit, two of the heuristics have higher predictive accuracy (Czerlinski, Gigerenzer, & Goldstein, 1999).

does not (e.g., noise). If one extracts too much information from the data, one will get a better fit (a higher *explained variance*), but one will mistake more noise for predictive information. The result can be a substantial decrease in one's predictive power. Note that both forms of simplifying—dispensing either with adding or with weighting—resulted in greater robustness. Minimalist, however, which dispensed with both weighting and adding, suffered from underfitting; that is, it extracted too little information from the data.

In general, the predictive accuracy of a model increases with its fit and decreases with its number of adjustable parameters, and the difference between fit and predictive accuracy diminishes with larger numbers of data points (Akaike, 1973; Forster & Sober, 1994). The lesson is *that in judgments under uncertainty, one has to ignore information in order to make good predictions.* The art is to ignore the right kind. Heuristics that promote simplicity by ignoring the dependencies between cues and using the best reason that allows one to make a decision have a good chance of focusing on the information that generalizes.

These results may appear counterintuitive. More information is always better; more choice is always better—so the story goes. This cultural bias makes contrary findings look like odd exceptions. Yet experts base their judgments on surprisingly few pieces of information (Shanteau, 1992), and professional handball players make better decisions when they have less time (Johnson & Raab, 2003). People can form reliable impressions of strangers from video clips lasting half a minute (Ambady & Rosenthal, 1993), shoppers buy more when there are fewer varieties (Iyengar & Lepper, 2000, but see Scheibehenne, 2008), and zero-intelligence traders make as much profit as intelligent people in experimental markets (Gode & Sunder, 1993). Last but not least, satisficers are reported to be more optimistic and have higher self-esteem and life satisfaction, whereas maximizers excel in depression, perfectionism, regret, and self-blame (Schwartz et al., 2002). Less can be more.

Design

A man is rushed to the hospital with serious chest pains. The doctors suspect acute ischemic heart disease (myocardial infarction) and need to make a decision, and they need to make it quickly: Should the patient be assigned to the coronary care unit or to a regular nursing bed with ECG telemetry? In a Michigan hospital, doctors sent 90 percent of their patients with severe chest pain to the coronary care unit. This "defensive" decision making led to overcrowding, decreased the quality of care provided, and became a health risk for patients who should not have been in the unit. Using an expert system with some 50 probabilities and a logistic regression, the physicians made better decisions than without it, but physicians dislike such systems because they are not transparent; that is, they don't understand them. How to design an efficient diagnostic instrument that physicians actually use? My answer is to base such a procedure on what we know about the structure of heuristics in the adaptive toolbox—such as search, stopping, and decision rules—and then flesh out the particulars with the empirical evidence available, in this case, with respect to heart disease. Following this approach, researchers at the University of Michigan Hospital (Green & Mehr, 1997) used the building blocks of take-the-best to design a classification heuristic in the form of a *fast and frugal tree* (figure 2.7, left). If a patient has a certain anomaly in his electrocardiogram (the so-called ST segment), he or she is immediately admitted to the coronary care unit. No other information is required. If that is not the case, a second variable is considered: whether the patient's primary complaint is chest pain. If this is not the case, the patient

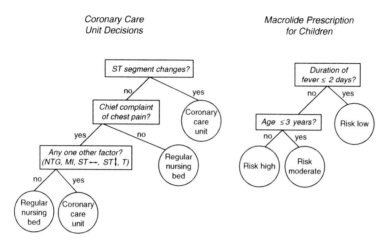

Figure 2.7: Fast and frugal trees for coronary care unit allocation (left; based on Green & Mehr, 1997) and macrolide prescription for children (right; based on Fischer et al. 2002). The first assists emergency unit physicians in deciding whether a patient with severe chest pain should be sent to the coronary care unit or to a regular nursing bed; the second assists pediatricians in diagnosing whether children are infected with Mycoplasma pneumoniae and should be treated with first-line antibiotic treatments (macrolides).

is immediately classified as low risk and assigned to a regular nursing bed. No further information is considered. If the answer is yes, then a final, composite question is asked to classify the patient.

Green and Mehr (1997) report that the fast and frugal tree was more accurate (as measured by the occurrence of myocardial infarction) than physicians' decisions. It had a higher sensitivity and a smaller false positive rate. The heuristic was also more accurate than a logistic regression that had all and more of the information contained in the fast and frugal tree. Note that the regression may have had an excellent fit in the clinical population in the East Coast where it was originally validated, but it was then applied in a Michigan hospital with a patient population that differed to an unknown extent. That is, unlike the situation in figure 2.6, where the training and test samples were drawn from the same population, robustness here refers to out-of population rather than out-of-sample prediction.

A fast and frugal tree is defined as a classification tree that allows for a classification at each level of the tree. It has $M + 1$ exits or end nodes (M is the number of variables or cues). It allows for a quick decision at each node of the tree (Martignon et al., 2003). In contrast, the number 2^M of end nodes of a complete tree increases exponentially, which makes complete trees computationally intractable for large numbers of variables. A fast and frugal tree has the same building blocks as take-the-best: ordered search, one-reason stopping rule, and one-reason decision making. It also orders the cues in the same frugal way, by ignoring dependencies between cues, which can enhance the robustness of the heuristic.

Fischer et al. (2002) designed a fast and frugal tree for macrolide prescription in children with community-acquired pneumonia (figure 2.7, right). These heuristics offer diagnostic procedures that can be applied rapidly and with limited information. Last but not least, they are transparent. Physicians are more willing to accept and actually use them than a logistic regression because heuristic tools correspond to their own intuitions and are easy to understand. Years after it was introduced, the fast and frugal tree for coronary care unit allocation is still used readily by physicians at the Michigan hospital. As Elwyn et al. wrote in the *Lancet* (2001: 574), "the next frontier will involve fast and frugal heuristics; rules for patients and clinicians alike." Systematic teaching of fast and frugal decision making is currently being introduced into medicine as an alternative to classical decision theory as well as an explication of the superb intuitions of master clinicians (Naylor, 2001).

Apart from designing strategies, one can also design human environments. Consider number representation. The Arabic number system proved superior to earlier systems in simplifying division. Unlike Roman numerals, it allows us to determine which of two numbers is larger in the same way as the take-the-best heuristic. Consider:

2,543,001

2,498,999.

Comparing the digits from left to right and stopping after the first two are different (5 > 4) supplies the answer. Traffic rules governing right-of-way and the FIFA soccer world championship rules are designed in the same lexicographic way. Relying on one good reason and making no trade-offs can promote safety and perceived fairness in human interaction. Recall the complaints over the American Bowl Championship Series formula that ranks college football teams by complex weighting and adding. External representations of risk that the mind can easily digest have improved risk communication in medicine, law, and AIDS counseling, and they are indispensable for informed consent and shared decision making (see chaps. 1 and 9). Applications in legal decision making are discussed by Gigerenzer and Engel (2006) and in marketing by Yee et al. (2007).

The Adaptive Toolbox

The study of heuristics is concerned with identifying (i) the building blocks of heuristics; (ii) the structures of environments that a given heuristic can exploit, that is, the kind of problems it can solve; and (iii) the design of heuristics and environments for specific applications. In other words, its first object is the study of the adaptive toolbox, and the second is that of ecological rationality. The study of the adaptive toolbox aims at description, including individual differences in the use of heuristics, and the change in the adaptive toolbox over the life course (Gigerenzer, 2003). Models of heuristics allow for qualitative predictions, such as whether players will catch a ball while running or the conditions in which hindsight bias will and will not occur. They also allow for quantitative predictions, such as the size of the less-is-more effect when using the recognition heuristic. Consistent with Bayesian model testing (MacKay, 1995), the strongest tests can be obtained from (i) counterintuitive predictions, such as the less-is-more effect in individual and group decision making, and (ii) models with zero adjustable parameters, such as the search, stopping, and decision rules of take-the-best.

The study of ecological rationality, in contrast, is descriptive and prescriptive. Its results concerning the match between heuristics and structures of environments can be used to derive hypotheses about people's adaptive use of heuristics. These results also carry prescriptive force. For instance, when the variability of cue weights is large, we can recommend a fast and frugal tree for classification, or take-the-best for paired comparison, because these heuristics will likely predict as well as more complex models, yet faster, more frugally, and more transparently. Most problems that worry our minds and hearts are computationally intractable—no machine or mind can find the optimal solution. The systematic study of fast and frugal heuristics can provide recommendations on an empirical basis, even when we can never know the best solution.

Chapter 3

Rules of Thumb in Animals and Humans

Simple heuristics correspond roughly to what behavioral biologists call rules of thumb. Our aim in this chapter is to relate research conducted by the Center for Adaptive Behavior and Cognition (ABC) to biological research on behavior. We seek to identify where behavioral biologists and ABC have used similar approaches or arrived at similar results but also to clarify exactly where the two schools disagree or diverge on tactics.

Examples of Fast and Frugal Heuristics in Humans

Take-the-Best

Consider the task of which of two alternatives to choose given several binary cues on some unobservable criterion. An example is predicting which of two mammals has the longer life span, given such cues as their brain weight, gestation time, and body weight. Gigerenzer and Goldstein (1996) proposed the take-the-best heuristic, described in the previous chapter. Its procedure is called lexicographic because it resembles the obvious way of setting two words in alphabetical order, by comparing the first letters and only considering the next letter if the first are identical. A hypothetical biological example might be a male bird that initially compares itself with a rival on the basis of their songs. If the songs differ in quality, the weaker rival leaves; only otherwise do both remain to compare one another on further successive cues, such as plumage or display. In general, the order of cues might have been individually estimated from a sample or learned by instruction or have evolved by natural selection.

This chapter is a revised version of J. M. C. Hutchinson and G. Gigerenzer, "Simple Heuristics and Rules of Thumb: Where Psychologists and Behavioural Biologists Might Meet," *Behavioral Processes* 69 (2005): 97–124. See also the comments to the original article and the authors' response in the same issue, pp. 125–163.

The predictive accuracy of take-the-best can be surprising, not only in comparison to multiple regression, as noted in the previous chapter. Figure 3.1 shows that the simple heuristic can outperform some of the most sophisticated statistical methods that have been proposed as models of cognitive processes, including neural networks, exemplar models, and decision trees (Brighton, 2006). Thus, a mind equipped with simple heuristics might have an advantage over one equipped with fancy, computationally expensive algorithms.

Take-the-best is fast and frugal in the information used, since usually not all cues are examined. It is simple in that it involves only comparisons of binary values rather than the additions and multiplications involved in the standard statistical solutions to the task. This degree of frugality and simplicity applies to the execution of the procedure. If the prior ranking of cues by validities has to be individually learned, counting is required, as is prior experience of the task with feedback. Nevertheless, it is still relatively much simpler to gauge the rank order of validities than the cue weights in a multiple regression equation, partly because validities ignore the correlations between cues. In natural biological examples, a good ordering of cues could have been achieved by natural selection or by individual learning through trial and error. Simulations show that performance remains high if the ordering of cues only roughly matches validity (Martignon & Hoffrage, 2002), or if the ordering is generated by a simple learning algorithm, itself a simple heuristic (Dieckmann & Todd, 2004).

The comparative analysis of the ecological rationality of take-the-best and tallying in the previous chapter makes clear that statements of the kind "This heuristic is good" are ill-conceived or at least incomplete. A heuristic is neither good nor bad per se; rather, some are better than others in specified environments (e.g., compensatory or noncompensatory) on specified criteria (e.g., predictive accuracy or frugality). It follows that although ABC has an overall vision that simple heuristics are the solution that the brain uses for many tasks, we envisage that the heuristics used for different tasks will vary and not be special cases of one universal calculus. This suggests a somewhat piecemeal research program, which need not be a weakness: The same piecemeal approach has certainly not held behavioral ecology back (Krebs et al., 1983). Incidentally, ABC also puts no general restrictions on the extent to which heuristics are innate or learned or applied consciously or unconsciously. Nor has our research so far focused on categorizing specific instances of heuristic use along these dimensions. We expect that in different circumstances the same heuristic might fall into more than one category.

A Fast and Frugal Tree in Action

A different decision task is to classify an object into one of two or more classes, as in legal and medical decisions. One of the initial decisions a legal system makes is whether to release a defendant on bail unconditionally or

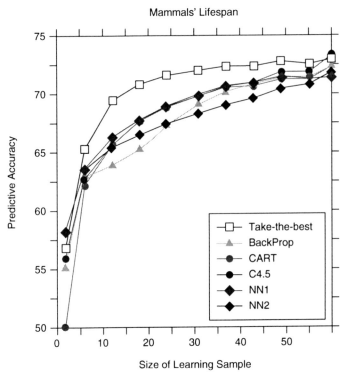

Figure 3.1: Which mammal lives longer? The task is to predict which of the two mammals has a higher life span, based on nine cues, such as brain weight, body weight, sleeping time, gestation time, and predation and danger indices. The x-axis shows the sample size (the number of mammals) on which each prediction algorithm is trained. The predictive accuracy is the model's performance in the test sample, that is, the mammals not included in the learning sample. Each point is averaged over 1,000 random selections of the learning set (subset). The complex strategies include: a three-layer feed-forward neural network trained using the back-propagation algorithm (BackProp), two decision trees designed to generalize well to new samples, CART (classification and regression tree: Breiman et al., 1984) and C4.5 (Quinlan, 1993), and two exemplar models, the basic nearest neighbor classifier (NN1) and a more elaborate model (NN2) based on the GCM model (Nosofsky, 1990). Note that the simple heuristic consistently leads to better predictions than each of these complex models, even though (or better: because) it ignores conditional dependencies between cues and relies on only one good reason to make the inference. Based on Brighton (2006).

punish him or her with curfew or imprisonment. In the English system, lay judges (magistrates) make some 2 million of these decisions every year. Figure 3.2 shows a model of a heuristic that predicts a very high proportion of the decision outcomes made by London magistrates whether to grant unconditional bail or to make a punitive decision, such as custody (Dhami, 2003). The heuristic is called a *fast and frugal tree*, and it has M + 1 exits (where M is the number of binary cues, in the present case: three), whereas a full decision tree has 2^M exits (chap. 2; Martignon et al., 2003). Just like take-the-best, this heuristic searches cues one at a time, can stop search after any cue, and the outcome depends on that cue alone. The tree in figure 3.2 is based on observations of court outcomes, whereas when magistrates were asked how they made their decisions, they reported a totally different process consistent with the official Bail Act, which specifies that they should consider many other cues, such as the severity of the crime and whether the defendant has a home. The simpler heuristic is likely used unconsciously.

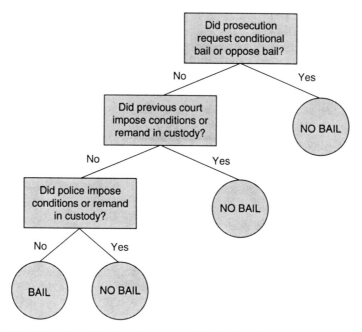

Figure 3.2: Should a defendant be granted bail? This fast and frugal decision tree is based on the bail decision outcomes of London magistrates (based on Dhami, 2003). Note that it does not include any characteristics of the defendant but "passes the buck" to the prosecution, a previous court, and the police. The tree shown here fitted 96 percent and predicted in cross-validation 92 percent of decisions correctly, better than a unit weight linear model that used 25 cues and achieved only 85 percent predictive accuracy.

Clever Cues

Some very simple heuristics perform well not because of the method of combining cues, but because they utilize a single "clever" cue. Loosely speaking, the heuristic lets the environment do much of the work. One example is the recognition heuristic, which relies on mere name, face, or voice recognition; another is the gaze heuristic and its relatives (chap. 2). Note that players are typically unaware of using this sort of heuristic even though it accurately accounts for their behavior. Biologist readers will probably already be asking whether other animals might also use similar heuristics: Indeed, maintenance of a constant optical angle between pursuer and target has been found in a variety of animals besides humans, including bats, birds, fish, and insects (Shaffer et al., 2004). Surely it is not the only heuristic that we share with animals.

Formal models of heuristics like take-the-best and fast and frugal trees have their roots in the work of Herbert Simon on satisficing and bounded rationality, but also in early models of heuristics for preferences, such as Tversky's (1972) elimination-by-aspects and work on the adaptive decision maker by Payne, Bettman, and Johnson (1993). Yet much recent work has abstained from formalizing heuristics or considering the conditions when they work well (Kahneman & Tversky, 1996). ABC's work also differs from those parts of cognitive psychology that are typically strong in modeling yet rely on versions of expected utility (no search or stopping rules; e.g., prospect theory: Kahneman & Tversky, 1979) or on Wald's (1947) sequential analysis (which has stopping rules, but relies on optimization). Whereas ABC's research explores the benefits of simplicity, other schools of psychology try to explain complex behavior by building equally complex cognitive models.

Some Simple Rules of Thumb from Biology

We now consider examples of rules of thumb from biology; there are many more that we could have chosen. Our aim in this section is to give a broad flavor of this area of biological research, and so we deliberately leave most comparisons with ABC's approach until later. The diversity of the biological examples and the lack of theoretical connections between many of them are parts of the picture we wish to convey.

A recently described example is the method by which the ant *Leptothorax albipennis* estimates the size of a candidate nest cavity (Mallon & Franks, 2000; Mugford, Mallon, & Franks, 2001). Natural nest sites are narrow cracks in rocks, typically irregular in shape. The ants' solution is first to explore the cavity for a fixed period on an irregular path that covers the area fairly evenly. While doing this an ant lays down an individually distinct pheromone trail. It then leaves. When it returns it again moves around but on a different irregular path. The frequency of encountering its old trail is used to judge size. This "Buffon's needle algorithm" is remarkably accurate: Nests half the area of others yielded reencounter frequencies 1.96 times greater.

Another example concerns how the wasp *Polistes dominulus* constructs its nest (Karsai & Pénzes, 2000). The nest is a tessellation of hexagonal cells that grows as each new cell is added. Up to the 15-cell stage only 18 arrangements of cells have been observed. These arrangements are all compact, which ensures that less new material is required and that the structure is strong. However, these optimality criteria are inadequate explanations of why just these 18 arrangements: Economy of material predicts 155 optimal arrangements, whereas not all the observed structures maximize compactness. A better explanation is a construction rule in which the wasp places each cell at the site where the sum of the ages of the existing walls is greatest. Age of wall might plausibly be judged by the concentration of pheromone added at the time of construction or the state of the larvae inside. This rule explains all observed arrangements, with one exception that plausibly follows from a small mistake in execution of the rule. Further unexpected forms appear as the nest grows beyond 15 cells, but then it is plausible that the wasp does not visit all potential building sites or that small differences in wall age get harder to judge as the structure gets older.

Social insects provide the richest source of rule of thumb examples (e.g., Müller & Wehner, 1988; Seeley, 1995; Camazine et al., 2001; Detrain & Deneubourg, 2002; Sato, Saito, & Sakagami, 2003). Some of these examples concern mechanisms that ensure that individual behavior is well integrated when perhaps there is some particular advantage of each individual rigorously following simple rules. But other examples do not concern coordination. Perhaps it is just that social insects are small animals with small nervous systems. This might matter because they really can only follow simpler rules than those followed by higher animals, but it could be merely that biologists are readier to view them as robotically following simple rules than larger animals that more closely resemble humans.

The two other areas of behavioral biology that make most frequent reference to rules of thumb are mate choice and patch-leaving. A paper by Janetos (1980) seems responsible for a tradition in behavioral ecology of modeling mate choice as a process of sequential assessment of candidate males. The two most discussed rules are for a female to accept the first male above a preset threshold ("satisficing") or for a female to view a preset number of N males and then return to the best ("best-of-N" rule). Janetos argued that animals follow simple rules that can achieve good but not optimal performance (Janetos & Cole, 1981). Other behavioral ecologists agreed that information constraints would restrict what sort of rule could be used but preferred to hypothesize that a rule's parameters were optimized for the environment (Real, 1990). However, neither of these two rules explains adequately the patterns of return typically observed nor effects of the quality of previously encountered males on acceptance decisions, so different heuristics or somewhat more complex rules may be necessary (Luttbeg, 1996; Wiegmann et al., 1996; Hutchinson & Halupka, 2004).

Patch-leaving rules represent more of a success for modeling. The idea is that food items occur in patches and that they are depleted by the forager, which should thus at some stage move to another patch. The question is when. The number of food items remaining is unknown to the forager, but it is indicated by the rate at which it finds items. An elegant optimality model derives how the rule of thumb should depend on the environment (Iwasa, Higashi, & Yamamura, 1981). In an environment in which all patches are of similar quality, finding a food item should decrease the tendency to stay because the patch has been depleted. In an environment in which some patches are very poor and some very good, finding a food item should increase the tendency to stay, because the success suggests that it is a better patch. Later, it was realized that if an independent cue was available indicating initial patch quality, even in the second type of environment the decremental decision rule can be better (Driessen & Bernstein, 1999). This fits empirical research on the parasitoid wasp *Venturia canescens,* which lays its eggs in caterpillars: The concentration of host scent sets the tendency to stay, this decreases through some sort of habituation response, but the effect of finding a host further decreases the tendency to stay (Driessen & Bernstein, 1999). Between similar parasitoid species there is much variation in whether finding a host increases or decreases the tendency to stay, but we do not yet know enough about the environmental structure in most of these examples to judge whether the theory explains these differences (van Alphen, Bernstein, & Driessen, 2003; Wajnberg et al., 2003).

Models of patch-leaving decision rules show a historical progression from unbounded rationality assuming omniscience toward more realistic assumptions of what information is available. At the omniscient end is the Marginal Value Theorem (Charnov, 1976) specifying that the optimal switching point is when the instantaneous rate of the reward falls to the mean rate in the environment under the optimal policy. But how should the animal know this mean rate without knowing the optimal policy already? McNamara and Houston (1985) proposed a simple iterative algorithm by which this might be learned while foraging efficiently. Another problem is that when prey are discrete items turning up stochastically, the underlying rate (= probability) of reward is not directly observable. The optimality models of Iwasa, Higashi, and Yamamura (1981) and others are one response to this situation, but another is the simpler rule, not derived from an optimality model, of giving up after a constant time without finding an item. If the giving-up time parameter is appropriate, the performance may come close to that of the optimum rule (Green, 1984). In the real world, in which environmental parameters are uncertain, it could be that the giving-up time rule works better than the optimum computed for a simple model of the environment. A more recent example concerns when a bee should leave one inflorescence for another; the problem is that bumblebees increasingly revisit flowers they have just emptied because they can only remember the last few visited. Goulson (2000) proposed that a good solution that agreed with bumblebees' observed behavior is to leave after two empty flowers are found.

The Attractions of Simplicity

The heuristics studied by ABC are simple in comparison with standard statistical procedures applied to the same task. Proposals by other psychologists as to how our minds tackle these tasks typically also involve more complex processes, such as Bayesian probability updating. Part of the reason why heuristics can be simple is that they can utilize evolved or highly trained abilities, such as recognition memory, that may involve complex data processing.

It is not just Occam's Razor that has made ABC favor simple models. But we will start off by mentioning the weakest reason. With simple heuristics we can be more confident that our brains are capable of performing the necessary calculations. The weakness of this argument is that it is hard to judge what complexity of calculation or memory a brain might achieve. At the lower levels of processing, some human capabilities apparently involve calculations that seem surprisingly difficult (e.g., Bayesian estimation in a sensorimotor context: Körding & Wolpert, 2004). So if we can perform these calculations at that level in the hierarchy (abilities), why should we not be able to evolve similar complex strategies to replace simple heuristics?

One answer is that simple heuristics often need access to less information (i.e., they are frugal) and can thus make a decision faster, at least if information search is external. Another answer—and a more important argument for simple heuristics—is the high accuracy that they exhibit in our simulations (e.g., see figure 3.1). This accuracy may be because of, not just in spite of, their simplicity. In particular, because they have few parameters they avoid overfitting data in a learning sample and, consequently, generalize better across other samples. The extra parameters of more complex models often fit the noise rather than the signal. Of course we are not saying that all simple heuristics are good; only some simple heuristics will perform well in any given environment.

It is tempting to propose that since other animals have simpler brains than humans they are more likely to use simple heuristics. But a contrary argument is that humans are much more generalist than most animals and that animals may be able to devote more cognitive resources to tasks of particular importance. For instance, the memory capabilities of small food-storing birds seem astounding by the standards of how we expect ourselves to perform at the same task (Balda & Kamil, 1992). Some better-examined biological examples suggest unexpected complexity. For instance, pigeons seem able to use a surprising diversity of methods to navigate, especially considering that they are not long-distance migrants (Wiltschko & Wiltschko, 2003; but cf. Wallraff, 2001). The greater specialism of other animals may also mean that the environments they deal with are more predictable and thus that the robustness of simple heuristics may no longer be such an advantage (cf. the argument of Arkes & Ayton, 1999, that animals in their natural environments do not commit various fallacies because they do not need to generalize their rules of thumb to novel circumstances).

A separate concern is that for morphological traits there are plenty of examples of evolution getting stuck on a local adaptive peak and not finding its way to the neatest solution. The classic example is the giraffe's recurrent laryngeal nerve, which travels down and then back up the neck, because in all mammals it loops round the aorta. Nobody knows how common such a situation might be with cognitive traits. It could be that humans' ability to learn through experience makes them more readily able to adopt simple heuristics than other animals that are more rigidly programmed and where natural selection alone is responsible for the adaptation.

By "adaptation" biologists imply not only that a trait fits the environment, but also that it has been shaped by the environment for that task. Therefore, claims of adaptation of heuristics are vulnerable to the arguments of the biologists Gould and Lewontin (1979), who were concerned about many claims of adaptation in biology being mere "just-so stories." Unfortunately, human psychologists are not able to utilize many of the lines of evidence that biologists apply to justify that a trait is adaptive. We can make only informed guesses about the environment in which the novel features of human brains evolved, and because most of us grow up in an environment very different to this, the cognitive traits we exhibit might not even have been expressed when our brains were evolving.

It thus would be a weak argument (which ABC avoids) to find a heuristic that humans use, then search for some environment in which that heuristic works well, and then claim on this basis alone that the heuristic is an adaptation to that environment. The heuristic may work well in that environment, but that need not be the reason why it evolved or even why it has survived. For instance, Schooler and Hertwig (2005) have constructed a model demonstrating that for the recognition heuristic it can be beneficial that we forget out-of-date information at a certain rate; but memory is used for a diversity of other purposes, so they rightly avoid claiming that this model explains the length of our memories. To claim adaptation, it is at least necessary to check that the heuristic is generally used only in environments in which it works well and better than other heuristics that we use in other contexts.

ABC avoids the difficult issue of demonstrating adaptation in humans by defining ecological rationality as the performance, in terms of a given currency, of a given heuristic in a given environment. We emphasize that currency and environment have to be specified before the ecological rationality of a heuristic can be determined; thus, take-the-best is more ecologically rational (both more accurate and frugal) than tallying in noncompensatory environments but not more accurate in compensatory ones (see figure 2.4). Unlike claiming that a heuristic is an adaptation, a claim that it is ecologically rational deliberately omits any implication that this is why the trait originally evolved, or has current value to the organism, or that either heuristic or environment occurs for real in the present or past. Ecological rationality might then be useful as a term indicating a more attainable intermediate step on the path to a demonstration of adaptation. There is nevertheless a risk that a demonstration of ecological rationality of a given heuristic in a given environment will mislead someone who uses this evidence alone to infer adaptation. Think of the Victorian habit of noting the most fanciful resemblance of an animal to a part of its environment as an adaptation. This reached its apogee in such ridiculous illustrations as pink flamingos camouflaged against pink sunsets (Gould, 1992, chap. 14; sexual selection is the real explanation for most bright plumage).

Why Not Use Optimality Modeling?

Optimality modeling is used in behavioral ecology mostly as a test of whether a particular adaptive argument explains a particular phenomenon. The model is constructed to include the components of the explanation (maximized currencies, constraints, trade-offs, etc.) and often a deliberate minimum of anything else. The next stage is to calculate the optimal behavior given these assumptions. If these predictions match empirical data, one can claim to have a coherent explanation for why that behavior occurs. Sometimes the match occurs only over a restricted range of a model parameter, in which case measuring or varying the corresponding characteristic in the real world offers a further empirical test. In the absence of a match, a new or modified explanation must be sought.

ABC's concern with adaptation to the environment might seem to ally it with optimality modeling. Much of our research has involved finding what decision rules work *well* in a model environment; optimality modeling involves finding what decision rules work *best* in a model environment. In both instances good performance is the basis of predictions, or even expectations, about the rules actually used. Optimality modeling has the attractions that there is no arbitrariness in deciding whether a heuristic works well enough and no uncertainty whether there might be another better heuristic that one had not thought of. Moreover, it has proved its practical utility in dominating the successful fields of behavioral ecology and biomechanics, making testable predictions that have not only stimulated empirical research but also strikingly often been well supported by the data. So why does ABC not take this road?

Typically one prediction of an optimality model is the policy, which describes what behavior is performed given any specified value of an individual's external environment and internal state. Although the policy can itself be viewed as a decision rule, it is the mechanisms generating policies that interest ABC and other psychologists. Behavioral ecologists do believe that animals are using simple rules of thumb that achieve only an approximation of the optimal policy, but most often rules of thumb are not their interest. Nevertheless, it could be that the limitations of such rules of thumb would often constrain behavior enough to interfere with the fit with predictions. The optimality modeler's gambit is that evolved rules of thumb can mimic optimal behavior well enough not to disrupt the fit by much, so that they can be left as a black box. It turns out that the power of natural selection is such that the gambit usually works to the level of accuracy that satisfies behavioral ecologists. Given that their models are often deliberately schematic, behavioral ecologists are usually satisfied that they understand the selective value of a behavior if they successfully predict merely the rough qualitative form of the policy or of the resultant patterns of behavior.

But ABC's focus on process means that it is concerned with a much more detailed prediction of behavior. A good model of the process can lead to predictions of behavior that differ from standard optimization models or for which optimization models are mute. For instance, the ball-catching heuristic described in chapter 2 predicts that the player catches the ball while running, the precise running speeds, and when players will run in a slight arc. All these predictions concern observable behaviors. The example of *Polistes* nest construction also showed how much more specific process models can be. Thus, we would encourage optimality modelers to consider decision processes to be interesting topics that their technique might address.

However, there remains a more fundamental reason for ABC's objection to the routine use of the optimality approach. There are a number of situations where the optimal solution to a real-world problem cannot be determined. One problem is computational intractability, such as the notorious traveling salesman problem (Lawler et al., 1985). Another problem is if there are multiple criteria to optimize and we do not know the appropriate way to convert them into a common currency (such as fitness). Thirdly, in many real-world problems it is impossible to put probabilities on the various possible outcomes or even to recognize what all those outcomes might be. Think about optimizing the choice of a partner who will bear you many children; it is uncertain what partners are available, whether each one would be faithful, how long each will live, etc. This is true about many animal decisions too, of course, and biologists do not imagine their animals even attempting such optimality calculations.

Instead the behavioral ecologist's solution is to find optima in deliberately simplified model environments. We note that this introduces much scope for misunderstanding, inconsistency, and loose thinking over whether "optimal policy" refers to a claim of optimality in the real world or just in a model. Calculating the optima even in the simplified model environments may still be beyond the capabilities of an animal, but the hope is that the optimal policy that emerges from the calculations may be generated instead, to a lesser level of accuracy, by a rule that is simple enough for an animal to follow. The animal might be hardwired with such a rule following its evolution through natural selection, or the animal might learn it through trial and error. There remains an interesting logical gap in the procedure: There is no guarantee that optimal solutions to simplified model environments will be good solutions to the original complex environments. The biologist might reply that often this does turn out to be the case; otherwise natural selection would not have allowed the good fit between the predictions and observations. Success with this approach undoubtedly depends on the modeler's skill in simplifying the environment in a way that fairly represents the information available to the animal. The unsatisfying uncertainty of how to simplify is often not appreciated. Bookstaber and Langsam (1985) argue that by choosing simple models with many of the uncertainties ignored, we introduce a bias in the optimal behavior predicted, favoring complex rules over coarser ones.

The same criticism about simplification of real environments can also be made of any simulation of a heuristic in a model environment, so much of ABC's research is as vulnerable to the argument as optimality modeling. ABC has tried to avoid the criticism by using data from a variety of real-world environments. This technique is rare in biology (but see Nakata, Ushimaru, and Watanabe's [2003] testing of web-relocation rules in spiders).

Environment Structure

It should already be clear that we have an interest in identifying what statistical properties of the environment allow particular heuristics to perform well. Their identification enables us to predict in which environments a heuristic is used. We might then go on to ask whether such statistical properties are easy to recognize and, hence, how a heuristic for selecting appropriate heuristics might work.

Three pertinent aspects of environment structure that take-the-best can exploit are (i) noncompensatory information (figure 2.4) or large variability of cue weights as the general case; (ii) scarce information; and (iii) redundancy, that is, moderate to high positive correlation between cues (Hogarth & Karelaia, 2005, 2006; chap. 2). If cues show many negative correlations with each other, a weighted linear model tends to perform better (Johnson, Meyer, & Ghose, 1989; Shanteau & Thomas, 2000). This is a different environment structure from the mammals' life spans (figure 3.1) and also perhaps from male traits used by females for mate choice, where quality variation might be expected to generate a positive correlation between all traits (which is observed in some examples, although others show no correlation: Candolin, 2003). Other aspects of environment structure that ABC has analyzed include the mean validity of the cues, the predictability of the criterion, and the skewness of frequency distributions (Hertwig, Hoffrage, & Martignon 1999; Martignon & Hoffrage, 2002).

Behavioral ecology has also considered what aspects of the environment favor different rules of thumb but often by using analytic techniques in combination with the optimality approach. We have already mentioned Iwasa, Higashi, and Yamamura's (1981) derivation of optimal patch-leaving rules, showing that how evenly prey are spread among patches determines whether a prey capture should make the predator more or less likely to move. Another example is McNamara and Houston's (1987) derivation of how the forgetting rate of a simple linear-operator memory rule should depend on the rate at which the environment changes.

Autocorrelation in food supply may be an important aspect of environment structure for animals. One would predict that nectar feeders would avoid returning to a flower immediately after exploiting it but return once it has had time to refill. Whereas bird species feeding on aggregated cryptic invertebrates remain in a good spot (win-stay), nectar-feeding birds indeed tend to "win-shift" in the short term (Burke & Fulham, 2003). Even naive captive-reared honeyeaters *Xanthomyza phrygia* more easily learned to win-shift than win-stay with short delays between feeding sessions but vice versa with long delays (Burke & Fulham, 2003). An easy rule to ensure returning at regular intervals to a resource is to follow the same route repeatedly; such trap-lining behavior is shown by nectar-feeding birds and insects as well as birds feeding on flotsam along stream edges (e.g., Davies & Houston, 1981; Thomson, 1996). Spatial, rather than temporal, autocorrelation may be the important statistical structure determining movement rules for species feeding on nonrenewing hidden food (e.g., Benhamou, 1992; Fortin, 2003).

How Biologists Study Rules of Thumb

Many behavioral ecologists are interested mostly in the ultimate function of behavior. To them rules of thumb may mostly seem important in providing a possible excuse if their optimality models fit only approximately. Then there are rare behavioral biologists who, very much like ABC, do have an interest in the adaptation of rules of thumb. They may use similar simulation techniques to compare the performance of different rules of thumb. For instance, Houston, Kacelnik, and McNamara (1982) considered how a forager should decide between two resources providing food items stochastically, each with an unknown reward rate (a "two-armed bandit"). Candidate rules of thumb included "Win-stay, Lose-shift," probability matching, and sampling each resource equally until one had yielded d more successes than the other. Which was the best rule depended on the environment, although the first two examples were generally the worst.

The simulation approach has the limitation that there is no guarantee that there are not simpler or better rules. One test is to give a real animal exactly the same task as the simulated agents and compare performance: Thus, Baum and Grant (2001) found that real hummingbirds did better in two of their three model environments than did any of the simulated simple rules of movement. Another check on the biological relevance of postulated rules of thumb is to compare behavior of the simulated agents with that of real animals. Some papers use the same simulation model to predict both behavior and performance (e.g., Wajnberg, Fauvergue, & Pons, 2000). In this example, the parameters of the patch-leaving rule were first estimated from experimental data but then were varied to examine which mattered for performance.

However, most biological research on rules of thumb has not involved computing but an experimental, bottom-up approach that starts by observing the animals and that usually is not driven by anything but the most intuitive theoretical expectations of what rules would work well. With this approach, rules of thumb are not the testable hypotheses with which one starts an investigation, but rather they emerge at the end of the process as broad summary descriptions of the more detailed patterns already discovered. The adaptive advantages of the observed mechanism over others may only appear as speculation in the discussion.

Some of the most elegant examples of this bottom-up approach come from the classic work of Tinbergen (1958), although for him ultimate function was certainly not always a peripheral issue. For instance, he was interested in how a digger wasp *Philanthus triagulum* finds its way back to its burrow. By building a circle of fir cones around the burrow and then moving them while the wasp was away, he showed that wasps use such objects as landmarks. He went on to examine what sorts of objects are used as landmarks, at what point they are learned, and how close landmarks interact with more distant ones. He also became interested in how the wasps found their prey. Using a variety of carefully presented models hanging from a thread he showed that what first alerted the wasps was the appearance of a smallish and moving object; they then approached closely downwind to check its scent, jumped on it, and then could use tactile or taste cues to further check its suitability. Although the right scent was necessary as a second stage, and although they could retrieve lost prey items by scent alone, without the initial movement stimulus a correctly smelling dead bee attracted no interest. Tinbergen was also surprised that, although homing wasps showed great sophistication in recognizing landmarks visually, hunting wasps were easily fooled into smelling a moving object that was visually very unlike their bee prey.

Some of this type of behavioral research has developed beyond the behavior to examine the neurological processes responsible. This can sometimes be uniquely illuminating with regards to rules of thumb. For instance, Römer and Krusch (2000) have discovered a simple negative feedback loop in the ear of a bushcricket, which adjusts the sensitivity of the ear according to the loudness of the signal. The consequence is that the female's brain is totally unaware of all but the loudest male cricket in the vicinity (or possibly two, if a different male is loudest in each ear). The consequence behaviorally is a rule of thumb for mate choice of simply heading toward the male that appears loudest (usually the closest). Whether this is adaptive has not been considered. Unfortunately, results at this almost physiological level of analysis are still largely restricted to perception, learning, and memory (e.g., Menzel, Greggers, & Hammer, 1993; Shettleworth, 1998; Menzel & Giurfa, 2001), not yet revealing much about cue integration or decision making.

In summary, although some biologists study rules of thumb in the same way that ABC studies heuristics, most of the results derive from experiments that have not been driven by theory. Such work often throws up surprises in the particulars, which one hopes theory can explain. In contrast, ABC aims at deducing surprising results from theories (such as less-is-more effects;

see chap. 2; Schooler & Hertwig, 2005) to provide some of the empirical surprises that its theories explain.

How Animals Combine Information from Multiple Cues

Much of ABC's research has been on the processing of multiple cues, so a disappointment about the biological research is that most papers examine a single cue. Often all other cues are held constant. When the interactions between cues have been investigated, and lots of such studies exist, most often the results are not related to those of other such studies. A few recent papers have reviewed how females integrate cues to male quality (Jennions & Petrie, 1997; Candolin, 2003; Fawcett, 2003: chap. 3), but results from many other domains of decision making could be connected (e.g., Partan & Marler, 1999). This is certainly somewhere that ABC can contribute to behavioral biology, by providing testable theory of what statistical structures of cues favor what methods of cue integration.

This is not the place for a thorough review of the empirical results, but a general conclusion is the diversity of methods used to combine cues. For instance, Shettleworth (1998: chap. 7) reviews how animals combine cues used in navigation (local and distant landmarks, path integration, sun compass, etc.). Experiments indicate clear cases both of a sequential application of cues and of averaging the locations pointed to by conflicting cues. However, even in those species that average, if there is too much conflict between cues, they tend to fall back on large-scale spatial cues, which in nature are the most constant and reliable. An interesting comparison is the rules for dealing with conflicting temporal cues (Fairhurst, Gallistel, & Gibbon, 2003).

We now focus in turn on sequential and nonsequential cue assessment, finding in each case that empirical results from biology might prompt new directions of research for ABC.

Sequential Cue Assessment

Most studies measure only how cue values and the availability of cues affect the outcome of choice, not the process, so we cannot readily tell whether assessment of cues is sequential. The exception is if there is an observable behavioral sequence in which different cues are seen to be inspected at each stage before others are available or where different cues predict breaking off the process at different stages. For instance, female sage grouse first assess males in a lek on the basis of their songs and then visit only those passing this test for a closer visual inspection of display rate (Gibson, 1996). Such a "layered" process of sexual selection seems extremely widespread (Bonduriansky, 2003), and clear sequences of cue inspection are similarly well known in navigation and food choice. Note, however, that a sequential process need not necessarily imply a fixed cue order or that cues observed at one stage are ignored in decisions at later stages. Thus, either visual or olfactory cues in isolation are sufficient to attract hawk moths to a flower, but both cues must be present to stimulate feeding (Raguso & Willis, 2002).

Even where the sequential aspect is not apparent, a clear ranking of importance of cues is at least compatible with a decision rule like take-the-best. For instance, honeybees trained to identify model flowers decide on the basis of color only if the odors of two alternatives match and on the basis of shape only if color and odor match (Gould & Gould, 1988: chap. 8). Gould and Gould explained this order on the basis of validity: Odor was the most reliable cue to the species of flower, color varied more from flower to flower, and shape varied depending on the angle of approach. They also are clear that by the time the bee gets close enough to sense flower odor, all three cues are available.

Whereas examining cues in order of decreasing validity may make good sense for search in memory or search on a computer screen, other factors seem more important in the biological examples. In mate choice the more reliable cues to quality tend to be examined last. In locating resources the cue giving the most exact location tends to be examined last. One reason is likely to be the cost of sampling each cue in terms of risk, energetic expenditure, or time. For instance, mock fighting another male may be the most reliable cue to which of the parties would win a real fight, but mock fighting has considerable dangers of damage and consequently is not attempted unless other safer displays have failed to make the difference in quality apparent (Wells, 1988; Enquist et al., 1990). Morphological cues may be judged at a glance, whereas behavioral traits may require time to assess. Fawcett and Johnstone (2003) consider the optimal order to assess cues differing in informativeness and cost. The other related reason for less valid cues to be assessed earlier is that some cues must necessarily appear before others. For instance, a deer stag cannot help but see the size of its rival before it starts fighting it, and the deepness of a roar may be available as a cue to size even before the animal gets close enough to judge size visually.

Paradoxically, in these situations a more noncompensatory environment may lead to examining cues in increasing order of validity (the reverse of take-the-best), at least in cases where the quantitative nature of cues means that cue values are unlikely to tie. As the chooser gets progressively closer or more willing to take risks, more cues become available; it should be adapted to read those new cues whose validities outweigh those of earlier cues, but less valid new cues are unlikely to provide useful additional information and so might be ignored. An interesting question is to what extent the orders in which cues are examined are adaptations. With sexual selection, it could often be that particular traits evolve as signals because of the stage of the assessment process in which they can be examined, rather than that the cue informativeness of preexisting signals has favored an order of inspection.

Nonsequential Cue Assessment

There are striking examples of an additive effect of different cues. By manipulating realistic computer animations of sticklebacks *Gasterosteus aculeatus,*

Künzler and Bakker (2001) showed that the proportion of choices for one image over another was linearly related to the number of cues in which it was superior (cf. tallying). Similarly, Basolo and Trainor (2002) showed in the swordtail fish *Xiphophorus helleri* that the time for a female to respond was explicable as the sum of the effects of each component of the sword (cf. weighted-additive). However, Hankinson and Morris (2003) pointed out an alternative explanation for such additive results, which depend on averaging the responses of many fish. An additive pattern need not be due to an additive integration of the cues in all individuals, but to each individual responding to different single cues—each extra cue persuades another subset of the population. We do know of cases of different individuals in the same population attending to different cues (e.g., Hill et al., 1999). The method of processing may differ between individuals too; older female garter snakes demand males that are good on two cues, whereas either cue alone satisfies younger females (Shine et al., 2003).

More complex interactions between cues are also observed. For instance, in the guppy *Poecilia reticulata,* color affected choice when both animations showed a low display rate but not when they both showed a high rate; conversely, display rates mattered when both animations displayed color but not an absence of color (Kodric-Brown & Nicoletto, 2001). Another complex pattern is suggested both in the work of Zuk, Ligon, and Thornhill (1992) and Marchetti (1998); female choice was unaffected by manipulations of single males' traits that earlier observational studies had suggested females were utilizing. One interpretation is that if one signal disagrees with all the other signals, it is ignored, which might be adaptive if accidental damage to single morphological characters is not indicative of quality. Some traits that we can measure independently may well be treated by the animal as composite traits, implying that complex integration of cues may happen at an almost perceptual level (Rowe, 1999; Calkins & Burley, 2003; Rowe & Skelhorn, 2004). One cue may alert the receiver to the presence of another (e.g., Hebets, 2005), or one cue may act as an amplifier for another (Hasson 1991; for instance, contrasting plumage coloration makes it easier for the receiver to judge display movements). The usual assumption is that amplifiers rely on constraints in the way perception works, but such multiplicative cue interactions arise through other mechanisms as well (Patricelli, Uy, & Borgia, 2003), and so it might be an adaptation to some particular environment structures. A multiplicative interaction favors two traits both being well developed over either one in isolation. Perhaps this is ecologically rational in negatively correlated environments (cf. Johnson, Meyer, & Ghose's [1989] finding of the benefits of including interaction terms in choice models in such environments).

Breaking Down Disciplinary Boundaries

In the preceding section we showed how empirical results on rules of thumb and ABC's theoretical approach could mutually illuminate each other. This short section examines further ways to develop the interaction.

ABC has already published research on heuristics used by animals. For instance, Davis, Todd, and Bullock (1999) simulated various rules that a parent bird might use to allocate food among its chicks (feed them in turn or feed the largest or hungriest, etc.). Other ABC papers have dealt with rules of thumb for mate choice, which relate both to animals and humans (Todd & Miller, 1999; Simão & Todd, 2002; Hutchinson & Halupka, 2004). The resulting papers fitted comfortably into the biological literature, emphasizing the similarities in approaches of the two schools.

Another way to break down the interdisciplinary barriers is to test theory developed in one school on the organisms (human or animal) of the other. ABC has already tested whether humans use the same patch-leaving rules known from animals (Wilke, Hutchinson, & Todd, 2004). One experimental context is a computer game modeled on a foraging task, but another consists of internal search in memory for solutions to a Scrabble-like word puzzle. It is known that different species use different patch-leaving rules, presumably in response to their environments (van Alphen, Bernstein, & Driessen, 2003; Wajnberg et al., 2003), but we will test whether, as a generalist species, individual humans can rapidly change the rule according to the environment structure encountered.

An equally valid research strategy would be to move in the opposite direction, testing whether animals use the heuristics that ABC has proposed that humans use. Demonstrating the parallel evolution of human heuristics in other lineages facing similar environmental structures would provide more stringent tests of their status as adaptations. Studying humans has some advantages, such as the possibility to use introspection to formulate plausible hypotheses about our heuristics, but animals provide many other advantages. In most nonhuman animals it is clearer what is their natural habitat, and it is still possible to study the animal's behavior and its consequences in that environment. Comparative studies can test whether the rules of thumb used by related species have adjusted to their differing environments. Analyzing the structure of the environment is usually easier than with humans because most species are more specialist. Shorter life cycles make it easier to relate the immediate consequences of a behavior to fitness. Practical considerations also allow far more complete manipulations of an animal's environment than with humans. Moreover, as Tinbergen found, it is often the case in animals that quite crude tricks suffice, itself perhaps a reflection of animals' greater reliance on simpler rules of thumb.

Conclusions

ABC has demonstrated that simple heuristics can be a surprisingly effective way of making many decisions, both in terms of frugality and accuracy. Research also shows that humans often use these simple heuristics in environments where they are ecologically rational. It lies ahead to discover how much of human cognition can be usefully understood in terms of heuristics.

How might ABC gain from a closer relationship with behavioral biology? Certainly biology considerably broadens the range of examples of heuristics, some of which will turn out to be shared between animals and humans. Some make particularly strong examples because they can be anchored in proven neurological mechanisms or because their adaptive value is less ambiguous than with humans. Animal examples may illuminate characteristics of natural environments that are less important to modern humans but to which our cognitive mechanisms are still adapted: An example is our suggestion that cue orders may have as much to do with costs and accessibility of each cue as with validity. We have also discussed how the tools of optimality modeling might be reapplied to the study of heuristics.

What might biology gain from a broader knowledge of ABC's work? Rules of thumb are already part of behavioral biology's vocabulary. And biologists already use the usual ABC approach of simulating candidate heuristics to judge their performance. However, although biological examples of rules of thumb and of cue integration are not so rare, they tend to be isolated curiosities in the literature. Can some of these different rules be classified by shared building blocks, just as with simple heuristics? The emphasis on decision rules might provide a useful impetus both to interpret further animal behaviors in such terms and then to expose commonalities between the examples. This is especially the case with cue integration, for which biology seems not to have developed an equivalent of ABC's theoretical framework explaining why particular methods of cue integration work well in particular types of information environments. Also largely missing from biology is the idea that simple heuristics may be superior to more complex methods, not just a necessary evil because of the simplicity of animal nervous systems (but see Bookstaber & Langsam, 1985; Real, 1992; Stephens & Anderson, 2001; Stephens, 2002). The shared assumption that performance is what matters should facilitate communication between biologists and ABC.

Chapter 4

I Think, Therefore I Err

> They all laughed at Wilbur and his brother,
> When they said that man could fly.
> They told Marconi wireless was a phony;
> It's the same old cry.
>
> —Ira Gershwin

Why do we make errors? Are they blunders caused by the limitations of our cognitive system? Or are errors an indispensable property of every intelligent system? From the first perspective, all errors are at best unnecessary and at worst harmful. Consider an error commonly made by children. When asked to find the sum of one-half and one-third, the answer is often two-fifths. This is called the *freshman error* of adding numerators and adding denominators (Silver, 1986). But such errors are not limited to children. After the invention of the telephone, a group of British experts concluded that it had no practical value, at least in their country: "The telephone may be appropriate for our American cousins, but not here, because we have an adequate supply of messenger boys" (Sherden, 1998: 175). In 1961, President John F. Kennedy is reported to have asked himself "How could I have been so stupid?" after realizing how badly he had miscalculated when he approved the Bay of Pigs invasion planned by the CIA (Janis & Mann, 1977: xv). Blunders like these seem to be both dispensable and embarrassing, and every intelligent system would surely work better without them. In this view, to err is not to think.

From the second perspective, there are errors that need to be made—that is, errors that are indispensable and functional. I call these "good" errors. Children are known for this. Consider a three-year-old who uses the phrase "I gived" instead of "I gave." A child cannot know in advance which verbs

This chapter is a revised version of G. Gigerenzer, "I Think, Therefore I Err," *Social Research* 72 (2005): 195–218 (www.socres.org).

are irregular; since irregular verbs are rare, the child's best bet is to assume the regular form until proved wrong. The error is "good"—that is, useful—because if the three-year-old did not try out new forms and occasionally make errors, but instead played it safe and used only those words it had already heard, it would learn a language at a slower rate. The characteristic of a good error is that a person is better off making it than not making it—for reaching a goal more quickly or for attaining it at all. In this view, every intelligent system has to make errors; making none would destroy the intelligence of the system. There is a close parallel to Darwinian theory, where random variability and mutation—copying errors—are essential for evolution by natural selection. Not making these errors would eliminate evolution. Trial-and-error learning, at the ontogenetic or evolutionary level, is one source of good errors in an uncertain world.

In this chapter, I deal with the study of human errors in experimental psychology. The problem that researchers try to resolve is this: How can one infer the laws of cognition—of perception, memory, and thought? One answer is to study the systematic errors people make. At first glance, this program looks like a straightforward extension of Francis Bacon's plan for studying nature's errors or of Freud's strategy of analyzing repressed memories, slips of tongue, and abnormal neurotic behavior. The idea is to catch nature when it does not pay attention—creating strange facts, such as blood rain in Bavaria and an Irish girl with several horns growing on her body (Daston & Park, 1998). However, there is an important difference. We can easily see what is wrong with a goat with two heads or a man with obsessive-compulsive hand washing and understand that it is not to the benefit of the animal or the human. Cognitive errors, however, are not as clear, as we will soon see. Here, one has to define what an error of judgment is, not simply observe it. In this chapter, I argue:

1. The study of cognitive errors has been dominated by a logical definition of errors. But this narrow norm tends to mistake forms of human intelligence that go beyond logic for stupid blunders and consequently fails to unravel the laws of mind.
2. An ecological analysis, in place of a logical one, can instead reveal the existence of good errors, which open a window into the mind. The prototype of an ecological analysis is the study of visual illusions.

I will document both points with illustrative examples.

Visual Illusions

Let us first see what a visual illusion is and what one can learn from it. Consider the dots on the left-hand side of figure 4.1. They appear concave, receding into the surface away from the observer. The dots on the right side, however, appear convex: They project up from the surface, extending toward the observer. When you turn the page upside-down, the concave dots

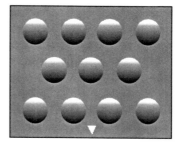

Figure 4.1: Perceptual illusion of "pop-out" dots. If you turn the page around, the concave dots will pop out and vice versa. The right picture is identical to the left, rotated by 180 degrees.

will turn into convex dots, and vice versa. But there is no third dimension, and there are no convex and concave dots. Seeing things that systematically deviate from the relevant physical measurements is called a *perceptual illusion*.

What can we learn from this illusion about how our brain works? First, that the world, from the perspective of our mind, is fundamentally uncertain. Our brain does not have sufficient information to know for certain what is out there, but it is not paralyzed by uncertainty. Second, the brain uses heuristics to make a good bet. Third, the bet is based on the structure of its environment or what the structure is assumed to be. The brain assumes a three-dimensional world and uses the shaded parts of the dots to guess in what direction of the third dimension they extend. By experimentally varying factors, such as the location of the light source and the shading, and documenting their effect on the illusion, Kleffner and Ramachandran (1992) concluded that the assumed ecological structures are:

1. light comes from above and
2. there is only one source of light.

These structures describe human (and mammalian) history, where the sun and moon were the only sources of light, and only one operated at a time. The first regularity also holds approximately for artificial light today, which is typically placed above us, as in the case of street lamps (although there are exceptions, such as car lights). The brain exploits these assumed structures by using a fast and frugal heuristic:

If the shade is in the upper part, then the dots are concave; if the shade is in the lower part, then the dots are convex.

Shading is phylogenetically one of the most primitive cues, and so is the principle of countershading that conceals animals' shapes from predators, as in the pale bellies of swarm fishes that neutralize the effects of the sun shining from above. Von Helmholtz (1856–1866/1962) used the term *unconscious inferences* for this type of heuristic, and he and his followers (e.g., Brunswik, 1934) thought that the cues were learned from individual experience; others have favored evolutionary learning (e.g., Shepard, 1987). The systematic study of this perceptual illusion has led to various insights and speculations about the mechanism of perception. These include that for the brain, "from above" means relative to retinal coordinates, not relative to the horizon or gravity, and that our brains seem to make the "default" assumption that objects are more likely to be convex rather than concave (Deutsch & Ramachandran, 1990).

Perceptual illusions are good errors, a necessary consequence of a highly intelligent "betting" machine (Gregory, 1974). Therefore, a perceptual system that does not make any errors would not be an intelligent system. It would report only what the eye can "see." That would be both too little and too much. Too little because perception must go beyond the information given, since it has to abstract and generalize. Too much because a "veridical" system would overwhelm the mind with a vast amount of irrelevant details. Perceptual errors, therefore, are a necessary part, or by-product, of an intelligent system. They exemplify a second source of good errors: Visual illusions result from "bets" that are virtually incorrigible, whereas the "bets" in trial- and-error learning are made in order to be corrected eventually. Both kinds of gambles are indispensable and complementary tools of an intelligent mind.

The case of visual illusions illustrates the general proposition that every intelligent system makes good errors; otherwise it would not be intelligent. The reason is that the outside world is uncertain, and the system has to make intelligent inferences based on assumed ecological structures. Going beyond the information given by making inferences will produce systematic errors. Not risking errors would destroy intelligence.

Logic and Blunders

Unlike in theories of perception, errors in the social sciences are typically seen as annoyances. The nuisance comes in many forms, such as observational and measurement error, and statistical techniques are employed to tame the error and extract the true values from all the noise. Economics, for instance, has long tried to ignore errors of measurement, possibly because of "the absence of any good cure for this disease" (Griliches, 1974: 975). The same negative attitude toward errors has shaped the program of studying errors of judgment, which emerged in the 1960s (Edwards, 1968; Wason, 1966). It became widely known through the heuristics-and-biases program (Tversky & Kahneman, 1974), invaded social psychology (Nisbett & Ross, 1980), and shaped the emerging field of behavioral economics in the 1980s (Camerer, 1995) as well as that of behavioral law and economics in the 1990s (Sunstein, 2000). Hundreds of studies have tried to document people's blunders in almost all domains of life: flawed intuitive notions of chance, the faulty intuitions of basketball coaches, patients' illogical judgments of pain, and people's moral errors. Oddly, the new program of studying useless errors was introduced in analogy to errors in perception, specifically to visual illusions.

Kahneman and Tversky (1982: 123) argued that one can determine an error in judgment exactly like an error in perception by using logic rather than physical measurement as the norm: "The presence of an error of judgment is demonstrated by comparing people's responses either with an established fact (e.g., that the two lines are equal in length) or with an accepted rule of arithmetic, logic, or statistics." Just as perceptual errors help to discover the laws of perception, it was assumed that errors of judgment help to discover the laws of higher-order cognition.

Psychologists were not the first to draw a parallel between perceptual and judgmental errors. In his chapter on illusion in probability estimation, Pierre Simon Laplace (1814/1951: 182) wrote that "the mind has its illusions, like the sense of vision." Yet before the 1950s and 1960s, few psychologists thought that logic or probability theory could reveal the laws of mind. On the contrary, Wilhelm Wundt (1912/1973), known as the father of experimental psychology, concluded that logical norms had little to do with thought processes and that attempts to apply them to learn about psychological processes had been absolutely fruitless.

The new focus on logic and probability was part of a larger movement. It occurred after inferential statistics was institutionalized in the social sciences during the 1950s (Gigerenzer et al., 1989), the revival of Bayesian statistics (Savage, 1954), and the emergence of theories that assumed logical structures as the basis of psychological processes (e.g., Piaget & Inhelder, 1951/1975).

Despite virulent disagreements with the experimental demonstrations of errors of judgment, Kahneman and Tversky's first major critic, the philosopher L. Jonathan Cohen (1981: 324), also relied on the analogy with perceptual illusions and even introduced a new fashionable term, describing errors of judgment "as cognitive illusions...to invoke the analogy with visual illusions." But what exactly does the analogy entail? An answer is strikingly absent in the literature. Recall that visual illusions are commonly understood as "good" errors, whereas errors of judgment are virtually always presented as disturbing fallacies that should not have occurred in the first place and often are suggested to be the cause of many a human disaster. Given this discrepancy, the content of the analogy is less than obvious. Its function, however, seems clear: The analogy served to persuade the scientific community that, like physical measurements, the laws of logic and probability were an uncontroversial norm for good thinking and that deviations would help to unravel the laws of thought.

In what follows, I will first argue that logic failed to realize the two goals: to define errors of judgment and to open a window into the human mind. I illustrate this argument with two logical principles, set inclusion and invariance. In the second part, I will argue that the analogy with visual illusions is actually the more promising program for attaining both goals: Kahneman, Tversky, and their followers were right in proposing the analogy, but they did not follow through on their original proposal.

Set Inclusion

In their book *The Early Growth of Logic in the Child*, Bärbel Inhelder and Jean Piaget (1959/1964: 101) reported an experiment in which they showed 5- to 10-year-old children pictures, 16 of which were flowers, and 8 of these 16 flowers were primulas. The children were asked a list of questions about class inclusion relations, one of which was: "Are there more flowers or more primulas"? Only 47% of the five- to seven-year-olds gave answers in accord with class inclusion—that is, that reflected an understanding that the flowers were more numerous because they included the primulas as a subset. Among eight-year-olds, however, a majority (82%) gave responses consistent with class inclusion. Later studies have confirmed this result, although some researchers suggest that the onset of class-inclusion reasoning may occur one or two years later (Reyna, 1991). Inhelder and Piaget (1959/1964: 117) concluded that "this kind of thinking is not peculiar to professional logicians since the children themselves apply it with confidence when they reach the operational level." The facts seemed to be settled: The adolescent and adult mind is an "intuitive logician."

Without reference to this earlier work, Tversky and Kahneman (1983) reached the opposite conclusion. They referred to set-inclusion problems as "conjunction problems." Consider the Linda problem:

> Linda is 31 years old, single, outspoken, and very bright. She majored in philosophy. As a student she was deeply concerned with issues of discrimination and social justice and also participated in anti-nuclear demonstrations.
> Which of two alternatives is more probable:
>
> Linda is a bank teller,
>
> Linda is a bank teller and is active in the feminist movement?

The majority of undergraduates (85%) chose the second alternative. Tversky and Kahneman argued that this is an error of judgment, a "conjunction fallacy," because it violates logic. "Like it or not, *A* cannot be less probable than (*A* and *B*), and a belief to the contrary is fallacious. Our problem is to retain what is useful and valid in intuitive judgment while correcting the errors and biases to which it is prone" (Tversky & Kahneman, 1982: 98). Numerous experiments replicated this result. The facts seemed to be, once again, settled, although in the opposite direction: The adult mind is not at all an intuitive logician. The conjunction fallacy was interpreted as a potential cause of general irrationality. "A system of judgments that does not obey the conjunction rule cannot be expected to obey more complicated principles that presuppose this rule, such as Bayesian updating, external calibration, and the maximization of expected utility" (Tversky & Kahneman, 1983: 313).

The error was afterward invoked to explain various economic and societal problems, including John Q. Public's unreasonable fear of technological risks, such as nuclear reactor failures (Stich, 1985), his imprudent spending on insurance (Johnson et al., 1993), and major blunders in U.S. security policy (Kanwisher, 1989). Stephen J. Gould (1992: 469) wrote:

> I am particularly fond of [the Linda] example, because I know that the [conjunction] is least probable, yet a little homunculus in my head continues to jump up and down, shouting at me, "but she can't just be a bank teller: read the description."...Why do we consistently make this simple logical error? Tversky and Kahneman argue, correctly I think, that our minds are not built (for whatever reason) to work by the rules of probability.

But why, we must ask, would eight-year-old children in Geneva not make this simple logical error, whereas American undergraduates consistently do? I argue that the irrationality is not to be found in adult reasoning, but in the logical norm. Consider what the norm is: The probability of an event A is larger than (or equal to) the probability of the events A and B, that is, $p(A) \geq p(A \& B)$. This conjunction rule is used as a content-blind norm for judgment; the content of the As and Bs is not considered relevant to evaluating good reasoning. All that counts is the mathematical probability p and the logical &, and correct judgment is attested when people use the English terms *probable* and *and* in this and only this way. This amounts to a purely syntactic definition of rational reasoning and, therefore, of an error in judgment. When a person takes account of the semantics, such as the content of A, or the pragmatics of the experimental situation, such as trying to find out what the experimenter wants to hear, and the resulting inference differs from the logical norm, then these forms of intelligence are counted as an error in judgment.

Are logical rules, used in a content-blind way, sound norms? I do not think so. Let us take the analogy with visual illusions seriously, specifically the aspect of uncertainty: Perception cannot know the right answer and therefore has to make an uncertain yet informed bet based on cues. One source of uncertainty in the Linda problem is the polysemy of the terms *probable* and *and*. The *Oxford English Dictionary* and its equivalents in other languages list various meanings of *probable*. A few, such as "what happens frequently," correspond to mathematical probability, but most, such as "what is plausible" and "whether there is evidence," do not. Perception solves this problem of underspecification by intelligent heuristics, and the same seems to be the case for higher-order cognition. For instance, according to Grice (1989), people rely on conversational heuristics, such as *relevance*. In the present context, the principle of relevance says that the description of Linda is relevant to finding the correct answer. Note that if a person treats the term *probable* as mathematical probability, then the principle of relevance is violated. You do not need to read the description of Linda to find the logical answer—Gould's homunculus understood this point.

Consider the following version of the Linda problem, Here the polysemy of the word *probable* is eliminated by using the phrase *how many:*

There are 100 persons who fit the description above (that is, Linda's). *How many* of them are:

Bank tellers?

Bank tellers and active in the feminist movement?

This change is sufficient to make the apparently stable cognitive illusion largely disappear. In one experiment, every single participant answered that there are more bank tellers (Hertwig & Gigerenzer, 1999; for similar results with other problems see Fiedler, 1988; Tversky & Kahneman, 1983). The experiment also showed that the majority of participants interpreted *how many* in the sense of mathematical probability but *more probable* as meaning "possible," "conceivable," or one of the other nonmathematical meanings listed in the *OED.* These results demonstrate intelligent context-sensitive reasoning (which no computer program can achieve at this point of time) rather than a rigid, content-blind application of logic (which is easy to program). The analysis also provides an answer to the question why children in Geneva made significantly fewer "errors" than American undergraduates. Inhelder and Piaget asked for *how many* rather than the ambiguous *probable,* and with this clarification, the triviality of the logical problem becomes clear and results become consistent for children and adults.

The same context-sensitivity was found for the cognitive processing of *and.* Consider this version of the conjunction:

Bank tellers and active feminists

The conjunction has been rephrased as a noun-plus-noun phrase, which should not matter from the point of view of logical norms. However, this noun-noun phrase leads to a substantial number of violations of the conjunction rule, even when *probable* is replaced by *how many.* This result was reported by Kahneman and Tversky (1996) to defend the "reality" of the conjunction error. However, the term *and* also has no single fixed meaning, and people are equipped with intelligent heuristics to infer the intended meaning from the semantic context, not only the syntax. Specifically, nounnoun phrases often refer to the disjunction, not the conjunction, of two elements or classes. For instance, the announcement "We invited friends and colleagues" does not refer to the intersection between the two groups, but to the joint set of both groups. Thus, the extension of the set *friends and colleagues* is larger than that of the set *friends,* which violates the conjunction rule. But that is not an error of judgment. Consistent with this analysis, when one replaces the noun-noun phrase by *bank tellers as well as active feminists,* which largely eliminates the interpretation in terms of a disjunction, the so-called conjunction fallacy again largely disappears (Mellers, Hertwig, & Kahneman, 2001).

The moral is that human intelligence reaches far beyond narrow logical norms. In fact, the conjunction problems become trivial and devoid of intellectual challenge when people finally realize that they are intended as a content-free logical exercise. This insight was driven home to me long ago when my daughter was eight years old, the age Inhelder and Piaget estimated that class inclusion emerges. I showed her the Primula and Linda problems that I had prepared for my students.

GG   Are there more flowers or more primulas?
CHILD   Primulas, but they all are flowers.
GG   (Question repeated).
CHILD   OK, more flowers. But why do you ask?
GG   Is Linda more likely a bank teller or a bank teller and active in the feminist movement?
CHILD   If she is in philosophy, she would not be a bank teller. Therefore, it must be bank teller and active in the feminist movement.
GG   Why?
CHILD   Because it is both. One cannot understand these questions.
GG   Why?
CHILD   Because they make no sense.

Let me summarize my argument. The use of logic and probability theory as a content-blind norm for good reasoning is widespread in recent experimental psychology. The Linda problem illustrates this norm and how it leads to misinterpreting intelligent semantic and pragmatic inferences as mental blunders. Even children have a much more differentiated understanding of language than logic provides; they rely on conversational axioms, invited inferences, and other forms of social intelligence (Fillenbaum, 1977; Sweetser, 1990). The interesting question is, how do we immediately know whether an "and" means a temporal, causal, or some other relation? My hypothesis is that we rely on heuristics similar to Grice's relevance axioms.

What have we learned from some 20 years and hundreds of experiments on the conjunction fallacy? We have learned more about the limits of logic as norms than about the workings of the mind. In fact, I do not know of any new deep insight that this activity has produced. Content-blind logical norms distract us from understanding intelligent behavior. Gould should have trusted his homunculus, and psychologists should trust psychological rather than logical analysis.

Framing

Framing is defined as the expression of logically equivalent information (whether numerical or verbal) in different ways. You may say that the glass is half full or that it is half empty. A physician may tell patients that they have a 10 percent chance of dying during an operation or a 90 percent change of surviving. In his classic *The Character of Physical Law* (1967: 53), Richard Feynman emphasized the importance of deriving different formulations for the same physical law, even if they are mathematically equivalent:

"Psychologically they are different because they are completely unequivalent when you are trying to guess new laws." Feynman used different frames in a positive way to elicit different thoughts.

In contrast to Feynman's insights, different reactions to logically equivalent formulations have been declared as normatively inappropriate, suspect of irrational thought. Consider Tversky and Kahneman's (1986: S253) normative principle of *invariance*: "An essential condition for a theory of choice that claims normative status is the principle of invariance: Different representations of the same choice problem should yield the same preference. That is, the preference between options should be independent of their description."

According to this account, it is normative to ignore whether your doctor describes the outcome of a possible operation as a 90 percent chance of survival (positive frame) or a 10 percent chance of dying (negative frame). It is logically the same (semantics and pragmatics are therefore not an issue for this view of rationality). But patients more often accept the treatment if doctors choose a positive frame (Edwards et al., 2001). Kahneman and Tversky interpret this to mean that people's mental machinery "is not adequate to perform the task of recoding the two versions . . . into a common abstract form" (Kahneman & Tversky, 1984: 346). From various demonstrations of framing effects, they (1984: 343) concluded that "in their stubborn appeal, framing effects resemble perceptual illusions more than computational errors." As with violations of the conjunction rule, framing effects are seen as blunders that should not happen to a rational person.

Does invariance amount to a normative principle of rational choice, and its violation to a judgmental error, as suggested? Feynman's insight contradicts this logical vision of rationality. But guessing new laws, or scientific discovery, one could argue, may be the exception to the rule. What about framing in everyday life? Consider the prototype of all framing stories:

The glass is half full.

The glass is half empty.

According to the invariance principle, (i) people's choices should not be affected by the two formulations, and (ii) if they are affected, then this violates rational choice. Should the description really not matter? Consider an experiment in which a full glass of water and an empty glass are put in front of a participant (Sher & McKenzie, 2006). The experimenter asks the participant to pour half of the full glass into the other glass and then asks the participant to select the half-empty glass. Which one does the participant choose? Most people chose the previously full glass. When they were asked, however, to select the half-full glass, most participants chose the previously empty one. This experiment reveals that the two statements are not pragmatically equivalent (see also McKenzie & Nelson, 2003). People extract surplus information from the framing of the question, and this surplus information concerns the dynamics or history of the situation, which helps to guess what is meant. They can "read between the lines." The principle of invariance is content-blind and not intelligent enough to "detect" this information.

Invariance and the conjunction rule are two instances of a large number of logical principles that have been used to define errors of judgment. Others include consistency (Berg & Gigerenzer, 2006), material conditional (chap. 1), transitivity, and additivity of probabilities, which I will not go into here. It is sufficient to say that the use of these logical rules as content-blind norms has led to the same problem: It eliminates the characteristics specific to human intelligence from the definition of good judgment. These include abilities that are yet unmatched by today's computer programs, such as inferring the meaning of polysemous terms from the semantic context and decoding information given "between the lines." As a consequence, research using content-blind norms has failed to unravel the nature of thinking or other cognitive processes. Inappropriate norms are not simply a normative problem. They tend to suggest wrong questions, and the answers to these can generate more confusion than insight into the nature of human judgment. This trap is known as a Type-III error: To find the right answer to the wrong question.

Good Errors

Why Do We Forget?

Jorge Louis Borges tells the tale of Ireneo Funes, whom he described as having been what every man was: He looked without seeing, heard without listening, and forgot virtually everything. One day Funes was bucked off a half-tamed horse, knocked unconscious, and left crippled. But his memory became clear and without limits. He was able to recall the forms of the clouds in the sky on any day, and reconstruct every dream. He even reconstructed an entire day, although this itself took an entire day. He checked his memory against the available facts and found that he never made an error. It irritated him that the dog of 3:14 p.m., seen in profile, should be named the same as the one seen a minute later, frontally. In Funes's world, everything was particular—which made it difficult for him to think because to think is to forget, generalize, and abstract.

Is there a truth in Borges's story? Research on memory suggests that the answer is yes. Evolution could have produced ideal memories and occasionally did so by mistake. The Russian psychologist A. R. Luria investigated the astounding memory of a man named Shereshevsky. Luria read to him as many as 30 words, numbers, or letters and asked him to repeat these. Whereas ordinary humans can correctly repeat about 7 plus or minus 2, this man recalled all 30. Luria increased the number to 50, to 70, but Shereshevsky recalled them all and even repeated them in reverse order. Luria could not find the limits of his memory. Some 15 years after their first meeting, Luria asked Shereshevsky to reproduce the series of words, numbers, or letters from that meeting. Shereshevsky sat, his eyes closed, and recalled the situation: They were sitting in Luria's apartment; Luria was wearing a gray suit sitting in a rocking chair and reading the series to him. Then, after all those years, Shereshevsky recited the series precisely. This was most remarkable at the time because Shereshevsky had become a famous mnemonist who performed onstage and had been exposed to a massive amount of information to memorize in each performance, which should have buried his old memories.

Is there a cost to such unlimited memory? Shereshevsky had detailed memories of virtually everything that had happened to him, both the important and the trivial. He could alter his pulse rate from some 70 to 100 by vividly remembering running after a train that had just begun to pull out. There was only one thing his brilliant memory failed to do. It could not forget. It was flooded by the images of childhood, which could cause him acute malaise and chagrin. With a memory composed entirely of details, he was unable to think on an abstract level. When he read a story, he could recite it word for word, but when asked to summarize the gist of the same story, he faltered.

In general, when a task required going beyond the information given, such as understanding metaphors, poems, synonyms, and homonyms, Shereshevsky was more or less lost. He complained about having a poor memory for faces. "People's faces are constantly changing," he said; "it's the different shades of expression that confuse me and make it so hard to remember faces" (Luria, 1968: 64). Details that other people would forget occupied his mind, making it hard to move from the flow of images and sensations to some higher level of awareness: gist, abstraction, and meaning. Similarly, autistic persons discriminate more accurately between true and false memories than the nonautistic do and can have spectacular rote memory abilities. But they also remember the gist of these events less well (Schacter, 2001: 193).

Is perfect memory desirable, without error? The answer seems to be no. The "sins" of our memory seem to be good errors, that is, by-products ("spandrels") of a system adapted to the demands of our environments. In this view, forgetting prevents the sheer mass of details stored in an unlimited memory from critically slowing down and inhibiting the retrieval of the few important experiences. Too much memory would impair the mind's ability to abstract, to infer, and to learn. Moreover, the nature of memory is not simply storing and retrieving. Memory actively "makes up" memories— that is, it makes inferences and reconstructs the past from the present (see figure 2.3). This is in contrast to perception, which also makes uncertain inferences but reconstructs the present from the past. Memory needs to be functional, not veridical. To build a system that does not forget will not result in human intelligence.

Benefits of Cognitive Limits

Cognitive limitations both *constrain* and *enable* adaptive behavior. There is a point where more information and more cognitive processing can actually do harm, as illustrated in the case of perfect memory. Built-in limitations can in fact be beneficial, enabling new functions that would be absent without them (Hertwig & Todd, 2003). Yet the possibility that less is more, that cognitive limitations could make sense, is hard to swallow; evidence is needed. The previous chapters have explicated some of the conditions where heuristics lead to better performance with less information and computation. Here are some further examples.

Newport (1990) argued that the very constraints of the developing brain of small children enable them to learn their first language fluently. Late language learners, in contrast, tend to experience difficulties when attempting to learn the full range of semantic mappings with their mature mental capacities. In a test of this argument, Elman (1993) tried to get a large neural network with extensive memory to learn the grammatical relationships in a set of several thousand sentences, yet the network faltered. Instead of taking the obvious step of adding more memory to solve the problem, Elman *restricted* its memory, making the network forget after every three or four words—to mimic the memory restrictions of young children who learn their first language. The network with the restricted memory could not possibly make sense of the long complicated sentences, but its restrictions forced it to focus on the short simple sentences, which it did learn correctly, mastering the small set of grammatical relationships in this subset. Elman then increased the network's effective memory to five or six words, and so on. By starting small, the network ultimately learned the entire corpus of sentences, which the full network with full memory had never been able to do alone.

Apart from limited memory at the beginning, language learning also needs sentences that are simply structured. If parents read the *New Yorker* to their babies, and only talked to them using its sophisticated vocabulary, the babies' language development would probably be impeded. Mothers and fathers know this intuitively; they communicate with their infants in "baby talk" rather than by using elaborate grammatical structures. Limited memory can act like a filter, and parents unconsciously support this adaptive immaturity by providing limited input in the first place.

A celebrated finding is Miller's (1956) estimate that the capacity of a short-term memory is limited to "seven-plus-or-minus-two" chunks, such as numbers or words. This cognitive limitation has inspired humbling speculations about the quality of human judgment and decision making. Few have asked whether this limit does anything for us. Kareev (2000, 2006) made an interesting argument and provided experimental evidence: Given the limit, people have to rely on small samples, which increases the chance of detecting correlations of events in the world. This is because a small sample is more likely than a larger sample to exhibit a magnified estimate of the true correlation in the population. Thus, the working memory limit enables contingencies to be detected early—after little sampling. When it outweighs the costs of the false alarms it generates, this advantage with respect to correlation detection would be particularly useful (see Juslin, Fiedler, & Chater, 2006).

As a final example, let me discuss three apparent errors that baseball players commit. First, some coaches scold players for taking unnecessary risks when they run to catch a ball at a slow pace (Gigerenzer, 2007). Second, studies with baseball outfielders showed that they often run toward the ball in an arc rather than in a straight line (Shaffer et al., 2004). Third, when balls were shot from various angles into the field where players were standing, the players performed poorly in estimating the location where the ball would hit the ground (Babler and Dannemiller, 1993; Saxberg, 1987). These three behaviors seem to be mistakes and the players performing them in need of training to improve performance. But, as in the case of the perceptual illusion, what if these phenomena are not errors that need to be corrected, but rather the outcomes of an intelligent rule of thumb? This raises the question whether players might use a heuristic rather than try to estimate the ball's trajectory. As explained in chapter 2, experienced players in fact use rules of thumb such as the gaze heuristic.

Now we can understand the nature of the three "errors." The gaze heuristic dictates the speed at which the player runs, which can vary from slowly trotting to running at top speed. Reduced speed is not an error in itself; rather, when players always run at top speed, they are often likely to miss the ball. Similarly, running in a slight arc is not a mistake; it is a consequence of using strategies similar to the gaze heuristic, and it can also be observed when a dog goes after a flying Frisbee—the dog runs so that its image of the disc is kept moving along a straight line (Shaffer et al., 2004). And, finally, the player does not need to be able to compute where the ball lands; the heuristic solves the problem without that knowledge. The three errors are good errors, the by-product of an efficient heuristic that solves the task. They only appear to be unnecessary errors if one does not pay attention to the underlying heuristics and assumes that players somehow compute the trajectory of the ball.

Every Intelligent System Makes Errors

By means of examples, I have dealt with a deep normative controversy in the cognitive and social sciences. Two visions are in conflict with one another. The first always sees errors negatively, as nuisances: The fewer one makes, the better. This negative view is implied by the reliance on logical principles for a general definition of rational behavior. I have argued that these "content-blind" norms fail to provide a reasonable general definition of error, and are inapt tools for unraveling the laws of the mind. In the second view, alongside errors of inattention and the like, good errors also exist. A good error is a consequence of the adaptation of mental heuristics to the structure of environments. This ecological view is illustrated by perceptual illusions. Not making good errors would destroy human intelligence. What is correct or erroneous is no longer defined by a syntactic principle but rather by the ecological rationality of a heuristic, that is, its success in the real world. Good errors can provide insights into the workings of the mind.

Descartes coined the dictum "I think, therefore I am" as a first step in demonstrating the attainability of certain knowledge. In an uncertain world, however, thinking as well as elementary perception involve making bets and taking risks. To err is not only human, it is also a necessary consequence of this kind of intelligence. I hope that Descartes will not mind my modifying his dictum accordingly: I think, therefore I err. Whenever I err, I know intuitively that I am.

Chapter 5

Striking a Blow for Sanity in Theories of Rationality

I took the title of this chapter from an e-mail Herbert A. Simon sent to me in May 1999. In it, he wrote a statement for the back cover of *Simple Heuristics That Make Us Smart* in which he commented: "I think the book strikes a great blow for sanity in the approach to rationality [and shows] why more than minor tampering with existing optimization theory is called for." But Herb wouldn't be Herb if he hadn't added: "and you wouldn't believe I had ever skimmed the volume if I didn't find SOMETHING to disagree with." And so he continued, pointing out that he hadn't found the expert/novice topic treated, that scientific discovery would have been a great example for ill-structured domains, that...

Bringing sanity into theories of rationality was a major guideline in Herbert Simon's scientific life. However, as he himself was prepared to admit, sanity in rationality entered his thinking as a negatively defined concept, a kind of black box that contained everything that was not optimization. What he opposed has various names: *full rationality, substantial rationality, maximization of expected utility, Homo economicus,* or simply *optimization.* What he proposed had its seeds in his revised dissertation, *Administrative Behavior* (1947), and eventually became termed *bounded rationality, satisficing,* or *procedural rationality.* Because of its initial vague definition, bounded rationality, however, came to mean many things to many people.

Bounded Rationality in the Plural

Simon's (1955, 1956) concept of bounded rationality has been claimed by three different programs. One of these Simon opposed, one he tolerated,

    This chapter is a revised version of G. Gigerenzer, "Striking a Blow for Sanity in Theories of Rationality," in *Models of a Man: Essays in Memory of Herbert A. Simon,* ed. M. Augier and J. G. March (Cambridge, MA: MIT Press, 2004), 389–409.

and one he embraced. I will call the three frameworks *optimization under constraints, cognitive illusions,* and *ecological rationality,* although I am not sure that Herb always wanted to distinguish between the latter two programs the way I do.

What Simon's Bounded Rationality Is Not: Optimization under Constraints

In models of full rationality, all relevant information is assumed to be available to *Homo economicus* at no cost. This classical version of *Homo economicus* has a distinctive Christian flavor: He is created in the image of an omniscient God. Real humans, however, need to search for information first. In an attempt to render economic theory more realistic, Stigler (1961) introduced constraints on full rationality, such as costs of information search. As described in chapter 1, the idea of optimization under constraints is to propose one or a few constraints (too many would make the mathematics too hard or even intractable) while retaining the ideal of optimization. In this view, a person who wants to buy a used car of a particular brand, for instance, stops search when the costs of further search—direct costs and opportunity costs—exceed those of its benefits. Introducing real constraints makes the approach more realistic, but maintaining the ideal of optimization, that is, calculating an optimal stopping point, does not. Such an ideal of optimization invokes new kinds of omniscience, that is, foreseeing the benefits and costs in further information search (Conlisk, 1996). There is little evidence that humans make decisions this way.

Lack of psychological reality was an objection Herb made time and again. The argument against his and others' concern with omniscience and psychological evidence has been the *as-if* conjecture: The question is not whether people actually optimize, with or without constraints, but whether they *act as if* they were doing so. As long as optimization predicts behavior, one need not be concerned with the actual motivations, emotions, and reasoning of people (Friedman, 1953). In the as-if view, the bounds in bounded rationality are just another name for constraints, and bounded rationality is merely a case of optimizing under constraints. Despite Herb's vehement protests, this message has become the doctrine. But this doctrine comes at a price: Retaining the ideal of optimization can make models of optimization under constraints more demanding than models of full rationality, both mathematically and psychologically. In the words of Thomas Sargent (1993: 2), a proponent of the view that bounded rationality means optimization under constraints: "Ironically, when we economists make the people in our models more 'bounded' in their rationality...*we* must be smarter, because our models become larger and more demanding mathematically and econometrically." In optimization under constraints, agents are re-created in the image of econometricians, one step above the gods. In personal conversation, Herb once remarked with a mixture of humor and anger that he had considered suing those authors who misuse his term of bounded rationality to construct ever more psychologically unrealistic models of human decision making.

Optimization, with or without constraints, has spread beyond economics. Psychologists often propose models of cognition that assume almost unlimited memory, storage capacities, and computational power. That is, many psychologists also build as-if models of behavior, as illustrated by various Bayesian approaches that model behavior but not cognitive processes (e.g., Oaksford & Chater, 2007). Over lunch, I once asked Herb about his impact on psychology:

GG   Do you think you had much effect on psychologists with "bounded rationality"?

HS   Yes. There is an abundant literature on recognition and search, for instance in Newell and Simon's *Human Problem Solving*.

GG   But what about exemplar models of categorization and the many other Laplacean demon models of cognition?

HS   Oh, these are of no relevance.

Why should we listen to Herb rather than build as-if models of optimization under constraints? Is there a problem with the program of making right predictions from wrong assumptions?

Optimization Is Intractable in Most Natural Situations

The ideal of as-if optimization is obviously limited because, in most natural situations, optimization is computationally intractable in any implementation, whether machine or neural. In computer science, these situations are called NP-hard or NP-complete; that is, the solution cannot be computed in polynomial time. "Almost every problem we look at in AI is NP-complete" (Reddy, 1988: 15). For instance, no mind or computer can apply Bayes's rule to a large number of variables that are mutually dependent because the number of computations increases exponentially with the number of variables. Probabilistic inference using Bayesian belief networks, for example, is intractable (Cooper, 1990; Dagum & Luby, 1993). In such situations, a fully rational Bayesian mind cannot exist. Even for games with simple and well-defined rules, such as chess and Go, we do not know the optimal strategy. Nevertheless, we do know what a good outcome is. In these situations, as-if optimization can only be achieved once the real situation is changed and simplified in a mathematically convenient way so that optimization is possible. Thus, the choice is between finding a good heuristic solution for a game where no optimal one is known and finding an optimal solution for a game with modified rules. That may mean abandoning our study of chess in favor of tic-tac-toe.

Optimization Is Not an Option with Multiple Goals

If optimization of a criterion is tractable, multiple goals nevertheless pose a difficulty. Consider the traveling salesman problem, where a salesman has to find the shortest route to visit N cities. This problem is intractable for large *N*s but can be solved if the number of cities is small, say if $N=10$, which results only in some 181,000 different routes the salesman has to compare (Gigerenzer, 2007). However, if there is more than one goal, such as the fastest, the most scenic, and the shortest route, then there is no way to determine to single best route. In this case there are three best routes. One might try to rescue optimization by weighting the three goals, such as $3x + 2y + z$, but this in turn means determining what the best weights would be, which is unclear for most interesting problems.

Optimization Is Not an Option with Imprecise, Subjective Criteria

Unlike physical distance, subjective criteria are often imprecise. Happiness, which means many things, is an obvious example. But the issue is more general. A colleague of mine is an engineer who builds concert halls. He informed me that even if he had unlimited amounts of money at his disposal, he would never succeed in maximizing acoustical quality. The reason is that although experts agree on the definition of bad acoustics, there is no consensus as to what defines the best. Hence he could try to maximize acoustical quality according to a single expert's judgment but not to unanimous agreement.

Optimization Is Unfeasible When Problems Are Unfamiliar and Time Is Scarce

In situations where optimization is in principle possible (unlike those under the first three points), a practical issue remains. Selten (2001) distinguishes between familiar and unfamiliar problems. In the case of a familiar problem, the decision maker knows the optimal solution. This may be due to prior training or because the problem is simple enough. In the case of an unfamiliar problem, however, the decision maker cannot simply employ a known method because the method that leads to the best result must first be discovered. In other words, the agent has to solve two tasks: level 1, employing a method that leads to a solution, and level 2, finding this method. Thus, two questions arise. What is the optimal method to be chosen? And what is the optimal approach to discovering that method? (There may be an infinite regress: level 3, finding a method for level 2, and so on.) At each level, time must be spent in deciding. Although Selten's argument concerning unfamiliar problems has not yet been cast into mathematical form, as the issue of combinatorial explosion has been, it strongly suggests that an optimizing approach to unfamiliar problems is rarely feasible when decision time is scarce.

Optimization Does Not Imply an Optimal Outcome

Some economists, biologists, and cognitive scientists seem to believe that a theory of bounded rationality must rely on optimization in order to promise optimal decisions. No optimization, no good decision. But this does not follow. Optimization needs to be distinguished from an optimal outcome. Note that the term *optimization* refers to a mathematical process—computing the maximum or minimum of a function—which does *not* guarantee optimal outcomes in the real world. The reason is that one has to make assumptions about the world in order to be able to optimize. These assumptions are typically selected by mathematical convenience, based on simplifications, and rarely grounded in psychological reality. If they are wrong, one has built the optimization castle on sand and optimization will not necessarily lead to optimal results. This is one reason why models of bounded rationality that do not involve optimization can often make predictions as good as those made by models that involve optimization (Gigerenzer & Selten, 2001b; Selten, 1998; March, 1978). A second reason is robustness. As described in chapter 1, asset allocation models that rely on optimization, Bayesian or otherwise, can perform systematically worse than a simple heuristic because parameter estimates are not robust.

A Good Fit, Per Se, Is Not a Good Empirical Validation of the Model

Friedman's (1953) argument in favor of as-if models was this: What counts is not descriptive accuracy, that is, the psychological validity of the axioms and assumptions, but rather the accuracy of the predictions a model makes. Despite Friedman's introductory example of the law of falling bodies, this explicit disinterest in a proper description of the underlying mechanisms would be unusual in physics, molecular biology, or genetics. (This does not mean that as-if models are never used; optimal foraging models in animal biology are an example.) The point I want to make here is that one needs to be careful in distinguishing between two kinds of statistical tests that have both been labeled "predictions." One is *data fitting,* that is, "explanations" of existing data; the other is *ex ante prediction,* that is, predictions of *new* observations.

In cognitive science and economics, the validity of a model is often reported in terms of its fit with *given* observations, such as what proportion of the variance a model explains. However, the belief that a good fit between model and data provides empirical evidence for the model is unfounded if the model has numerous free parameters. For instance, introducing more and more relevant constraints into models of optimization increases the number of adjustable parameters, which can make the resulting model too "powerful" to allow for falsification by empirical data. In these situations, a model can fit almost all possible data, including data produced by two logically inconsistent theories. Here, a good fit is a mathematical truism, not an empirical result. Utility maximization models often have many adjustable parameters—such as the utilities and utility functions in each particular case (Simon, 1986). This problem of robustness, or overfitting, is not specific to optimization models, but rather occurs in any statistical model that has a relatively large number of adjustable parameters, including neural networks (Geman, Bienenstock, & Doursat, 1992). If smart enough, one can likely find parameters so that the model fits a given situation. The problem of overfitting becomes particularly stringent in the as-if philosophy because the only empirical test for a model concerns its predictive power. Models of bounded rationality that dispense with optimization and also, for the most part, with utilities and probabilities reduce this validation problem in two ways. First, they model the underlying mechanisms of choice and inference and thereby provide a second source for testing their validity (process and outcome; see chap. 2; Brandstätter, Gigerenzer, & Hertwig, 2006). Second, they are simple and robust so that their predictions show consistently less overfitting than optimizing models.

These points highlight some limits of as-if optimization. There are other well-known problems, such as the "infinite regress" problem of determining how much information to gather in order to determine the cost of information. Last but not least, there is the class of ill-defined problems that by definition exclude optimization. Finding the best husband or the meaning of life are examples of naturally ill-defined problems. There are also intentionally ill-defined situations, such as legal contracts, which do not try to list all consequences for all possible actions of each party, since this might destroy trust, and absolutely watertight contracts rarely exist in the first place. These issues indicate that, despite its mathematical beauty, optimization under constraints is not the last word. Bounded rationality needs a different intellectual home—but which?

What Simon's Bounded Rationality Is Not: Cognitive Illusions

Optimization with decision costs taken into account is one misreading of Herb's concept of bounded rationality. It is not the only one. Others assume that the study of bounded rationality is the study of cognitive limitations and systematic errors in judgment and decision making (e.g., Rabin, 1998). Surprisingly, this second meaning amounts to something like the converse of the first: the cognitive illusions program aims at demonstrating that people's judgments and decisions do not follow the predictions of as-if optimization.

For instance, in his article "Bounded Rationality in Individual Decision Making," Camerer (1998: 179) reviews anomalies in decisions and errors in judgments and calls this the "exploration of procedural (bounded) rationality of individuals." Kaufman (1999: 141) gives the example of a gay man who practiced unsafe sex with multiple partners and "is now HIV positive and admits to his bounded rationality." This view that the study of bounded rationality is the study of systematic errors in judgment and decision making has spread from psychology into economics and law, shaping new research areas, such as behavioral economics and behavioral law and economics (e.g., Jolls, Sunstein, & Thaler, 1998). In Camerer's (1995: 588) words, "the goal is to test whether normative rules are *systematically* violated and to propose alternative theories to explain any observed violations." The products of this research are well known: a list of cognitive illusions, such as base rate neglect, overconfidence bias, and the sunk-cost effect.

The cognitive illusions program assumes bounded rationality to mean that humans have cognitive limitations, which express themselves in errors in judgment and decision making; therefore, the study of errors is the study of bounded rationality. Compared to optimization under constraints, this second interpretation of bounded rationality is relatively new. Its origins seem to be a reference to Simon's work on bounded rationality in the preface of Kahneman, Slovic, and Tversky's 1982 anthology. Since there are no citations at all to Simon in the early influential papers of Kahneman and Tversky, which were reprinted in the anthology, it was probably intended more as an acknowledgement to a distinguished figure than as an intellectual debt (Lopes, 1992). Nevertheless, the notion that bounded rationality is the study of cognitive illusions has since become widespread.

Herb applauded the demonstrations of systematic deviations from expected utility by Kahneman, Tversky, and others. But what did he think when the followers of Kahneman and Tversky labeled these demonstrations the study of "bounded rationality?" I asked him once, and his response was, "That's rhetoric. But Kahneman and Tversky have decisively disproved economists' rationality model." Herb was surprised to hear that I held their notion of cognitive illusions and biases to be inconsistent with his concept of bounded rationality. I think he liked their results so much that he tended to overlook that these experimenters accepted as normative the very optimization theories that Herb so fought against, at least when the results were interpreted as cognitive illusions. A true theory of bounded rationality does not cling to optimization theories, neither as descriptions nor as norms of behavior. (I gave reasons for the normative limits in the previous section.) We once discussed this issue on a walk through the beautiful Carnegie Mellon campus in the spring of 1997. A systematic deviation from an "insane" standard should not automatically be called a judgmental error, should it? "I hadn't thought about it in this way," Herb replied.

Why is bounded rationality not the same as irrationality? Herb has given the answer in the form of an analogy. Bounded rationality is like a pair of scissors: The mind is one blade, and the structure of the environment is the other. To understand behavior, one has to look at both, at how they fit. In other words, to evaluate cognitive strategies as rational or irrational, one also needs to analyze the environment because a strategy is rational or irrational only with respect to a particular physical or social environment. The study of cognitive illusions and errors, however, studies only the cognitive blade and compares it with laws of probability rather than with the structure of the environment. One blade alone does not cut well.

I will illustrate the differences between these three visions of bounded rationality by using a problem introduced in chapter 2. A company wants to design a robot that can catch a fly ball. For the sake of simplicity, we will only consider the case where a ball comes in high behind or in front of a player, not to his left or right.

One team of engineers, whom I call the optimizing team, proceeds by programming the family of parabolas into the robot's brain, given that, in theory, balls fly in parabolas. To select the proper parabola, the robot needs to be equipped with instruments that can measure the distance from where the ball was thrown or shot as well as its initial velocity and projection angle. Yet in a real game, balls do not fly in parabolas because of air resistance and wind. Thus, the robot would require further instruments that can measure the speed and direction of the wind at each point of the ball's flight in order to compute the resulting path. In addition, further factors, such as spin, affect the flight of the ball. The optimizing team eventually succeeds in producing a lengthy equation that, given all these measurements, specifies the trajectory of the flight and the spot where the ball will land. Note that this equation is an as-if model—the team is not concerned with the actual mechanisms that real players or robots use—and, consequently, the equation does not inform us how to actually build a robot. The optimizing team responds that their task is not "robot psychology," that is, to understand how a robot actually does, or could do, the job. Their claim is that the model will predict the point to which real players and robots would run to catch the ball.

A subgroup within the optimizing team objects that there is no time for the robot to make the proposed measurements and computations, given that the ball is only in the air for a few seconds. A fully rational robot would just sit on the field, measuring and calculating and thus missing every ball. The more precise the measurements are, the longer they take and the less time the robot has left to run to the spot where the ball is supposed to land. The real constraint, they argue, is not money but time. Instead of trying to model an omniscient robot, the team proposes building one that optimizes under constraints. After some deliberation, the subgroup puts forward a number of constraints on the robot's ability for information search. Finally, the members of this subgroup design a sophisticated formula that optimizes the outcome under the given constraints, a mathematical masterpiece. The hard-core members of the optimizing team, however, object that this formula is even more complex than the first one and that the robot will sit even longer on the field, measuring and calculating when it should stop measuring and calculating.

A second team enters the field and argues that in order to design a robot, one first needs to understand the players' cognitive processes and find out what they actually do. One should experimentally study real players and create situations in which they systematically demonstrate judgmental errors, that is, deviations from the optimizing model. These errors will be the window for the underlying cognitive processes. This group calls itself the cognitive illusions team. After a phase of trial and error, they find a task in which the players show a bias. A player is positioned on a fixed point in the field, a ball is shot in high, and the player is asked to predict how many yards in front or behind his position the ball will hit the ground (Babler & Dannemiller, 1993; Saxberg, 1987). The surprising result is that the players don't predict very well but consistently underestimate the distance between their position and the point where the ball will land. This systematic error is called the "optimistic bias" in baseball, cricket, and soccer because underestimating the distance suggests to players that they might actually get the ball even when they can't. A debate opens on whether this judgmental error could be adaptive, since in a real game, not trying to run for a ball that could in fact have been reached is a more costly error than trying without success. The cognitive illusions team claims that the optimizing team's model has been descriptively disproved; actual players show systematic errors, whereas the optimizing model doesn't predict any. The optimization team responds that they will nevertheless maintain their model; a model that can at least approximately predict the data is better than no model. After all, they argue, the notion of an "optimistic bias" is only a redescription of the data; the bias team hasn't put forward any alternative model of the underlying cognitive mechanisms or of how to build the robot.

A third team is called in. They agree with the second that humans may not be able to compute the point where the ball will land. However, they argue that the negative goal of disproving the optimization team's predictions does not directly lead to positive models of the underlying cognitive processes. For instance, the notion of an "optimistic bias" does not describe how a player actually catches a ball, but only how his judgment deviates from the actual landing point. The third team proposes opening what they call the adaptive toolbox. What do players actually do in order to catch a ball, given that they do not seem to perform the measurements and calculations that the optimization team proposes? The adaptive toolbox team conducts experiments that show that experienced players rely on several heuristics, the simplest one being the *gaze heuristic*:

> *Fixate your gaze on the ball, start running, and adjust your running speed so that the angle of gaze remains constant.*

As mentioned in chapter 2, the gaze heuristic works in situations where the ball is already high in the air. If this is not yet the case, the player does not need a completely new strategy but only to change the last of its three "building blocks" (Shaffer et al., 2004):

> *Fixate your gaze on the ball, start running, and adjust your running speed so that the image of the ball rises at a constant rate.*

One can intuitively see its logic. If the player sees the ball rising from the point it was hit with accelerating speed, he had better run backward because the ball will meet the ground behind his present position. If, however, the ball rises with decreasing speed, he needs to run toward the ball instead. If the ball rises at a constant speed, the player is in the right position. Both versions of the heuristic ignore all causally relevant variables for computing the trajectory and pay attention to only one piece of information.

The optimizing team responds that it may be very interesting to know how actual players do the job, but it is not really relevant. The successful player will run exactly to the same point that can be calculated from our equations, the team maintains, and so the player acts "as if" he were optimizing. Not exactly, the adaptive toolbox team replies, for there are two important advantages to realistic process models. First, the omniscient, optimizing player exists only "as if" and therefore does not lead to instructions on how to build a robot or how to teach human beginners. The necessary information and computation will most likely lead to computational explosion; that is, the model is impossible to implement in any human or computer hardware. In contrast, the gaze heuristic can be taught to inexperienced players, and it may eventually be possible to build a robot that uses it. Second, with a good model of the heuristics a person uses, it is possible to make more precise predictions than with an as-if model, including behaviors that an as-if model cannot foresee. For instance, the gaze heuristic predicts that the player will catch the ball while running. Optimization models would not predict this behavior. Similarly, knowing the heuristics players use helps to predict what players cannot do. Remember that the cognitive illusions team showed that even experienced players fail to predict where the ball will land. Knowing the heuristic, we understand why this is in fact not a requirement for successfully catching a ball. The gaze heuristic succeeds without this ability. Thus, what looks like a serious judgmental bias in need of de-biasing turns out to be irrelevant for good ball catching.

There is a final point in this example. Rationality is said to be a means toward an end. But the end is *dependent on* the interpretation of bounded rationality being taken. For optimization under constraints, the end is to estimate the point at which the ball will land; the cognitive illusions program shares this view but with the additional claim that players miscalculate this point because of their cognitive limitations. Knowing the cognitive process can inform us, however, that the end might be a different one. In the case of the gaze heuristic, the player's goal is not to predict the landing point, but to be there where the ball lands. The rationality of heuristics is not simply a means to a given end; the heuristic itself can define what the end is.

Homo heuristicus

This thought experiment illustrates the program of ecological rationality: to study (i) the heuristics people actually use to solve a class of tasks, (ii) the structure of the task environment, and (iii) what environmental structure a heuristic can exploit. The corresponding methodologies used to investigate these issues are experimental research, analytical proofs, and computer simulations. The aim of such research is to establish a "periodic system" of heuristics and their building blocks as well as a conceptual language to describe the structures of relevant real-world environments. This program develops Herbert Simon's ideas of studying the rational principles that underlie the behavior of real people, who do not optimize and, for the most part, do not calculate utilities and probabilities. Recall that this program differs from the optimizing program in that it analyzes the actual process—the heuristics—rather than constructing as-if models based on a convenient mathematical structure. Unlike the cognitive illusions program, it directly analyzes the decision process rather than trying to demonstrate violations of the assumptions underlying as-if models. The various heuristics in the adaptive toolbox consist of a small number of building blocks, including rules for information search, stopping, and decision.

In *Bounded Rationality: The Adaptive Toolbox* (2001: i), Reinhard Selten and I started out with the goal "to promote bounded rationality as the key to understanding how actual people make decisions without utilities and probabilities." The adaptive toolbox signifies a radical departure from the classical "repair program" of adjusting economic theories, where one variable, such as regret, is added to the expected utility calculus or where one tinkers with the functions for probabilities or utilities, as in prospect theory. In contrast, our starting point is empirically rooted knowledge about the human mind and its capabilities. Quantitative probabilities, utilities, and optimization appear to play little role in actual judgment and decision making, whereas fast and frugal processes, such as name recognition, aspiration levels, imitation learning, sequential search, stopping rules, and one-reason decision making, do. The models of heuristics typically have zero adjustable parameters, which makes it easier to empirically test and falsify them. In statistical terms, heuristics err on the side of "bias" rather then "variance" (Geman, Bienenstock, & Doursat, 1992). This work on the adaptive toolbox and on ecological rationality will, I hope, provide a positive alternative to the investigation of rational choice: the study of how *Homo heuristicus* makes decisions in an uncertain world.

The term *adaptive toolbox* is not Herb's, although it is in his spirit. The rationality of the adaptive toolbox is ecological and refers to the match between a heuristic and the structure of an environment, which is the essence of Simon's own analogy of a pair of scissors. When heuristics are able to exploit the structure of environments, they can avoid a trade-off between accuracy and effort and instead be both more accurate and more frugal. Whereas the used car buyer in Stigler's classical example typically does not get the best buy, because information search costs limit attempts at an exhaustive search, situations exist in which a smart heuristic can solve a task perfectly, as illustrated by the gaze heuristic. Studying ecological rationality—the match between heuristics and environments—is important for freeing the concept of heuristics from the flavor of always being the second-best solution. The issue can be posed with a different twist. If one has a good model of the mechanism, what is the additional value of an as-if model? "As if" may well turn out to be the second-best solution.

Epilogue

Herb is no longer among us. But his spirit is. His struggle with the concept of bounded rationality will stay with us, and I believe that if he could see how his ideas are being developed he would be enthusiastic, even though we are only beginning to develop a general theory. Let me end with his own words:

Dear Gerd:

I have never thought of either bounded rationality or satisficing as precisely defined technical terms, but rather as signals to economists that they needed to pay attention to reality, and a suggestion of some ways in which they might. But I do agree that I have used bounded rationality as the generic term, to refer to all of the limits that make a human being's problem spaces something quite different from the corresponding task environments: knowledge limits, computational limits, incomparability of component goals. I have used satisficing to refer to choice of "good enough" alternatives (perhaps defined by an aspiration level mechanism) or "best-so-far" alternatives to terminate selective search among alternatives—the latter usually not being given in advance, but generated sequentially. So one might apply "satisficing" to the "good-enough criterion" or to any heuristic search that uses such a criterion to make its choice.

Final remark on this point, going from most general to most specific, we have bounded rationality, then heuristic search, then satisficing. Further, on the same level as heuristic search, we have a second class of methods, very important in the theory of expertise: problem solution by recognition. Currently, that is my taxonomy of decision and problem solution methods. You can decide better than I can where you want to place fast-and-frugal in this rough classification. I would tend to regard it as a class of heuristics, hence on the same level as satisficing.

I guess a major reason for my using somewhat vague terms—like bounded rationality—is that I did not want to give the impression that I thought I had "solved" the problem of creating an empirically grounded theory of economic phenomena. What I was trying to do was to call attention to the need for such a theory—and the accompanying body of empirical work to establish it—and to provide some examples of a few mechanisms that might appear in it, which already had some evidential base. There still lies before us an enormous job of studying the actual decision making processes that take place in corporations and other economic settings. . . .

End of sermon—which you and Reinhard [Selten] don't need. I am preaching to believers.

Cordially,

Herb

Chapter 6

Out of the Frying Pan into the Fire

The 9/11 Commission's report unfolded the chronology of the terrorist attacks on September 11, 2001, which cost the lives of some three thousand people and billions of dollars in property damage (National Commission on Terrorist Attacks upon the United States, 2004). It focused on how al-Qaeda terrorism evolved, the possible failures of intelligence agencies to detect and avoid the attack, and potential diplomatic, legal, and technological measures to prevent future attacks. The report concerned the origins and prevention of what I refer to as *direct damage,* that is, the immediate consequences of terrorist action. Here I deal with a second source of harm caused by terrorist action, which I refer to as *indirect damage.* Indirect damage is not under the control of terrorists; it is mediated through the minds of citizens. In the case of September 11, known indirect damages include the financial damages in the aviation industry fueled by many people's anxiety about flying, the job loss in the tourism industry, and peculiar consequences, such as the increase in criminal suspects being involuntarily examined for psychiatric hospitalization (Catalano et al., 2004). Note that these misfortunes are not a necessary consequence of terrorist action; they are of psychological origin and could in principle be prevented, once individuals and institutions realize that terrorists target minds as well as bodies.

Dread Risks

Low-probability, high-damage events in which many people are killed at one point in time are called *dread risks.* As opposed to situations in which

This chapter is a revised version of G. Gigerenzer, "Out of the Frying Pan into the Fire: Behavioral Reactions to Terrorist Attacks," *Risk Analysis* 26 (2006): 347–351; reprinted with kind permission of Blackwell Publishing.

a similar number of people or more are killed over a longer period of time, people tend to react to dread risks with strong emotions (Slovic, 1987). The unconscious heuristic process seems to be: *If there is a danger of many people dying at one point in time, avoid the situation.*

The crash of the four planes in the terrorist attack on September 11 exemplifies such a catastrophic event. In contrast, the estimated 44,000 to 98,000 people who die every year in U.S. hospitals because of documented and preventable medical errors do not constitute a dread risk (Kohn, Corrigan, & Donaldson, 2000). Even after learning about the dangers, few people would avoid hospitals, since patients generally do not all die at one point in time but scattered across time. One potential evolutionary account of this specialized avoidance behavior is in terms of preparedness; that is, human minds are prepared to learn the association between dread risk and avoidance behavior in one trial. A possible reason is that for our evolutionary ancestors, living in small bands of hunter-gatherers, the loss of many members at one point of time could have brought the group beyond a critical threshold that threatened their survival. A further explanation is the lack of proper information about risks among the general public of many Western societies. For instance, few people are aware that the probability of losing one's life is about the same for driving 12 miles by car as for a nonstop flight, say, from New York to Detroit (Sivak & Flannagan, 2003). That is, if one arrives safely by car at the airport, the most dangerous part of the trip may be over (figure 6.1). A third account is in terms of control: people fear terrorist attacks because they have no control, whereas people believe they are in control while driving. While there is some truth in each of these accounts, none by itself seems to be sufficient (for instance, although the driver has some control, the person sitting next to the driver has little control, yet he or she typically also feels little fear). My point here is not to provide an explanation for the tendency to avoid dread risks but rather to draw attention to avoidance behavior as a potential cause for the indirect damages of terrorism, mediated through our minds.

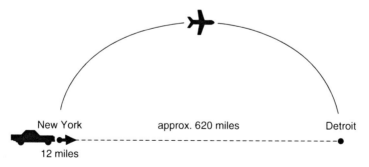

Figure 6.1: Fly or drive? The risk of losing one's life during a nonstop flight is approximately the same as when driving 12 miles by car.

Avoidance Behavior after September 11

I investigate a possible mediated death toll of the attack on September 11. This possibility has gone virtually unnoticed, although it was hypothesized shortly after the attack (Myers, 2001). In earlier research, I collected preliminary data limited to 3 months after the attack (Gigerenzer, 2004a; see also Sivak & Flannagan, 2004); here, I provide a comprehensive analysis of the 18 months after the attack. My hypothesis is as follows: If (i) Americans reduced their air travel after the attack, and (ii) a proportion of those who did not fly instead drove to their destination, then (iii) a number of Americans died on the road in the attempt to avoid the fate of the passengers who were killed in the four fatal flights. I call this the *dread hypothesis,* for short. Is there evidence for such a mediated toll of lives?

The first part of the dread hypothesis—the reduction in air travel following the attacks—is well documented. Millions of Americans reduced their air travel, which left airlines and travel agencies flying into the red. For instance, the national revenue passenger miles decreased by 20 percent, 17 percent, and 12 percent, in October, November, and December 2001, respectively, compared with the same months in 2000 (U.S. Department of Transportation, 1996–2003). Data for the second part of the dread hypothesis, in contrast, is difficult to obtain because there is no record of how many people decided not to fly and took their car instead. Indirect evidence can be obtained from the Office of Highway Policy Information, which reports the number of vehicle miles driven before and after the attack. To establish whether there was an increase in driving, three conditions must be met. First, there must be a sudden increase in the individual monthly miles traveled in the months following the attack compared to the monthly miles of the previous year. Second, this increase must not be observed in the months before the attack. Finally, the increase must fade away at some point, when the pictures of the attack fade out of people's minds.

In the eight months before the attack (January to August 2001), the individual monthly vehicle miles traveled in 2001 (all systems) were on average 0.9 percent higher than in 2000—which is normal given that miles traveled increase from year to year in the United States. Immediately after the attack and in the 12 months following, the miles traveled increased substantially. In the three months after the attack (October to December 2001), the increase tripled to 2.8 percent. In the first three months of 2002, the increase was 3.1 percent and then 2.9 percent in the subsequent six months (April to September 2002), compared to the previous year. Thereafter, in the next six months (October 2002 to March 2003), this figure declined to 0.5 percent; that is, the increase in road traffic after September 11 diminished after one year.

The hypothesis that more people chose to drive rather than fly after the attack has another testable implication. The increase in miles driven should be most pronounced in the rural interstate highways, where much of long-distance driving occurs, rather than in urban areas. Specifically, before the attack, the increase in the rural interstate highways should be similar to the

0.9 percent increase on all road systems but thereafter rise above it. Consistent with this hypothesis, the increase in the eight months before the attack was similar to that for all traffic systems, 1 percent. In the three months following the attack, the vehicle miles increased by 5.2 percent. In the first three months of 2002, the increase (compared to the previous year) was 3.7 percent; in the following six months, 2.2 percent. One year after the attack, the increase in miles driven on rural interstate highways stopped and even reversed to a slight decrease of an average of −0.2 percent in the six months following (October 2002 to March 2003). Thus, vehicle miles increased after September 11, most strongly on rural interstate highways, for a period of about 12 months.

Did this change in travel behavior go hand in hand with a surplus in fatal road accidents? To test the third part of the dread hypothesis, I compare the fatal road accidents after September 11 with two baselines: first with the average number of fatal road accidents in the five years preceding the attack (1996–2000, the zero line in figure 6.2) and, second, with the number of fatal crashes in 2001 before the attack. The first baseline is meaningful because the number of fatal traffic accidents had been very stable over those five years. The total monthly number of fatal traffic accidents varied between about 2,500 in February and 3,500 in August, while the maximum deviation from these figures during the five years was, averaged across all months, only about 115 accidents, which amounts to 3–4 percent of the monthly average. The second baseline, January through August 2001, shows that in the months before the attack, the number of fatal accidents consistently followed the pattern of the preceding five years. On average, there were only nine(!) additional fatalities per month (out of some 2,500 to 3,500 each month), and the number of fatal accidents always remained within the minimum and maximum values of the five previous years.

This regularity broke down in the months following September 2001 (figure 6.2). For a period of 12 months, October 2001 to September 2002, the number of fatal accidents exceeded the five-year baseline every month as well as the baseline adjusted by the average increase of nine fatal crashes in pre–September 2001. In the majority of months, the surplus exceeds the maximum value of the preceding five years, as shown by the bars in figure 6.2. This is exactly the same period in which the passenger miles showed a marked increase. The surplus death toll was highest in January and March of 2002. After one year, fatal crashes returned to the baseline before the attack, at the same point in time when the road traffic returned to normal (see above). This consistent pattern after the attacks provides support for the hypothesis that the terrorist attacks caused a mediated secondary death toll.

How many fatalities resulted from people's decrease in flying and increase in driving? To estimate this number, I will use the five-year baseline as the comparison standard, corrected by the average increase of nine fatalities per month. For the 12 months following the attack, one obtains a surplus of 317

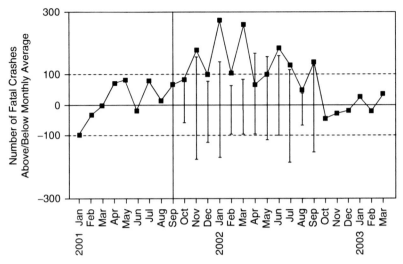

Figure 6.2: The number of fatal traffic accidents in the United States increased after the terrorist attacks on September 11, 2001, for a period of 12 months. Numbers are expressed as deviations from the five-year baseline 1996–2000 (the zero line). The bars (shown for the 12 months following the terrorist attacks) specify the maximum and the minimum number for each month of the baseline. Before September 11, the average of the monthly numbers of fatal traffic accidents for 2001 was close to the zero line, and the monthly values were always within the maximum and minimum of the previous five years. Yet in the 12 months following the terrorist attacks (October 2001 to September 2002), the number of fatal traffic accidents every month was higher than the zero line, and in most cases it exceeded the maximum of the previous years.

Data taken from U.S. Department of Transportation, Federal Highway Administration (2002/2003).

fatal crashes for October through December 2001 and of an additional 1,188 for January through September 2002, which totals 1,505 fatal crashes. Given that the ratio between fatalities and fatal traffic accidents in 2001 and 2002 was consistently 1.06, the total estimated number of Americans who lost their lives on the road by trying to avoid the risk of flying is 1,595. I want to emphasize that this number is an estimate, since a nonexperimental study cannot control for all alternative explanations. This estimate is six times higher than the total number of passengers (256) who died in the four fatal flights.

The Madrid Attacks

Does the dread hypothesis generalize to other cultures? On March 11, 2004, exactly two and a half years after 9/11, the bombings of four commuter trains during the Madrid rush hour killed about 200 people and wounded 1,460. The evolutionary preparedness hypothesis would predict that Spaniards would then avoid riding trains. And indeed, Spaniards reduced their train travel after the bombing, although the effect was smaller and shorter (only two months) than the American reaction after September 11 (López-Rousseau, 2005). But there are two other parts to the dread hypothesis. The second, an increase in highway traffic, did not happen in Spain; in fact, there was a decrease. As a consequence, the fatal highway accidents also decreased rather than increased, and no secondary loss of lives mediated through Spaniards' minds was observed. Like Americans, the Spaniards avoided the dread risk, but unlike Americans, they did not take the next step and jump into their cars. Why is that? One possible factor is that there is less of a car culture in Spain than in the United States. A second is the availability of a better-developed public transport system that allowed Spaniards to resume train travel quickly. A final possible reason is that Spain has been exposed to decades of terror attacks so that one terror attack provides less of a dread risk and more of a calculated risk instead.

Counterterrorism Should Address Reduction of Mediated Damages

How to react to the emerging global terrorism? As a response, the National Commission's *9/11 Report* (2004: ci–cii) demands "the use of all elements of national power: diplomacy, intelligence, covert action, law enforcement, economic policy, foreign aid, public diplomacy, and homeland defense." A national counterterrorism center should coordinate these means and strive for defeating terrorism anywhere in the world. The present analysis indicates that there is a second goal, to defeat the effects of terrorism acting through our minds. Terrorist attacks are hard to prevent, even with costly diplomatic and military strategies and controversial surveillance systems. It would be comparatively easier and less expensive to invest at least part of the efforts in reducing the mediated death toll. The first measure to achieve this goal is to make the issue an issue. The psychological aspect has not yet entered public policy awareness to the same degree that the technological side of fighting terrorism has. Yet there are a number of measures that can be taken and tested, from making people aware of the fact that terrorists can strike a second time through their minds to disseminating relevant information to the public, such as that a dozen miles of driving result in the same risk of dying as one nonstop flight. Factual information will not change everyone's behavior, but by knowing the facts, people can understand their immediate emotional reactions and better control them. Such an extended counterterrorism policy can save lives. Otherwise, history may repeat itself after the next attack, if another should happen.

Summary

A low-probability, high-damage event in which many people are killed at one point in time is called a *dread risk*. Dread risks can cause direct damage and in addition, indirect damage mediated though the minds of citizens. The behavioral reactions of Americans to the terrorist attacks on September 11, 2001, provide evidence for the dread hypothesis: (i) Americans reduced their air travel after the attack; (ii) for a period of one year following the attacks travel on interstate highways increased, suggesting that a proportion of those who did not fly instead drove to their destinations; and (iii) for the same period, in each month the number of fatal highway crashes exceeded the baseline of the previous years. An estimated fifteen hundred Americans died on the road in the attempt to avoid the fate of the passengers who were killed in the four fatal flights.

Chapter 7

What's in a Sample?

A Manual for Building Cognitive Theories

In his *Opticks,* Isaac Newton (1704/1952) reported experiments with prisms to demonstrate that white light consists of spectral colors. Newton did not sample, nor was he interested in means or variances. In his view, good experimentation had nothing to do with sampling. Newton was not antagonistic to sampling, but he used it only when he thought it was appropriate, as in quality control. In his role as the master of the London Royal Mint, Newton conducted routine sampling inspections in order to determine whether the amount of gold in the coins was too little or too large. Just as in Newton's physics, experimentation and statistics were hostile rivals in nineteenth-century physiology and medicine. The great experimenter Claude Bernard used to ridicule the use of samples; his favorite example was that it is silly to collect the urine of one person, or of even a group of persons, over a 24-hour period because it is not the same before and after digestion and because averages are reifications of unreal conditions (Gigerenzer et al., 1989: 129). When B. F. Skinner demonstrated the effects of reinforcement schedules, he used one pigeon at a time, not two dozen. Although Skinner did not sample pigeons, his theory assumed that his pigeons sampled information about the consequences of their behavior, as William Estes (1959) pointed out.

These cases illustrate some of the perplexing faces of sampling. What's in a sample? Why coins but not prisms or urine? Why did we come to believe that sampling and experimentation are two sides of the same coin, whereas Newton, Bernard, and Skinner did not? Why did Skinner not sample pigeons but implicitly assumed that pigeons sample information? In this chapter, I try to put some order into the puzzling uses and nonuses of sampling. Fiedler and Juslin (2006) distinguished various forms of cognitive sampling, such as

This chapter is a revised version of G. Gigerenzer, "What's in a Sample? A Manual for Building Cognitive Theories," in *Information Sampling and Adaptive Cognition,* ed. K. Fiedler and P. Juslin (New York: Cambridge University Press, 2006), 239–260.

internal versus external sampling (e.g., memory versus the Internet), and the unit size of the objects of sampling. In contrast, I will focus on the evolution of the ideas of sampling—from the statistical toolbox to theories of mind.

I argue that the sampling tools that have been proposed and accepted as descriptions of how the mind works were mostly those that researchers happened to be familiar with as research tools. Other tools had little chance of being considered. Furthermore, the very idea that the mind samples information—from memory or from the environment—became prominent only after psychologists began to emphasize the role of sampling in their research methods. What I hope to achieve with this chapter is not a complete taxonomy of sampling, but rather motivation to take a look into the toolbox and rethink the possibilities of sampling when building theories of mind.

Who Samples?

I begin with the observation that the answer to the question of *who* samples information is different in the cognitive sciences than in the fields from which statistical sampling theory actually emerged: astronomy, agriculture, demographics, genetics, and quality control. In these noncognitive sciences, the researcher alone may sample (figure 7.1). For instance, an astronomer may repeatedly measure the position of a star, or an agricultural researcher may fertilize a sample of plots and measure the average number of potatoes grown. Sampling concerns objects that are measured on some variable. Why would that be different in the cognitive sciences?

In the cognitive sciences (in contrast to the natural sciences), there are two "classes" of people who can engage in sampling: researchers and the participants of their studies (figure 7.2). Whether and how researchers draw samples is generally seen as a methodological question. Whether and how researchers think that the minds of their participants engage in sampling of information is treated as a theoretical question. The labels "methodological" and "theoretical" suggest that both questions are unrelated and should be answered independently. After all, what do theories of cognitive processes have to do with the methods to test these theories?

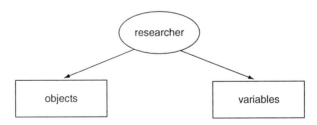

Figure 7.1: The structure of the potential uses of sampling in the noncognitive sciences. Researchers may sample objects (such as electrons) to measure these on variables (such as location and mass).

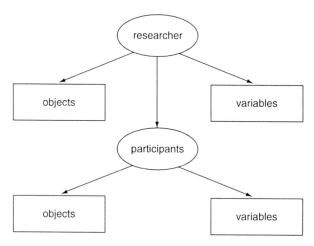

Figure 7.2: The structure of the potential uses of sampling in the cognitive sciences. Researchers may sample stimulus objects, participants, or variables, and their participants may themselves sample objects and variables.

I do not believe that these two issues are independent of each other. My hypothesis is that there is a significant correlation (not a one-to-one relation) in cognitive psychology between researchers' sampling practices and the role of sampling in their theories of mind. This hypothesis is an extension of my work on the tools-to-theories heuristic. The general tools-to-theories thesis is twofold (Gigerenzer, 1991):

> *Discovery:* New scientific tools, once entrenched in a scientist's daily practice, suggest new theoretical metaphors and concepts.
> *Acceptance:* Once proposed by an individual scientist (or a group), the new theoretical concepts are more likely to be accepted by the scientific community if their members are also users of the new tool.

Note that Sigmund Freud, I. P. Pavlov, and the Gestalt psychologists, as well as the "father" of experimental psychology, Wilhelm Wundt, did not sample participants, and sampling played no role in their theories of mind. All this changed after the unit of investigation ceased to be the individual person and instead became the group mean—a process that started in the applied fields, such as educational psychology (Danziger, 1990). Harold Kelley (1967), for instance, who used sampling and Fisher's analysis of variance to analyze his data, proposed that the mind attributes a cause to an effect in the same way, by sampling information and an intuitive version of analysis of variance. The community of social psychologists who also used analysis of variance as a routine tool accepted the theory quickly, and for a decade it virtually defined what social psychology was about. In contrast, R. Duncan Luce (1988: 582) rejected routine use of analysis of variance as "mindless hypothesis testing in lieu of doing good research," and his theories of mind differed as a consequence. For instance, being familiar with the statistical tools of Jerzy Neyman and Egon S. Pearson and their doctrine of random sampling, Luce (1977) proposed that the mind might draw random samples and make decisions just as Neyman-Pearson theory does.

In summary, I propose that if researchers sample, they are likely to assume in their theories that the mind samples as well. If they do not sample, their view of cognitive processes typically also does not involve sampling. Moreover, the specific kind of sampling process that researchers use is likely to become part of their cognitive theories.

What's in a Sample?

In the cognitive sciences, the object of sampling can be threefold: participants, objects, and variables. Researchers can sample participants, stimulus objects, or variables. Today, participants are sampled habitually, objects rarely, and variables almost never. In addition, the minds under study can sample objects and variables. In cognitive theories, minds mostly sample objects but rarely variables. This results in five possible uses of sampling in psychology (figure 7.2).

My strict distinction between the cognitive and noncognitive sciences is an idealization; in reality there are bridges. The astronomers' concern with the "personal equation" of an observer illustrates such a link. Astronomers realized that researchers had systematically different response times when they determined the time a star travels through a certain point. This led to the study of astronomers' personal equations, that is, the time that needed to be subtracted to correct for their individual reaction times. In this situation, the object of sampling was both the researchers and their objects, such as stars (Gigerenzer et al., 1989).

Why Sampling?

I distinguish two goals of sampling: hypothesis testing and measurement. Take significance tests as an example, where a sample statistic—such as t or F—is calculated. Significance tests were already being used by astronomers in the early nineteenth century (Swijtink, 1987). Unlike present-day psychologists, astronomers used the tests to reject data (so-called outliers), not to reject hypotheses. At least provisionally, the astronomers assumed that a hypothesis (such as normal distribution of observational errors around the true position of a star) was correct and mistrusted the data. In astronomy, the goal was precise measurement, and this called for methods to identify bad data. In psychology, researchers trusted the data and mistrusted the hypotheses; that is, following the influence of Fisher, the goal became hypothesis testing, not measurement.

Hypothesis testing and measurement are concepts taken from statistical theory, and the obvious question is whether they are also good candidates for understanding how the mind works. Whatever the right answer may be, hypothesis testing has been widely assumed to be an adaptive goal of cognition, including in numerous studies that tried to show that people make systematic errors when testing hypotheses. Note that measurement has not been as extensively considered and studied as a goal of cognition (with some exceptions, such as the work of Brunswik, 1955), which is consistent with the fact that researchers tend to use their sampling tools for hypothesis testing rather than measurement.

How to Sample?

Sampling is not sampling. I distinguish four ways of how to sample, beginning with the nonuse of sampling.

Study Ideal Types, Not Samples

Newton thought that the science of optics was close to mathematics, where truth can be demonstrated in one single case, and he loathed researchers who replicated his experiments. Similarly, the most influential psychologists achieved their fame by studying one individual at a time. Freud's Anna O., Wundt's Wundt (the "father" of experimental psychology served as experimental subject), Pavlov's dog, Luria's mnemonist Shereshevsky, and Simon's chess masters are illustrations. They represent ideal types, not averages. They may also represent distinct individual types, such as brain patients with specific lesions. Note that the ideal type approach does not mean that only one individual is studied. There may be several individuals, such as Freud's patients or Skinner's pigeons. The point is that the fundamental unit of analysis is $N = 1$, the singular case.

It is of a certain irony that Fisher's only psychological example in his influential *Design of Experiments* (1935) concerns the analysis of a lady who claimed that she could tell whether the tea fusion or the milk was poured first into a cup of tea. This single-case study of extraordinary sensory abilities did not become the model for experimental research. Fisher sampled objects, not participants, as in figure 7.1. Psychologists generally interpreted his methodology to be about sampling participants, not objects.

In his seminal book *Constructing the Subject* (1990), Danziger argued that the reason why American psychologists turned away from studying individuals in the 1930s and 1940s and embraced means as their new "subject" had little to do with the scientific goals of our discipline. In contrast, this move was largely a reaction to university administrators' pressure on professors of psychology to show that their research was useful for applied fields, specifically educational research, which offered large sources of funding. The educational administrator was interested in such questions as whether a new curriculum would improve the *average* performance of pupils and not the study of the laws of the individual mind. Danziger provided detailed evidence that sampling of participants started in the applied fields but not in the core areas of psychology, and in the United States rather than in Germany, where professors of psychology were not, at that time, under pressure to legitimize their existence by proving their practical usefulness. Some of these differences continue to prevail: Social psychologists tend to sample dozens or hundreds of undergraduates for five to ten minutes, whereas perceptual psychologists tend to study one or a few participants, each individually and for an extended time.

Convenience Sampling

In the 1920s, Ronald A. Fisher (1890–1962) was chief statistician at the agricultural station in Rothamsted. Before Fisher, agricultural researchers had little sense for sampling. For instance, in the mid-nineteenth century, the British agriculturist James F. W. Johnston tried to determine which fertilizer was the best for the growth of turnips. He fertilized one plot, which yielded 24 bushels, and compared this result with those from three plots without fertilizer, which respectively yielded 18, 21, and 24 bushels of grain. Johnston understood that turnips naturally show up to 25 percent variation from plot to plot and that the average difference of about 10 percent that he observed was therefore not indicative of a real improvement. What Johnston did not understand was the importance of sample size—that this variability becomes less and less important as the number of plots on which the average is based increases (Gigerenzer et al., 1989: chap. 3).

Fisher's major contribution was to unite the rival practices of scientific experimentation and statistics. From Newton to Bernard to Skinner, this connection, as mentioned, had not existed. Fisher turned the two rival practices into two sides of the same coin and introduced randomized trials to agriculture, genetics, and medicine. By way of parapsychology and education, his ideas also conquered experimental psychology. The marriage between statistics and experimentation also changed statistics, from the general emphasis on large samples to Fisher's small-sample statistics. The idea of basing inferences on small samples—as in the typical experiment—was highly controversial. The statistician Richard von Mises (1957: 159) predicted that "the heyday of small sample theory ... is already past." It was not past, however; Fisher prevailed.

Fisher's position emphasized some aspects of sampling—sample size, significance, and random assignment—and left out others. Most importantly, the concept of random sampling from a defined population had no place in Fisher's (1955) theory. Fisher's samples were not randomly drawn from a defined population. There was no such population in the first place. A sample whose population is not known is called a *convenience sample*. Fisher's liberal interpretation of how to sample became entrenched in psychology: The participants in psychological experiments are seldom randomly sampled, nor is a population defined.

Fisher did not think that convenience samples were a weakness. He held that in science there is no known population from which repeated sampling can be done. In a brilliant move, Fisher proposed to view any sample as a random sample from an *unknown hypothetical infinite population*. This solution has puzzled many statisticians: "This is, to me at all events, a most baffling conception" (Kendall, 1943: 17). However, Fisher's ideas about sampling were not the last word. Fisher had two powerful rivals, the Polish statistician Jerzy Neyman and the British statistician Egon S. Pearson, the son of Karl Pearson.

Random Sampling

The earliest quasi-random sampling procedure I know of is the trial of the Pyx (Stigler, 1999). The trial is a ceremony that goes back to the Middle Ages, the final stage of a sampling inspection scheme for production quality control at the London Royal Mint. The word *Pyx* refers to the box in which the sample of coins was collected, in order to determine whether the coins were too heavy or too light and contained too much or too little gold. As mentioned before, Newton served as master at the Royal Mint from 1699 until his death in 1727. The same Newton who did not use sampling for scientific experimentation supervised sampling for the purpose of quality control. The trial of the Pyx employed a form of sampling that is different from a convenience sample. It used a random sample drawn from a defined population, the total production of the Mint in one or a few years.

In the twentieth century, hypothesis testing that used random sampling from a defined population was formalized by Neyman and Pearson. In their theory of hypothesis testing, one starts with two hypotheses (rather than one null hypothesis) and the probabilities of the two possible errors, Type I and Type II, from which the necessary sample size is calculated. A random sample is then drawn, after which one of the two hypotheses is accepted, and the other is rejected (in Fisher's scheme, the null can only be rejected, not accepted). Neyman and Pearson believed that they had improved the logic of Fisher's null hypothesis testing. Fisher (1955) did not think so. He thought that those who propose sampling randomly from a defined population and calculating sample size on the basis of cost-benefit trade-offs mistake science for quality control. He compared the Neyman-Pearsonians to Stalin's five-year plans, that is, to Russians confusing technology with producing knowledge.

Sequential Sampling

A third line of sampling is sequential sampling, which had the status of a military secret during World War II and was later made public by Abraham Wald (1947). In comparison to Fisher's and Neyman and Pearsons's theories, sampling is sequential, not simultaneous. Whereas the sample size in

Neyman-Pearson tests is fixed, calculated from a desired probability of Type I and Type II error, there is no fixed sample size in sequential sampling. Rather, a stopping criterion is calculated on the basis of the desired probabilities of Type I and Type II errors, and one continues to sample until it is reached. Sequential sampling has an advantage. It generally results in smaller sample sizes for the same alpha and power. Fisher was not fond of sequential sampling and for the same reasons he despised Neyman-Pearson's theory. Although sequential sampling can save time and money, researchers in psychology rarely know and use it.

Which of these ideas of sampling have shaped psychological methods and theories of mind? I will now discuss each of the five possibilities for sampling in figure 7.2.

Do Researchers Sample Participants?

Do psychologists use individuals or samples as the unit of analysis? In the nineteenth and early twentieth centuries, the unit of analysis was clearly the individual. This changed in the United States during the 1920s, 1930s, and 1940s, when experimental studies of individuals were replaced by the treatment group experiment (Danziger, 1990). The use of samples of individuals began in the applied fields, such as education, and spread from there to the laboratories. The strongest resistance to this change in research practice came from the core of psychological science, perceptual research, where to the present day one can find reports of individual data rather than averages. Nonetheless, sampling participants has largely become the rule in psychology, and its purpose is almost exclusively hypothesis testing, or more precisely, null hypothesis testing. Using samples to measure parameters is comparatively rare.

How do researchers determine the size of the sample? Psychologists generally use rules of thumb ("25 in each group might be good enough") rather than the cost–benefit calculation prescribed by Neyman and Pearson. For instance, Cohen (1962) analyzed a volume of a major journal and found no calculation of sample size depending on the desired probabilities of Type I and Type II errors. When Sedlmeier and Gigerenzer (1989) analyzed the same journal 24 years later, nothing had changed: Sample size was still a matter of convenience, and as a consequence, the statistical power was embarrassingly low—a fact that went unnoticed.

Do researchers draw random samples of participants from a defined population? Experimental studies in which first a population is defined, then a random sample is drawn, and then the members of the sample are randomly assigned to the treatment conditions are extremely rare (e.g., Gigerenzer, 1984). When is sequential sampling of participants used? Virtually never. In summary, when researchers sample participants, they have perfectly internalized Fisher's ideas about sampling—except that, as mentioned above, Fisher sampled objects, not participants.

This almost exclusive reliance on convenience samples and Fisher's analysis of variance creates many of the problems that other uses of sampling tried to avoid. Researchers do not know the power of their tests; measuring constants and curves does not seem to be an issue; they waste time and money by never considering sequential sampling; and when they conclude that there is a true difference in the population means, nobody knows what this population is.

Why sample participants and analyze means if there is no population in the first place? Why not analyze a few individuals? In 1988, I spent a sabbatical at Harvard and had my office next to B. F. Skinner's. I asked him over tea why he continued to report one pigeon rather than averaging across pigeons. Skinner confessed that he once tried to run two dozen pigeons and feed the data into an analysis of variance, but he found that the results were less reliable than with one pigeon. You can keep one pigeon at a constant level of deprivation, he said, but you lose experimental control with 24. Skinner had a point, which W. Gosset, the inventor of the *t*-test, made before: "Obviously the important thing...is to have a low real error, not to have a 'significant' result at a particular station. The latter seems to me to be nearly valueless in itself" (quoted in Pearson, 1939: 247). The real error can be measured by the standard deviation of the measurements, whereas a *p*-value reflects sample size. One can get small real errors by increasing experimental control, rather than by increasing sample size. Experimental control can reveal individual differences in cognitive strategies that get lost in aggregate analyses of variance (e.g., Gigerenzer & Richter, 1990).

To summarize, psychologists' sampling of participants follows Fisher's convenience samples. Alternative sampling procedures are practically nonexistent. I believe that it is bad scientific practice to routinely use convenience samples and their averages as units of analysis. Rather, the default should be to analyze each individual on its own. This allows researchers to minimize the real error, to recognize systematic individual differences, and—last but not least—to know their data.

Do Researchers Sample Objects?

Fisher made no distinction between the analysis of participants and objects. Do researchers sample stimulus objects in the same way they sample participants? The answer is no: The classic use of random sampling for measurement in psychophysics has declined, and concern with sampling of objects is rare compared with sampling of participants.

In the astronomer's tradition, the use of random sampling for measurement is the first major use of sampling in psychophysics. In Fechner's work, samples were used to measure absolute and relative thresholds. In Thurstone's (1927) law of comparative judgment, an external stimulus corresponds to an internal normal distribution of subjective values, and a particular encounter with the stimulus corresponds to a randomly drawn subjective value from this distribution. The goal of repeated presentation of the same stimuli is to obtain psychological scales for subjective quantities. As Luce (1977) noted, there is a close similarity between the mathematics in Thurstone's law of comparative judgment and that in signal detection theory but a striking difference in the interpretation. Thurstone used random variability for measurement, whereas in signal detection theory the mind is seen as an intuitive statistician who actively samples objects (Gigerenzer & Murray, 1987). The use of sampling for measurement has strongly declined since then, owing to the influence of Stevens and Likert, who promoted simple techniques, such as magnitude estimation and rating scales, that dispensed with the repeated presentation of the same stimulus. A tone, a stimulus person, or an attitude question is presented only once, and the participant is expected to rate it on a scale from, say, one to seven. Aside from research in perception and measurement theory, sampling of objects for the purpose of measuring subjective values and attitudes has been largely driven out of cognitive psychology (see Wells & Windschitl, 1999).

As a consequence, Egon Brunswik (e.g., 1955) accused his colleagues of practicing a double standard by being concerned with the sampling of participants but not of stimulus objects. He argued that "representative" sampling of stimuli in natural environments is indispensable for studying vicarious functioning and the adaptation of cognition to its environment (Kurz & Tweney, 1997). For Brunswik, representative sampling meant random sampling from a defined population. In a classic experiment on size constancy, he walked with individual participants through their natural environment and asked them at random intervals to estimate the size of objects they were looking at.

Like Fechner and Thurstone, Brunswik was concerned with measurement but not with the construction of subjective scales. He understood cognition as an adaptive system and measured its performance in terms of "Brunswik ratios" (during his Vienna period, e.g., for measuring size constancy) and later (while at Berkeley) by means of correlations. He was not concerned with repeated presentations of the same object or with random sampling from any population, but with random sampling of objects from a natural population. Brunswik was influenced by the large-sample statistics of Karl Pearson. Pearson, who together with Galton invented correlation statistics, was involved in an intense intellectual and personal feud with Fisher. The clash between these two towering statisticians replicated itself in the division of psychology into two methodologically opposed camps: the large-sample correlational study of intelligence and personality, using the methods of Galton, Pearson, and Spearman, and the small-sample experimental study of cognition, using the methods of Fisher. The schism between these two scientific communities has been repeatedly discussed by the American Psychological Association (e.g., Cronbach, 1957) and still exists in full force today. Intelligence is studied with large samples; thinking is studied with small samples. The members of each community tend not to read and cite what the others write. Brunswik could not persuade his colleagues from the experimental community to take the correlational statistics of the rival discipline seriously. His concept of representative sampling died in the no-man's-land between the hostile brothers. Even since the Brunswikian program was revived a decade after Brunswik died (Hammond, 1966), the one thing that is hard to find in neo-Brunswikian research is representative sampling (Dhami, Hertwig, & Hoffrage, 2004).

But does it matter if researchers use random (representative) sampling or a convenience sample that is somehow selected? The answer depends on the goal of the study. If its goal is to measure the accuracy of perception or inaccuracy of judgment, then random sampling matters; if the goal is to test the predictions of competing models of cognitive mechanism, random sampling can be counterproductive because tests will have higher power when critical items are selected. For claims about cognitive errors and illusions, the sampling of stimulus objects does matter. Research on the so-called overconfidence bias illustrates the point.

In a large number of experiments, participants were given a sample of general knowledge questions, such as, "Which city has more inhabitants, Hyderabad or Islamabad?" Participants chose one alternative, such as "Islamabad," and then gave a confidence judgment, such as "70 percent," that their answer was correct. Average confidence was substantially higher than the proportion correct; this was termed "overconfidence bias" and attributed to a cognitive or motivational flaw (see table 1.2, second entry). How and from what population the questions were sampled was not specified in these studies. As the story goes, one of the first researchers who conducted these studies went through almanacs and chose the questions with answers that surprised him. However, one can always demonstrate good or bad performance, depending on the items one selects. When we introduced random sampling from a defined population (cities in Germany), "overconfidence bias" largely or completely disappeared (Gigerenzer, Hoffrage, & Kleinbölting, 1991). The message that one of the most "stable" cognitive illusions could largely be due to researchers' sampling procedures was hard to accept, however, and was debated for years (e.g., by Griffin & Tversky, 1992). Finally, Juslin, Winman, and Olsson (2000) published a seminal review of more than one hundred studies showing that "overconfidence bias" is practically zero with random sampling but substantial with selected sampling. They (2000: 384) concluded that there was "very little support for a cognitive processing bias in these data." The bias was in the sample, not in the mind.

In summary, whereas sampling of participants has become institutionalized in experimental psychology, sampling of stimulus objects has not. Except for a few theories of measurement, which include psychophysics and Brunswik's representative design, it is not even an issue of general concern.

Do Researchers Sample Variables?

Now we enter no-man's-land. Why would a researcher sample variables, and what would that entail? Few theories in psychology are concerned with how the experimenter samples the variables on which participants judge objects. One is personal construct theory (Kelly, 1955). The goal of the theory is to analyze the "personal constructs" people use to understand themselves and their world. George Kelly's emphasis on the subjective construction of the world precludes using a fixed set of variables, such as a semantic differential, and imposing it on all participants. Instead, Kelly describes methods that elicit the constructs relevant for each person. One is to present triples of objects (such as mother, sister, and yourself) and to ask the participant first which of the two are most similar, then what it is that makes them so similar, and finally what makes the two different from the third one.

Unlike when sampling participants and objects, situations in which a population of variables can be defined are extremely rare. In Kelly's attempts to probe individual constructs, for instance, the distinction between convenience samples and random or representative samples appears blurred. If the goal of the research is to obtain statements about the categories or dimensions in which people see their world, then the researcher needs to think of how to sample the relevant individual variables.

I turn now to theories of how minds sample. According to our scheme, minds can sample along two dimensions: objects and cues (variables).

Do Minds Sample Objects?

Consistent with the tools-to-theories heuristic, the idea that the mind samples objects to compute averages or variances or to test hypotheses emerged only after inferential statistics in psychology was institutionalized. From Fechner to Thurstone, probability was linked with the measurement of thresholds and the construction of scales of sensation but not with the image of the mind as an intuitive statistician who draws samples for *cognitive inferences* or *hypothesis testing*. One of the first and most influential theories of intuitive statistics was signal detection theory (Tanner & Swets, 1954), which transformed Neyman-Pearson theory into a theory of mind.

There seem to be two main reasons for this late emergence of the view that the mind actively engages in sampling. The first is described by tools-to-theories: Only after a combination of Fisher's and Neyman-Pearson's statistical tools became entrenched in the methodological practices of psychologists around 1950 did researchers begin to propose and accept the idea that the mind might also be an intuitive statistician who uses similar tools (Gigerenzer, 1991). The second reason is the influence of Stanley S. Stevens, who rejected inferential statistics as well as Thurstone's concern with variability and probabilistic models. For instance, in the first chapter of his *Handbook of Experimental Psychology* (1951: 44–47), Stevens included a section entitled "Probability," the only purpose of which seems to be warning the reader of the confusion that might result from applying probability theory to anything, including psychology. He was deeply suspicious of probabilistic models on the grounds that they can never be definitely disproved.

Like David Krech and Edwin G. Boring, Stevens stands in a long tradition of psychologists who are determinists at heart.

Yet many current theories in cognitive and social psychology still do not incorporate any models of sampling. Consistent with this omission, most experimental tasks lay out all objects in front of the participants and thereby exclude information search in the first place. This tends to create cognitive theories with a blind spot for how people sample information and when they stop. This in turn creates a blind spot for the situations in which the mind does and does not sample, including when there might be evolutionary reasons to rely only on a single observation.

When Is It Adaptive Not to Sample?

Although Skinner did not sample pigeons, as mentioned before, his view about operant conditioning can be seen as a theory of information sampling. Specifically, this interpretation is invited by his variable reinforcement schedules, where an individual repeatedly exhibits a behavior (such as pecking in pigeons and begging in children) and samples information about consequences (such as food). Skinner's laws of operant conditioning were designed to be general-purpose, that is, to hold true for all stimuli and responses. This assumption is known as the *equipotentiality* hypothesis. Similarly, after Thorndike found that cats were slow in learning to pull strings to escape from puzzle boxes, he concluded that learning occurs by trial and error and hoped that this would be a general law of learning. If all stimuli were equal, minds should always sample information in order to be able to learn from experience. The assumption that all stimuli are equal is also implicit in many recent versions of reinforcement learning (e.g., Erev & Roth, 2001). Consider William Estes (1959: 399), one of the first to formulate Skinner's ideas in the language of sampling:

> All stimulus elements are equally likely to be sampled and the probability of a response at any time is equal to the proportion of elements...connected to it....On any acquisition trial all stimulus elements sampled by the organism become connected to the response reinforced on that trial.

Is the assumption of the equivalence of stimulus objects in sampling correct? Are there stimulus objects that an organism does not and should not sample? John Garcia is best known for his challenge of the equipotentiality hypothesis. For instance, he showed that in a single trial a rat can learn to avoid flavored water when it is followed by experimentally induced nausea, even when the nausea occurs two hours later. However, the same rat has great difficulty learning to avoid the flavored water when it is repeatedly paired with an electric shock immediately after the tasting:

> From the evolutionary view, the rat is a biased learning machine designed by natural selection to form certain CS-US associations rapidly but not others. From a traditional learning viewpoint, the rat was

an unbiased learner able to make any association in accordance with the general principles of contiguity, effect, and similarity (Garcia y Robertson & Garcia, 1985: 25).

The evolutionary rationale for one-trial learning as opposed to sampling stimulus objects is transparent. Learning by sampling and proportionally increasing the probability of response can be dangerous or deadly when it comes to food, diet, and health. To avoid food poisoning, an organism can have a genetically inherited aversion against a food or a genetically coded preparedness to learn a certain class of associations in one or a few instances.

Genetically coded preparedness shows that sampling cannot and should not be an element of all cognitive processes. Rather, whether an organism samples (a so-called bottom-up process) or does not (a top-down process) largely depends on the past and present environmental contingencies. A mind can afford to learn some contingencies but not all—sampling can be overly dangerous. One-trial learning amply illustrates the adaptive nature of cognitive processes, which codes what will be sampled and what will not.

Convenience Sampling

One class of models developed after the inference revolution assumes that the mind samples information to test hypotheses, just as researchers came to do. Consider the question of how the mind attributes a cause to an event, which has been investigated in the work of Piaget and Michotte. In Michotte's (1946/1963) view, for instance, causal attribution was a consequence of certain spatiotemporal relationships; that is, it was determined "outside" the mind and did not involve inductive inference based on samples of information. After analysis of variance became institutionalized in experimental psychology, Harold Kelley (1967) proposed that the mind attributes a cause to an event just as researchers test causal hypotheses: by analyzing samples of covariation information and calculating F-ratios (F for Fisher) in an intuitive analogy to analysis of variance. Note that the new ANOVA mind used the tests for rejecting hypotheses while trusting the data, parallel to the way researchers in psychology use ANOVA. If Kelley had lived a century and a half earlier, he might have instead looked to the astronomers' significance tests. As pointed out earlier, the astronomers assumed (at least provisionally) that the hypothesis was correct but mistrusted the data. If this use of sampling had been taken as an analogy, the mind would have appeared to be expectation-driven rather than data-driven.

Kelley's causal attribution theory illustrates how Fisher's ANOVA was used to model the mind's causal thinking, assuming that the mind uses convenience samples for making inductive inferences about causal hypotheses.

As clear as the distinction between convenience and random sampling is in statistical theory, it is less so in theories that assume that the mind samples objects. Is the sample of people a tourist encounters on a trip to Beijing a random sample or a convenience sample? It may depend on whether the tour guide has planned all encounters ahead, or whether the tourist strolls through the city alone, or whether the tour guide has picked a random sample of Beijing tenth-graders to meet with.

Random Sampling

Psychophysics has been strongly influenced by Neyman-Pearson theory. Under the name of signal detection theory, it became a model of how the mind detects a stimulus against noise or a difference between two stimuli, and it replaced the concepts of absolute and relative thresholds. Neyman's emphasis on random sampling from a defined population, as in quality control, became part of the cognitive mechanisms. For instance, Luce (1977; Luce & Green, 1972) assumed that a transducer (such as the human ear) transforms the intensity of a signal into neural pulse trains in parallel nerve fibers and that the central nervous system (CNS) draws a random sample of all activated fibers. The size of the sample is assumed to depend on whether or not the signal activates fibers to which the CNS is attending. From each fiber in the sample, the CNS estimates the pulse rate by either counting or timing, and these numbers are then aggregated into a single internal representation of the signal intensity. In Luce's theory, the mind was pictured as a statistician of the Neyman-Pearson school, and the processes of random sampling, inference, decision, and hypothesis testing were freed of their conscious connections and seen as unconscious mechanisms of the brain.

Sequential Sampling

Former first lady Barbara Bush is reported to have said, "I married the first man I ever kissed. When I tell this to my children they just about throw up" (quoted in Todd & Miller, 1999). Is one enough, just as in Garcia's experiments, or should Barbara Bush have sampled more potential husbands? After Johannes Kepler's first wife died of cholera, he immediately began a methodological search for a replacement. Within two years he investigated eleven candidates and finally married Number 5, a woman who was well educated but not endowed with the highest rank or dowry. Are eleven women a large enough sample? Perhaps too large, because the candidate Number 4, a woman of high social status and with a tempting dowry, whom friends urged Kepler to choose, rejected him for having toyed with her too long. Swiss economists Frey and Eichenberger (1996) asserted that people do not sample enough when seeking a mate, taking the high incidence of divorce and marital misery as evidence. In contrast, Todd and Miller (1999) argued that given the degree of uncertainty—one never can know how a prospective spouse will turn out—the goal of mate search can only be to find a fairly good partner, and they showed that under certain assumptions, Kepler's sample was large enough.

Mate search is essentially sequential for humans, although there are female birds that can inspect an entire sample of males lined up simultaneously. Since sequential sampling has never become part of the statistical tools used by researchers in psychology, one might expect from the tools-to-theories heuristic that minds are not pictured as performing sequential sampling either. This is mostly but not entirely true.

Cognitive processes that involve sequential sampling have been modeled in two different ways: optimizing models and heuristic models. Optimizing models are based on Abraham Wald's (1947) statistical theory, which has a stopping rule that is optimal relative to given probabilities of Type I and Type II errors (e.g., Anderson, 1990; Busemeyer & Rapoport, 1988). Many of these models have been applied to psychophysical tasks, such as judging which of two lines is longer. In the case of a binary hypothesis (such as line *A* or *B;* marry or not marry), the basic idea of most sequential models is the following: Thresholds are calculated for accepting one or the other hypothesis, based on the costs of the two possible errors, such as wrongly judging line *A* as larger or wrongly deciding that to marry is the better option. Each reason or observation is then weighted, and sampling of objects is continued until the threshold for one hypothesis is met, at which point search is stopped and the hypothesis is accepted. These models are often presented as as-if models, the task of which is to predict the outcome rather than the process of decision making, although it has been suggested that the calculations might be performed unconsciously.

Heuristic models of sequential sampling assume an aspiration level rather than optimization. Their goal is to model the process and the outcome of judgment or decision making. For instance, in Herbert Simon's (1955) models of satisficing, a person sequentially samples objects (such as houses or potential spouses) until encountering the first one that meets an aspiration level. In Reinhard Selten's (2001) theories of satisficing, the aspiration level can change with the duration of the sampling process.

Can sequential sampling ever be random? In statistical theory, the answer is yes. One draws sequentially from a population until the stopping rule applies. In the case of mental sampling, it is much harder to decide whether a sequential search process should count as random. Consider for instance, a satisficer who sequentially encounters potential spouses or houses until finding one that exceeds the aspiration level. In most cases, the sequential sample will be a convenience sample rather than a random sample from a defined population.

The relative rarity of sequential sampling in models of the mind goes hand in hand with the preference experimenters have for tasks that do not provide an opportunity for the participants to sample objects: All objects are already displayed in front of the participant. Few experiments address the questions: (i) When does the mind sample simultaneously versus sequentially? (ii) Is there an order in sequential search; that is, is the search random or systematic? (iii) How is sequential search stopped; that is, what determines when a sample is large enough?

Does the Mind Sample Variables?

Satisficing refers to a class of heuristics that apply to situations in which an aspiration level is given and the objects or alternatives are sampled sequentially. Alternatively, the objects can be given and the variables (cues, reasons, or features) need to be searched. Examples include choosing between two job offers (paired comparison) and classifying patients as high-risk or low-risk (categorization). As I mentioned, cognitive theories that model how minds sample objects are few, but those that model how minds sample variables are even more rare. For instance, models of similarity generally assume that the variables (features, cues, etc.) are already given and then postulate some way in which individual features are combined to form a similarity judgment—city block distance and feature matching are illustrations of this. However, in everyday situations, the features are not always laid out in front of a person but need to be searched for, and since there is typically a large or infinite number of features or cues, cognition may involve sampling features. Sampling cues or features can occur inside or outside of memory (e.g., on the Internet).

Unlike for sequential sampling of objects, for sampling of variables there seem to be no optimizing models but only heuristic models. There are two possible reasons. First, it is hard to think of a realistic population of variables, in contrast to a population of objects. Two job candidates, for instance, can vary on many different cues, and it is hard to define a population of cues. Second, the large number of cues makes optimizing models such as Bayes's rule or full classification trees computationally intractable because the number of decision nodes increases exponentially with the number of cues in a full tree. Thus, even optimizing models need to use heuristic simplifications, as in Bayesian trees (Martignon & Laskey, 1999).

Heuristic models of sequential sampling include two major classes: one-reason decision making and tallying (chap. 2). Each heuristic consists of a search rule that specifies the direction of sampling, a stopping rule that specifies when sampling is terminated, and a decision rule. Take-the-best is an example of a heuristic that employs ordered search and one-reason decision making; it typically samples a small number of cues. Tallying, in contrast, relies on adding but not on weighing; it searches for cues in random order and stops search after m ($1 < m \leq M$) cues have been inspected. M refers to the total number of cues, and m refers to the number of cues searched for. Versions of tallying have been discussed in the literature, such as unit-weight models in which all cues ($m = M$) or the m significant cues are looked up (Dawes, 1979; Einhorn & Hogarth, 1975).

In summary, cognitive sampling of cues or variables is a process that has been given little attention. However, just as for sampling of objects, heuristic models exist that formulate stopping rules to determine when such a sample is large enough.

What's in a Sample?

Shakespeare has Juliet ask, "What's in a name?" What's in a name uncovers what the name means to us, and by analogy, what's in a sample reveals what sampling means to us. The taxonomy proposed in this chapter distinguishes two subjects of sampling (experimenter versus participant), two purposes of sampling (measurement versus hypothesis testing), three targets of sampling (participants, objects, and variables), and four ways of how to sample ($N = 1$, i.e., no sampling; convenience sampling; random sampling; and sequential sampling). As in Brunswik's representative design, these dimensions do not form a complete factorial design; for instance, participants do not sample participants. Among the logically possible uses of sampling, some are realized in practice, whereas others are not or are only realized by a minority. Is the resulting picture of the actual uses and nonuses of sampling one of chaos, orderly chaos, or reasonable choice? Is the overreliance on Fisher's convenience sampling in methodology a good or bad thing, and is the relative neglect of sequential sampling in both methodology and cognitive theories realistic or unrealistic? Why is so little attention paid to the mind's sampling of features?

Whatever the reader's evaluation, a toolbox can open one's eyes to the missed opportunities or blind spots of sampling. There may be other paths to a toolbox of methods for sampling; the present one has a deliberate bias toward the evolution of the various ideas of sampling and the intellectual inheritance we owe to competing statistical schools. This historical window allows us to understand the current patchwork of sampling in both methodology and theory along with the possibilities of designing new theories of mind that overcome the historical biases we inherited.

Chapter 8

A 30 Percent Chance of Rain Tomorrow

Predicting weather is an age-old problem of statistical inference. Harvesting, warfare, and outdoor sporting events depend on it. Before the Grand Prix, one of Ferrari's most-discussed decisions is which weather forecaster to hire because reliable forecasts are key to choosing the right tires—and to winning the race. Over most of human history, forecasts of precipitation (rain or snow) were given in a deterministic form, such as, "It will rain tomorrow," sometimes modified by "it is likely." In the mid–twentieth century, however, the advent of computers turned forecasting into a probabilistic science (Shuman, 1989) and later influenced the way forecasts were communicated to the public. In 1965, American laypeople became the first to be exposed to probabilities of precipitation in mass media weather forecasts (Monahan & Steadman, 1996).

But how does the public understand a quantitative probability of rain? In 1980, Murphy, Lichtenstein, Fischhoff, and Winkler reported that the majority of 79 residents of Eugene, Oregon, mostly college students, "misunderstood" what "a precipitation probability forecast of 30 percent" means. The authors concluded that the real cause of the students' confusion was not a misunderstanding of probabilities per se, but rather of "the event to which the probabilities refer" (Murphy et al., 1980: 695). They recommended that the National Weather Service initiate a program to educate the general public in this regard and to study laypeople's understanding of probabilistic forecasts.

Our investigation starts where Murphy et al. left off in 1980, extending their study in two respects. First, we examine how the general public in five countries—three of which have adopted probabilistic weather forecasts on

This chapter is a revised version of G. Gigerenzer, R. Hertwig, E. van den Broek, B. Fasolo, and K. V. Katsikopoulos, "'A 30% chance of rain tomorrow': How Does the Public Understand Probabilistic Weather Forecasts?" *Risk Analysis* 25 (2005): 623–629; reprinted with kind permission of Blackwell Publishing.

a wide scale—understands probabilities of rain. Second, we argue that the confusion is largely due to the public not being informed about the reference class to which a probability of rain refers.

To What Class of Events Does a Probability of Rain Refer?

A forecast, such as "There is a 30 percent chance of rain tomorrow," conveys a single-event probability, which, by definition, does not specify the class of events to which it refers. In view of this ambiguity, the public will likely interpret the statement by attaching more than one reference class to probabilities of rain and not necessarily the class intended by meteorologists. Consequently, laypeople may interpret a probability of rain very differently than intended by experts. This problem has been pointed out before (National Research Council, 1989); here, we provide an empirical test.

The National Weather Service defines the probability of precipitation as "the likelihood of occurrence (expressed as a percentage) of a measurable amount of liquid precipitation...during a specified period of time at any given point in the forecast area" (National Weather Service Tulsa, 1998). In practice, the accuracy of "the rain forecast is the percentage correct of those days when rain was forecast" (Thornes, 1996: 69). Thus, a 30 percent chance of rain does not mean that it will rain tomorrow in 30 percent of the area or 30 percent of the time. Rather, it means that in 30 percent of the days for which this prediction is made, there will be at least a minimum amount of rain (such as .2mm or .01 in.).[1] We refer to this as the "days" definition of rain probability. It implies only a possibility of rain tomorrow—it may or may not rain—whereas the "time" and "region" definitions mean that it will rain tomorrow for certain, the only question being where and for how long. If people want to know where, at what time, and how much it will rain, they might not naturally think of the "days" interpretation.

Given the ambiguity of single-event probabilities, the fact that weather forecasts rarely clarify the definition of rain probability led us to two hypotheses. According to the first hypothesis, the public has no common understanding of what a probability of rain means; rather, different people have different interpretations. The second hypothesis specifies where we can expect a higher or lower degree of confusion. It is reasonable to expect that various attempts to inform and educate the public—such as Web sites by meteorological institutes—will be more effective the longer they have been in place. Specifically, the confusion should be lower and the prevalence of the days interpretation should be higher (1) among people in countries that have been exposed to probabilistic weather forecasts

1. Meteorologists do not always agree on a single definition of probabilities of rain. Here we cite three definitions (National Weather Service Tulsa, 1998; Murphy & Winkler, 1971; Murphy et al., 1980), which are all couched in different terms, such as single-event probabilities or betting quotients. No matter how these definitions are phrased, the accuracy of the forecast is measured in a more consistent way, as the percentage correct of days when rain was forecast (i.e., the days interpretation).

for a longer period (national exposure) and (2) among people who have been exposed to probabilistic weather forecasts for a larger proportion of their lives (individual exposure).

Method

To test these hypotheses, we surveyed citizens living in five cities of five countries that together reflect the full range of exposure to probabilistic weather forecasts. Probabilities of rain were introduced into mass media weather forecasts in New York in 1965, in Amsterdam in 1975, and in Berlin in the late 1980s; in Milan, they have been introduced only on the Internet; and in Athens, they are not reported in the mass media at all. Respondents were surveyed in public places and were paid for their participation. The Berlin sample was the only one that included both members of the general public and university students; the results for the two groups were pooled in the analysis because their responses did not differ. All respondents were asked to indicate their age. The survey was conducted in the fall of 2002.

Participants were told to imagine that the weather forecast, based on today's weather constellation, predicts: "there is a 30 percent chance of rain tomorrow." They were asked to indicate which of the following alternatives is the most appropriate and which of the following alternatives is the least appropriate interpretation of the forecast:

1. It will rain tomorrow in 30 percent of the region.
2. It will rain tomorrow for 30 percent of the time.
3. It will rain on 30 percent of the days like tomorrow.

We refer to these as the "region," "time," and "days" interpretations, respectively. Each of these phrases is an abbreviation of the longer statement: If the weather conditions are like today, at least a minimum amount of rain will fall in 30 percent of the region, 30 percent of the time, or 30 percent of the days. In half of the Berlin sample, the order of these alternatives was counterbalanced, while in the other half the alternatives were listed in the order above. The order was found to have no effect on responses, and thus we used the above order for all other cities. Participants were then requested to provide their own interpretation of the statement in a free-response format. Finally, they were asked: "Assume that you have to run an errand and it will take you about an hour to walk to the store and to return. At what probability of rain will you take an umbrella with you?" The total number of participants was 750.

What Do People Think a 30 Percent Chance of Rain Means?

Figure 8.1 shows that, as the correct interpretation, two-thirds of the respondents in New York chose days, about one-quarter chose time, and a few chose region. In none of the European cities, in contrast, did a majority of

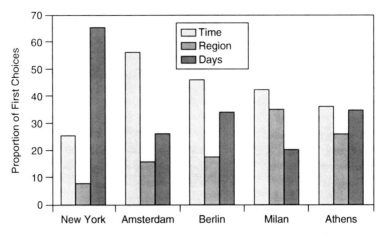

Figure 8.1: First choice. Citizens of New York ($n = 103$), Amsterdam ($n = 117$), Berlin ($n = 219$), Milan ($n = 203$), and Athens ($n = 108$) were asked what the statement "There is a 30 percent chance of rain tomorrow" refers to. The three alternatives were "It will rain tomorrow for 30 percent of the time," "in 30 percent of the region," and "on 30 percent of the days on which the prediction is made."

respondents select the days interpretation. The favored interpretation in Amsterdam, Berlin, Milan, and Athens was time.

As figure 8.2 reveals, the days interpretation is polarizing. It is often judged as the best (in New York) or the worst (in the European cities) but rarely as the second-best. For instance, consider the different distributions of first and last choices among the participants in Athens. Their first choices (figure 8.1) were fairly uniformly distributed, consistent with Greeks' lack of exposure to probabilities of rain in weather forecasts. However, it is the days interpretation (figure 8.2) that makes least sense to the participants in Athens, and the same holds for the other three European cities. As one Milanese expressed it, "A percentage of days is most absurd." Many people thought that the forecast refers to when, where, or how much it will rain tomorrow. Figures 8.1 and 8.2 illustrate that lay interpretations of rain probability in the European cities diverge substantially from the meaning intended by meteorologists.

Does the prevalence of the days interpretation increase with a country's length of exposure to weather forecasts that include rain probability? Figure 8.1, which orders the cities according to exposure, shows that the prevalence of the days interpretation in the five countries is not positively correlated with length of national exposure. Only the high frequency in New York fits the national-exposure hypothesis.

To test the individual-exposure hypothesis, we measured the proportion of each participant's life during which he or she had been exposed to weather forecasts expressed in probabilistic terms. This continuous measure ranged from 0 for all respondents in Greece and Italy (where probabilistic

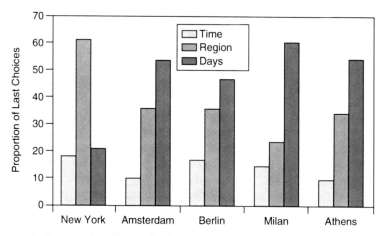

Figure 8.2: Last choice. For each alternative, the percentage of people is shown who chose it as the least appropriate one.

forecasts have not been introduced into the mass media) to 1 for people who both resided in the United States, the Netherlands, or Germany (where probabilities are routinely reported in mass media weather forecasts) and who were born after probabilities of rain were introduced (e.g., for New Yorkers, after 1965). Consistent with the individual-exposure hypothesis, the proportion of individual exposure was positively related to choosing the days interpretation ($r=0.2$, $p=0.0001$), negatively related to choosing the region interpretation ($r=-0.2$, $p=0.0001$), and unrelated to choosing the time interpretation ($r=-0.02$). Although these correlations are statistically significant, they are small in magnitude, indicating that exposure to probabilities of rain per se affords little opportunity to learn what they really mean.

When people answered the open question, they often simply restated the probability (e.g., "a 3 in 10 chance of raining tomorrow"). If they referred to a reference class, they mostly referred to time, region, and days, but a few referred to other classes of events. Several people in New York and Berlin, for instance, thought that the rain probability statement means "3 out of 10 meteorologists believe it will rain." A woman in Berlin said, "Thirty percent means that if you look up to the sky and see 100 clouds, then 30 of them are black." Participants in Amsterdam seemed the most inclined to interpret the probability in terms of the amount of rain. "It's not about time, it indicates the amount of rain that will fall," explained a young woman in Amsterdam. Some people seemed to intuitively grasp the essence of the "days" interpretation, albeit in imaginative ways. For instance, a young woman in Athens in hippie attire responded, "If we had 100 lives, it would rain in 30 of these tomorrow." One of the few participants who pointed out the conflict between various interpretations observed, "A probability is only about whether or not there is rain, but does not say anything about the time and region." Another said, "It's only the probability that it rains at all, but not about how much."

Many participants acknowledged that, despite a feeling of knowing, they were incapable of explaining what a probability of rain means. Borrowing Judge Potter Stewart's remark in a landmark U.S. Supreme Court case, a 74-year-old New York man explained, "It's like with pornography; you can't define it, but you know it when you see it."

Do people who interpret probabilities of rain differently have different thresholds for taking an umbrella? Across all cities, the average threshold among respondents who chose the days interpretation was 55.9 percent; the time interpretation, 53.5 percent; and the region interpretation, 50.6 percent. In terms of effect sizes, the differences between the thresholds for days as opposed to region and time are small ($d=0.25$, $d=0.11$). This result is consistent with the fact that the days interpretation implies only a possibility of rain; it may not rain at all. To someone who makes the region or time interpretation, in contrast, the only uncertainty is where and for how long it will rain.

Why Does the General Public Still Not Understand?

Twenty-three years after Murphy et al.'s (1980) study, some two-thirds of the New Yorkers we surveyed interpreted a probability of rain as intended by meteorologists, but only one-third to one-fifth of respondents in Amsterdam, Berlin, Milan, and Athens did so. The inclusion of quantitative probabilities in weather forecasts has been advocated because probabilities can "express the uncertainty inherent in forecasts in a precise, unambiguous manner, whereas the crude measure of uncertainty represented by traditional forecast terminology is subject to a wide range of misinterpretations" (Murphy et al., 1980: 695). If probabilities are really unambiguous, one may ask why probabilistic forecasts are still so widely misunderstood. Our data point to some potential explanations.

Missing and Conflicting Information from Meteorological Authorities and Mass Media

In each of the European countries represented in this study, we consulted representatives of local meteorological authorities and perused weather forecasts in daily newspapers. Consider the Dutch case first.

In the Netherlands, chances of rainfall have been communicated to the public since 1975, when an automated prediction model began to be used by meteorological experts. On television and to some extent in newspapers, however, forecasts are mostly presented in terms of the amount of rain expected (e.g., "1 mm rain expected tomorrow") rather than in terms of a probability. Often, the expected time of day when the rain will start is also presented, as in the following newspaper report: "In the morning it will remain dry, but during the afternoon, there is a fair chance that some showers will occur locally." This statement appeared next to a table with expected chances (60 percent) and expected amount of rain (2 mm). When quantitative probabilities are used, they are sometimes accompanied by a verbal explanation. Consider how the official weather forecast Web site of the Dutch Meteorological Institute (KNMI, 2002) explains what a probability of rain means:

> If the chance exceeds 90 percent, then one can count on rain in every region in Holland. The higher the percentage, the more certain the meteorologist is that it will rain. Some examples:

10–30%	Almost none	Almost nowhere
30–70%	Possible	In some places
70–90%	There's a fair chance	In almost all the regions

Note that the introductory text refers to meteorologists' degree of certainty while the descriptive labels refer to the number of regions in which it will rain, thus misleadingly suggesting that probabilities of rain pertain to meteorologists' degree of certainty and to the size of the affected region. As Robert Mureau of the Royal Dutch Meteorological Institute explained: "We are aware of the fact that probabilities are not very well understood by the general public. We ourselves have not been very clear about the terminology definitions either, which might have caused even more confusion. We do sometimes ask people, including meteorologists, about their understanding of the forecasts, and the confusion about probabilities is striking—people mention the portion of time, region, or 1 out of 10" (personal communication, 2002; see also Floor, 1992). These observations illustrate that the Dutch public is exposed to various aspects of rain forecasts—including amount and meteorologists' confidence—but that efforts to clarify which aspects a probability of rain refers to have been confusing.

Although television, radio, and newspaper weather forecasts in Italy are largely devoid of probabilities, we found Italian Web sites that aim to explain what probabilities of rain mean and explicitly warn of the potential for reference class confusion. The Web site of Sirmione, a town on Lake Garda, for example, says: "The probability of precipitation does not specify the duration and quantity of the precipitation, nor its exact location. A probability of 70 percent does not mean that it will rain for 70 percent of the time or that there will be rain in 70 percent of the region, but rather that somewhere in this region there are 7 out of 10 chances of rain." Another site cautions: "A probability of rain specified for the entire day and for the whole region does not coincide with the probability that it will rain only in the morning in a smaller part of the region" (Comune di Prato, n.d.). Although these authorities make an effort to spell out what probability of rain is not, the responses of our Italian participants indicate that they had only limited impact. Why are mass media weather forecasts in Italy probability-free? An Italian meteorologist explained that the media abhor uncertain predictions. When a meteorologist provides percentages, Italian journalists dichotomize the percentages into "it will rain or it will not rain."

In Germany, the use of probability in mass media weather forecasts is only somewhat more advanced. We found that a few of the major German newspapers report probabilities of precipitation; the same holds for radio and television stations. And when probabilities of rain are reported, their meaning is rarely explained. For instance, the *Berliner Morgenpost* reports the probability of precipitation every day using a pictorial representation of a dial, but there is neither an explanation of it nor any reference to this probability in the weather section in which it appears. Similarly, infoRadio, the major Berlin news station, broadcasts probabilities of rain without explanation. In the words of Kirk and Fraedrich (n.d.) from the Meteorological Institute of the University of Hamburg: "Today, probabilities of precipitation have become entrenched in the daily forecasts in the press and radio. However, they are not unproblematic, because we are lacking a unique definition of probabilities of precipitation, and in most cases, it is only a subjective estimate of the consulting meteorologist. Furthermore, the probability is often confused with a spatial or temporal frequency distribution."

According to two experts of the General Secretary for Civil Protection of the Greek Ministry of Internal Affairs, Greek meteorologists rarely use numerical probabilities: "There is considerable disagreement among meteorologists about what numerical probabilities of rain might mean or how they could be derived.... It is not uncommon that, just before the time the forecast has to be broadcast on TV, a number of meteorologists meet to discuss and debate their opinions and finally reach a consensus about the forecast."

These interviews and media analyses reveal three practices that fuel the public's confusion about what probabilities of rain mean. First, in countries such as Greece, probabilities of rain are simply not provided to the public. Note that this also holds to some degree in other countries, where only some mass media use probabilities. Second, when probabilistic weather forecasts are provided, they are typically presented without explaining what class of events they refer to. Third, in the rare cases where an explanation is presented, it sometimes specifies the wrong reference class. The way to resolve these confusing and contradictory signals is straightforward: Always communicate the reference class to which probabilities of precipitation pertain.

A Comparison with Murphy et al.'s (1980) Analysis

In response to the question of whether the public is "confused about the meaning of probabilities or about the definition of the event to which the probabilities refer," Murphy et al. (1980: 695) concluded that the event, not the probabilities, is misunderstood. Consistent with this conclusion, a majority of participants in our study correctly rephrased the probability portion of the statement as a relative frequency ("it will rain in 3 out of 10 days"), a single-event probability ("a 3 in 10 chance of raining tomorrow"), or odds ("odds are 7 to 3 that it won't rain"). Only a few of them confused probabilities with odds ("the odds are 3 to 10"; on odds see Thornes & Stephenson, 2001).

Although we agree with Murphy et al. on what is not the problem, our results and interpretation of what is the problem differ from theirs. Murphy et al. asked students what a "precipitation probability forecast of 30 percent means" and gave four choices. One of them corresponded to the time interpretation and another to the area interpretation. The other two were (Murphy et al., 1980: 700):

> *At any one particular point in the forecast area (for example, at your house) there is a 30 percent chance that there will be measurable precipitation and a 70 percent chance that there will be no measurable precipitation during the forecast period.*

and

> *There is a 30 percent chance that measurable precipitation will occur somewhere (i.e., in at least one place) in the forecast area during the forecast period, and a 70 percent chance that it will not occur anywhere in the area during the period.* (italics in the original)

Based on their finding that 39 percent and 56 percent of the students, respectively, thought that the alternatives quoted verbatim above were correct, Murphy et al. concluded that the problem was the lack of distinction between "precipitation at a particular point in the forecast area" and "precipitation somewhere in the forecast area." Whereas they identified the first one as correct, the majority of students opted for the second one. The "time" and "area" interpretations were each chosen by only 3 percent of their college students.

Why were these results so different from ours? It may have to do with the difference between college students and the general public or with the simple fact that the two options endorsed most frequently in Murphy et al.'s study were longer and more elaborately phrased (they added clarifications in parentheses) than the "time" and "area" alternatives. Also, if we compare our New York sample with Murphy et al.'s data, the difference is smaller than in the international comparison.

For Murphy et al., the problem lies in the definition of the event. In their interpretation (Murphy & Winkler, 1971: 241), "a probability of 3/10 means that the forecaster is indifferent between receiving three dollars for sure and receiving ten dollars if measurable precipitation occurs. This forecast is for the unique situation...not for a large collection of similar situations.". Yet the accuracy of a weather forecaster is measured on a class of events, such as all days where a minimal amount of rain was predicted (Thornes, 1996). Thus, the problem may not only be in the definition of the event, but also with the specification of the class of events, as we propose. In the two interpretations cited above, the events are singular ("at any one particular point...") and it is not immediately clear to John Q. Public what reference class, if any, this definition refers to.

Reference Classes in Risk Communication

In 1995, the World Meteorological Organization (WMO) estimated the global budget for weather services at approximately $4 billion (Sherden, 1998). We have shown that, despite impressive technologies that allow meteorologists to produce these probabilities, the public understands probabilities of rain in multiple ways, such as referring to "days," "regions," "time," or "meteorologists." The present analysis suggests a simple solution to the problem. Misunderstandings can be easily reduced if a statement specifying the intended reference class is added. For instance, the rain forecast might say, "There is a 30 percent probability of rain tomorrow. This percentage does not refer to how long, in what area, or how much it rains. It means that in 3 out of 10 times when meteorologists make this prediction, there will be at least a trace of rain the next day."

The ambiguity of a single-event probability and the resulting possibility of miscommunication about risks are not limited to weather forecasts. Far-reaching consequences arise, for instance, when single-event probabilities are used by expert witnesses to explain DNA evidence in court (Koehler, 1996a), by clinical psychologists and psychiatrists to predict the possibility that a mental patient will commit violent acts (Slovic, Monahan, & MacGregor, 2000), and by medical organizations to communicate the benefits and risks of treatments (Gigerenzer, 2002a).

Many risk experts and meteorologists promote quantitative probabilities because they believe that numbers are more precise and convey more information to the public than qualitative risk statements. This is only partly true. Quantitative probabilities will continue to confuse the public as long as experts do not spell out the reference class when they communicate with the public.

Chapter 9

Understanding Risks in Health Care

The science fiction writer H. G. Wells predicted that in modern technological societies statistical thinking will one day be as necessary for efficient citizenship as the ability to read and write. How far have we got, seventy years later?[1] A glance at the literature reveals a shocking lack of statistical understanding of the outcomes of modern technologies, from standard screening tests for HIV to DNA evidence. For instance, physicians with an average of 14 years professional experience were asked to imagine using the Haemoccult test to screen for colorectal cancer (Hoffrage & Gigerenzer, 1998). The prevalence of cancer was 0.3 percent, the sensitivity of the test was 50 percent, and the false positive rate was 3 percent. The doctors were asked: What is the probability that a person

This chapter is a revised version of G. Gigerenzer and A. G. K. Edwards, "Simple Tools for Understanding Risks: From Innumeracy to Insight. *British Medical Journal* 327 (2003): 741–744.

1. Many authors have cited Wells's prediction championing statistical literacy. For example, in the classic *How to Lie with Statistics,* one of the epigraphs reads: "Statistical thinking will one day be as necessary for efficient citizenship as the ability to read and write." The quote is attributed to Wells but without an exact reference. In fact, none of the dozens of books where I saw this quote provided the source. When using the quote in my book *Calculated Risks* (2002; UK edition: *Reckoning with Risk),* I added a footnote explaining that I had been unable to locate its source (Wells wrote more than 100 books) and that it might have even been fabricated. I received various letters in response, including one article (Tankard, 1979) that argued that Wells's prediction was about the role of mathematics, not statistics, and that statisticians might have misrepresented this to promote their own cause. Tankard quotes Wells calling for "sound training in mathematical analysis" and saying: "it is as necessary to be able to compute, to think in averages and maxima and minima, as it is now to be able to read and write" (Tankard, 1979: 30–31). Tankard also cited Lovat Dickson, one of Well's biographers, who could not recall another place in his writing that dealt specifically with statistics.

Just as I was prepared to accept this account, I received a letter from Geoffrey Hunt, a British librarian who appended a copy of Wells's *World Brain* (1938/1994). And here it was: "A certain elementary training in statistical method is becoming necessary for everyone living in this world of today as reading and writing" (141). That verifies the essence, if not the exact wording, of this popular quote.

who tests positive actually has colorectal cancer? The correct answer is about 5 percent. However, the physicians' answers ranged from 1 percent to 99 percent, with about half estimating the probability as 50 percent (the sensitivity) and 47 percent (sensitivity minus false positive rate). If patients knew about this degree of variability and statistical innumeracy they would be justly alarmed.

Statistical innumeracy has been attributed to problems inside our minds. We disagree: The problem is not simply internal, but lies in the external representation of information, and hence an external solution exists. Every piece of statistical information needs a representation—that is, a form. Some forms tend to cloud minds, while others foster insight. Clearly, medical students, physicians, and patients should be taught representations that foster insight. We know of no medical institution that teaches the power of representations; even worse, writers of information brochures for the public seem to prefer confusing representations (Slaytor & Ward, 1998).

Bad presentation of medical statistics, such as the risks associated with a particular intervention, can lead to patients making poor decisions on treatment. How can doctors improve the presentation of statistical information so that patients can make well-informed decisions? Here we deal with three numerical representations that foster confusion: single-event probabilities, conditional probabilities (such as sensitivity and specificity), and relative risks. In each case we show alternative representations that promote insight (table 9.1). These "mind tools" are simple to learn. Finally, we address questions of the framing (and manipulation) of information and how to minimize these effects.

Single-Event Probabilities

The statement "There is a 30 percent chance of rain tomorrow" is a probability statement about a singular event: It will either rain or not rain tomorrow. Single-event probabilities are a steady source of miscommunication because, by definition, they leave open the class of events to which the probability refers. As demonstrated in the previous chapter, some people will interpret this statement as meaning that it will rain tomorrow in 30 percent of the area, others that it will rain 30 percent of the time, and a third group that it will rain on 30 percent of the days where this prediction is made. Area, time, and days are examples of *reference classes,* and each class gives the probability of rain a different meaning.

The same ambiguity occurs in communicating clinical risk, such as the side effects of medication. A psychiatrist prescribes fluoxetine (Prozac) to his mildly depressed patients. He used to tell them that they have a "30 percent to 50 percent chance of developing a sexual problem," such as impotence or loss of sexual interest (Gigerenzer, 2002a). Hearing this, patients became anxious. After learning about the ambiguity of single-event probabilities, the psychiatrist changed how he communicated risks. He now tells patients that out of every 10 people to whom he prescribes Prozac, 3 to 5 will experience a sexual problem. Patients who were informed in terms of frequencies were

Table 9.1: How to represent statistical information so that patients and physicians are likely to be confused (left) or show insight (right)

How to foster confusion	How to foster insight
Use single-event probabilities— e.g., "you have a 30% chance of suffering a side effect from the medication."	*Specify reference class*, then use single-event probabilities; or, *use frequency statements*—e.g., "3 out of every 10 patients will suffer a side effect from the medication."
Use conditional probabilities— e.g., "the probability of a positive test result if the patient has the disease" (sensitivity) or "the probability of a negative test result if the patient does not have the disease" (specificity) or "the probability of the disease if the patient has a positive test result" (positive predictive value).	*Use natural frequencies*—e.g., in table 9.2.
Use relative risks— e.g., randomized trials indicated that out of every 1,000 women (age 40 and older) who did not participate in mammography screening, 4 died of breast cancer, whereas among those who participated, 3 died. This result is often presented in the form of relative risks: "Participation in mammography screening reduces the mortality of breast cancer by 25%."	*Use absolute risks* (perhaps together with relative risks)—e.g., "Among 1,000 women who participated in screening, we can expect that 1 will be saved from dying of breast cancer." *Use number needed to treat or harm* (NNT/NNH)—e.g., "To prevent one death from breast cancer, 1,000 women need to undergo screening for 10 years."

less anxious about taking Prozac. Only then did the psychiatrist realize that he had never checked what his patients had understood by "a 30 percent to 50 percent chance of developing a sexual problem." It turned out that many had assumed that in 30 percent to 50 percent of their sexual encounters, something would go awry. The psychiatrist and his patients had different reference classes in mind: The psychiatrist thought of his patients, but the patients were thinking instead of their own sexual encounters.

Frequency statements always specify a reference class (although it may not specify it precisely enough). Thus, misunderstanding can be reduced by two mind tools: specifying a reference class before making a single-event probability or only using frequency statements.

Conditional Probabilities

The chance of a test actually detecting a disease is typically communicated in the form of a conditional probability, the sensitivity of the test: "*If a woman has breast cancer, the probability that she will have a positive result on mammography is 90 percent.*" This statement is often confused with: "*If a woman has a positive result on mammography, the probability that she has breast cancer is*

90 percent." That is, the conditional probability of A given B is confused with that of B given A (Casscells, Schoenberger, & Grayboys, 1978). Despite years of medical training, many physicians have trouble distinguishing between a test's sensitivity, specificity, and positive predictive value—three conditional probabilities. Again, the solution lies in the representation.

Consider the question "What is the probability that a woman with a positive mammography result actually has breast cancer?" Table 9.2 shows two ways to represent the relevant statistical information: in terms of conditional probabilities and natural frequencies. The information is the same (apart from rounding), but with natural frequencies the answer is much easier to calculate. Only 7 of the 77 women who test positive (70 + 7) actually have breast cancer, which is 1 in 11, or 9 percent. Natural frequencies correspond to the way humans have encountered statistical information during most of their history. They are called "natural" because, unlike conditional probabilities or relative frequencies, they all refer to the same class of observations (Gigerenzer & Hoffrage, 1999). For instance, the natural frequencies "7 women" (with a positive mammogram and cancer) and "70 women" (with a positive mammogram and no breast cancer) both refer to the same class of 1,000 women, whereas the conditional probability "90 percent" (the sensitivity) refers to the class of 8 women with breast cancer, but the conditional probability "7 percent" (the specificity) refers to a different class of 992 women without breast cancer. This switch of reference classes tends to confuse the minds of physicians and patients alike.[2]

Table 9.2: Representation of the same statistical information in conditional probabilities and natural frequencies

Conditional probabilities
The probability that a woman has breast cancer is 0.8%. If she has breast cancer, the probability that a positive mammogram will show a positive result is 90%. If a woman does not have breast cancer, the probability of a positive result is 7%. Take, for example, a woman who has a positive result. What is the probability that she actually has breast cancer?

Natural frequencies
Eight out of every 1,000 women have breast cancer. Of these eight women with breast cancer, seven will have a positive result on mammography. Of the remaining 992 women who do not have breast cancer, some 70 will still have a positive mammogram. Take, for example, a sample of women who have positive mammograms. How many of these women actually have breast cancer?

Note that numbers may vary across populations and age groups.

2. Numbers are based on Nyström et al. (1996) and differ slightly from those used in chapter 1, where they were simplified to make it easier to calculate the probability of cancer given a positive mammogram. This probability is about 1 out of 10 no matter which numbers are used.

Figure 9.1 shows the responses of 48 physicians, whose average professional experience was 14 years, to the information given in table 9.2, except that the statistics were a base rate of cancer of 1 percent, a sensitivity of 80 percent, and a false positive rate of 10 percent (Hoffrage & Gigerenzer, 1998). Half the doctors received the information in conditional probabilities and half in natural frequencies. When asked to estimate the probability that a woman with a positive result actually had breast cancer, physicians who received the information in conditional probabilities gave answers that ranged from 1 percent and 90 percent— very few gave the correct answer of about 8 percent. In contrast, most of the physicians who were given natural frequencies gave the correct answer or were close to it; only five concluded that the chance of breast cancer would be over 50 percent. Simply stating the information in natural frequencies turned much of the physicians' innumeracy into insight, helping them understand the implications of a positive test result as it would arise in practice. Presenting information in natural frequencies is a simple and effective mind tool to reduce the confusion resulting from conditional probabilities (Hoffrage, Lindsey et al., 2000). This is not the end of the story regarding risk communication (which requires adequate exploration of the significance of the risk to the individual concerned, its implications, and its burden, as is described elsewhere; see Paling, 2003), but it is an essential foundation.

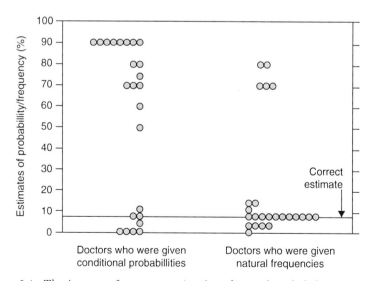

Figure 9.1: The impact of representation (conditional probabilities versus natural frequencies) on breast cancer diagnosis. Each point represents one doctor. The ordinate axis shows physicians' estimates of the probability or frequency of breast cancer given a positive mammogram (from Gigerenzer, 2002a).

Relative Risks

Women are told that undergoing mammography screening over age 50 reduces their risk of dying from breast cancer by 25 percent. Women in high-risk groups are told that bilateral prophylactic mastectomy reduces their risk of dying from breast cancer by 80 percent (Hartmann et al., 1999). These numbers are relative risk reductions. The confusion produced by relative risks has received more attention in the medical literature than that of single-event or conditional probabilities (Sarfati et al., 1998; Wright, 2001). Nevertheless, few patients realize that the impressive 25 percent figure means an absolute risk reduction of only 1 in 1,000: Of 1,000 women who do not undergo mammography screening, about 4 will die from breast cancer within 10 years, whereas out of 1,000 women who participate, 3 will die (Nyström et al., 1996). Similarly, the 80 percent figure for prophylactic mastectomy refers to an absolute risk reduction of 4 in 100: 5 of 100 high-risk women who do not undergo prophylactic mastectomy will die of breast cancer, compared with 1 in 100 women who have had a mastectomy. Again, this benefit can be reported as 80 percent or 4 percentage points; both are technically correct. One reason why women tend to misunderstand relative risks is that they think that the number relates to women like themselves who take part in screening or who are in a high-risk group. But relative risks relate to a different class of women, to those who die of breast cancer without having been screened.

The confusion caused by relative risks can be avoided by using absolute risks (such as "1 in 1,000") or the number needed to treat or be screened to save one life (the NNT, which is the reciprocal of the absolute risk reduction and thus essentially the same representation as the absolute risk). However, health agencies typically inform the public in the form of relative risks. Transparent representations have not been encouraged by health authorities, who themselves sometimes exhibit innumeracy, for example, when funding proposals that report benefits in relative risks because the numbers look larger (Fahey, Griffiths, & Peters, 1995). For such authorities making decisions on allocating resources, the population impact number (the number of people in the population among whom one event will be prevented by an intervention) is a better means of putting risks into perspective (Heller & Dobson, 2000).

The Reference Class

In all these representations, the ultimate source of confusion or insight is the reference class. Single-event probabilities leave the reference class open to interpretation. Conditional probabilities, such as sensitivity and specificity, refer to different classes (the class of people with and without illness, respectively), which makes their mental combination difficult. Relative risks often refer to reference classes that differ from those to which the patient belongs, such as the class of patients who die of cancer versus those who participate in screening. Using such transparent representations as natural frequencies clarifies the reference class.

Framing

Framing is the expression of logically equivalent information (numerical and verbal) in different ways (Wilson, Purdon, & Wallston, 1988). Studies of the effects of verbal framing on interpretations and decision making initially focused on positive versus negative framing and on gain versus loss framing (Kahneman & Tversky, 1979). Positive and negative frames refer to whether an outcome is described, for example, as a 97 percent chance of survival (positive) or a 3 percent chance of dying (negative). The evidence from health care settings is that positive framing is more effective than negative framing in persuading people to take risky treatment options (Edwards et al., 2001; Kühberger, 1998). However, gain-and-loss framing is perhaps even more relevant to communicating clinical risk, as it concerns the individual implications of accepting or rejecting tests. Loss framing considers the potential negative effects from not having a test. In HIV testing, for example, these might include transmitting the virus to sexual partners because of unawareness of the infection. Loss framing appears to influence the uptake of screening more than gain framing (the gains from taking a test, such as maintenance of good health; see Edwards, Elwyn, & Mulley, 2002).

Visual representations may substantially improve comprehension of risk (Lipkus & Hollands, 1999). They may enhance the time efficiency of consultations. Doctors should use a range of pictorial representations (graphs, population figures) to match the type of risk information the patient most easily understands.

Manipulation

It may not seem to matter whether the glass is half full or half empty, yet different methods of presenting risk information can have important effects on outcomes among patients. That verbal and statistical information can be represented in two or more ways means that an institution or screening program may choose the one that best serves its interests. For instance, a group of gynecologists informed patients in a leaflet of the benefits of hormone replacement therapy in terms of relative risk (large numbers) and of the harms in absolute risk (small numbers). Women with no training in framing are misled to believe that the benefits strongly outweigh the harms (Gigerenzer, 2002a).

Pictorial representations of risk information are not immune to manipulation either. For example, different formats, such as bar charts and population crowd figures, could be used (Schapira, Nattinger, & McHorney, 2001), or the representation could appear to support short-term benefits from one treatment rather than long-term benefits from another (Mazur & Hickam, 1994). Furthermore, within the same format, changing the reference class may produce greatly differing perspectives on a risk, as illustrated in figure 9.2, which relates to the effect of treatment with aspirin and warfarin in patients with atrial fibrillation. On the left side of the figure, the effect of treatment on a particular event (stroke or bleeding) is depicted relative to the class of people who suffer an event and have not had the treatment (as in relative risk reduction). On the right side, the patient can see the treatment effect relative to a class of 100 untreated people who have not had a stroke or bleeding (as in absolute risk reduction). The choice of representation can generate different decisions or interpretations by patients.

The wide room for manipulating representations of statistical information is a challenge to the ideal of informed consent. Where there is a risk of influencing patient outcomes and decisions, professionals should consistently use representations that foster insight and should balance the use of verbal expressions—for example, both positive and negative frames or gain-and-loss frames.

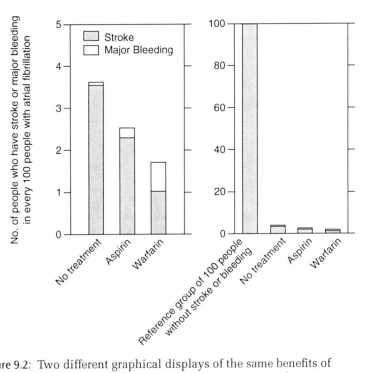

Figure 9.2: Two different graphical displays of the same benefits of treatment. The display on the left side is likely to persuade patients to accept treatment, whereas the one on the right side is less likely to do so. Risks are for patients without further risk factors for stroke or bleeding.

Table 9.3: Summary points

Summary points:
• The inability to understand statistical information is not a mental disease of physicians or patients but is largely due to poor representations of the information.
• Poorly presented statistical information may cause erroneous communication of risks, with serious consequences.
• Single-event probabilities, conditional probabilities (such as sensitivity and specificity), and relative risks are confusing because they make it difficult to understand to what class of events a probability or percentage refers.
• For each confusing representation there is at least one alternative, such as natural frequency statements, which always specify a reference class and therefore avoid confusion, fostering insight.
• Simple representations of risk can help professionals and patients move from innumeracy to insight and make consultations more time-efficient.
• Instruction in efficient communication of statistical information should become part of medical curricula and the continuing education of doctors.

Conclusion

The dangers of patients being misled or making uninformed decisions in health care are countless. One of the reasons is the prevalence of poor representations that invite drawing the wrong inferences. Such confusion can be reduced or eliminated with simple mind tools. Human beings have evolved into fairly adept intuitive statisticians and can gain insight but only when information is presented simply and effectively (Cosmides & Tooby, 1996). This insight is then the platform for informed discussion about the significance, burden, and implications of risks for the individual or family concerned. It also facilitates clear explanation of diseases and their treatment. Instruction in how to communicate statistical information efficiently should be part of medical curricula and continuing education for doctors.

Chapter 10

The Evolution of Statistical Thinking

Statistical thinking—learning to live with uncertainty—is one of the most important mathematical tools in everyday life. Thinking means calling certainties into question. It can be learned through good examples, the best of which are the problems that actually influenced the historical development of statistical thinking. These are the focus of this chapter.

The origins of the mathematical theory of probability go back to 1654. Unlike most great ideas, which had already been developed in Greek antiquity, the concept of mathematical probability was an unusually late discovery. The philosopher Ian Hacking called this a "scandal in philosophy." The history of probability is therefore relatively short and has been documented extensively (e.g., Daston, 1988; Gigerenzer et al., 1989; Hacking, 1975, 1990). My intention is not to simply renarrate this development, but instead to present a light and brief history in the form of classical problems and outline the meaning of statistical thinking as the basis of skeptical thinking, then and now. I begin with a notorious gambler and two distinguished mathematicians.

The Chevalier's Wager

Antoine Gombaud, chevalier de Méré, was a passionate gambler who lived in France in the seventeenth century. He used to bait his fellow gamblers by wagering even money that he would throw at least one six after four rolls of a die. As far as we know, his dice were not rigged; nonetheless the chevalier regularly earned money with this game. Either he no longer found any

This chapter is a revision and translation of G. Gigerenzer, "Die Evolution des Statistischen Denkens" ["The Evolution of Statistical Thinking"], *Unterrichtswissenschaft* 32 (2004): 4–22, translated by Rona Unrau. Published with permission of Juventa Verlag.

willing victims or the game grew too monotonous with time: whatever the reason, he thought up a new version that was intended to be equally lucrative. The chevalier's new game was as follows:

Double-six: A pair of dice are rolled 24 times. If at least one double-six is thrown, I win; otherwise you win.

Would you accept the offer? De Méré's intuition is transparent. He knew from experience that it is advantageous to bet that at least one six is thrown in a series of four rolls. However, a double-six is six times as rare as a single six. Therefore, he assumed that it would be advantageous to bet that he would throw a double-six in 24 (six times four) rolls. Fortune, alas, stopped smiling on the chevalier; he began to lose. Was he unlucky in spite of thinking correctly, or was he unlucky because he thought incorrectly? The chevalier had no answer to this question; his intuition spoke for the first explanation but his experience for the second.

De Méré turned to the renowned mathematicians Blaise Pascal and Pierre Fermat, who exchanged a series of letters in 1654 on this and similar problems and developed a joint solution (Pascal, 1713/1970). For that reason, 1654 is accepted as the date when the mathematical theory of probability came into being. The chevalier de Méré's letdown gave occasion to one of the greatest intellectual revolutions. Here is a recount of Pascal and Fermat's analysis, using modern terminology. Let's begin with the first game. How high is the probability of at least one six in a series of four rolls?

The probability p(six) of one six in a roll of a fair die is one-sixth.

The probability of "no six" is therefore p(no six) = five-sixths.

The probability of "no six" in a series of four rolls is therefore: p(no six in four rolls) $= (5/6)^4 = (5/6)(5/6)(5/6)(5/6) = .482$.

Hence the probability p(at least one six in four rolls) $= .518$.

Now we understand why de Méré made money on this first game. His chances of winning were higher than 50 percent. The same logic can be applied to the double-six game. If you don't yet know the answer, don't give up; remember that we are now solving a problem that, as far we know, no one managed to solve before 1654. Once again, the question is: how high is the probability of throwing at least one double-six in 24 rolls?

The probability p(double-six) in one roll with a pair of dice is 1/36.

The probability of "no double-six" is p(no double-six) = 35/36.

The probability of "no double-six" in a series of 24 rolls is therefore: p(no double-six in 24 rolls) $= (35/36)^{24} = .509$.

Hence the probability of throwing at least one double-six in 24 rolls is .491.

Now we see that the chance of winning the double-six game is in fact slightly below 50 percent. The reason why de Méré lost had nothing to do with bad luck, but with a wrong intuition. Nonetheless, the exactitude of his observations at the gambling table is fascinating. He must have been able to find plenty of other players and spend hours playing the game in order to have noticed this small divergence from 50 percent. It was this contradiction between exact experience and wrong intuition that inspired Pascal and Fermat to search for and find the laws of probability. Here they are, in modern terminology:

1. The probability of an impossible event is 0 and of a certain event is 1.
2. The sum of the probabilities of all possible events is 1.
3. If A and B are independent events, the probability $p(A\&B)$ of A and B happening is equal to the product of individual probabilities: $p(A\&B) = p(A)p(B)$.

For example, the probability of rolling a seven with a regular die is 0 and that of rolling a number between one and six is 1. The total sum of all probabilities for rolling one to six is 1, and the probability of rolling a six on the first throw and a one on the second, two independent events, is 1/6 times 1/6, which results in 1/36.

Pascal's Wager

The laws of probability were a response to experiences at the gambling table but also have other origins. Thinking in probabilities was to a greater degree part of a large intellectual revolution, which ensued from abandoning the ideal of certain knowledge and developing forms of rationality in dealing with an uncertain world.

Plato divided our world into two realms—the heavenly world of immutable categories and fixed knowledge and the disordered world full of changes and uncertainties. For hundreds of years mathematicians as well as theologians and their devoted followers believed that they lived in a world of absolute certainty. However, the Reformation and the Counter-Reformation eroded this realm of certainty to a large extent. Gradually, a more modest ideal prevailed. It was accepted that knowledge with absolute certainty is unreachable for mortals, but nonetheless it was held that in theory and practice, the available amount of knowledge suffices for guiding reasonable people.

Religious convictions, whether held by believers or atheists, have always been tinged with emotional certainty. We are absolutely sure that God exists. Or we know beyond a doubt that God does not exist. In *Pensées*, however, Pascal (1669/1962, 2:141–155) turns the question of God completely around. Instead of emotional truth, rational expectancy is now the issue. Expectancy, like a wager, is uncertain. Pascal's wager can be summarized as follows:

> Pascal's wager: *I don't know if God exists. But I know that if I believe in him and he doesn't exist, I will miss out on some moments of worldly lust and vice. On the other hand, if I don't believe in him and he*

nonetheless exists, the price I will pay is eternal damnation and agony. What should I wager on?

For Pascal, the answer is simple. Even if someone holds the possibility of God existing for slight, should God indeed exist, the consequences are immeasurably far-reaching: The blissfulness of the redeemed is as infinite as the agony of the damned. Under these circumstances, argues Pascal, our rational self-interest demands that we sacrifice our certain but limited worldly pleasures for the uncertain but infinite gains of redemption.

Pascal's wager illustrated a radically new way of thought that accompanied the theory of probability. Being religious is a question of expectancy, not of unconditional belief, and this expectancy is uncertain. It is no coincidence that as this new way of thinking in probabilities and expectancies took root, the use of torture in Europe declined. During the Inquisition, torture was a tool used to find out the unequivocal truth, an end that justified the means.

Pascal's fundamental term was not truth, but expectancy, which would later be calculated as the production of the probability p_i of the event i and its value x_i:

$$E = \Sigma p_i x_i \qquad (10.1)$$

For example, the probabilities of "red" and "black" on a roulette table are 18/37 each, and of "green" (zero) 1/37. If you bet $100 on red, the expectancy amounts to 18/37 × $200 + 18/37 × $0 + 1/37 × $0 = $97.79. Thus, in the long range, you can expect to lose. Defining rational behavior through expectancy was the basis of the new understanding of addressing uncertainties rather than denying them and living with false certainties. But the definition of rational behavior as the maximization of expectancy was not the end of the story. Mathematical expectancy soon ran into unexpected difficulties.

The St. Petersburg Paradox

The St. Petersburg paradox introduced the first serious conflict between the concept of rational expectation and common sense (Jorland, 1987). The Swiss mathematician Nicholas Bernoulli was the first to identify this problem in a letter to Pierre Remond de Montmort, who published it in the second edition of *Essai d'analyse sur les jeux de hazard* (1713). Daniel Bernoulli, Nicholas's cousin, published a possible solution in the annuals of the Petersburg Academy (1738/1954), after whom the problem is named.

St. Petersburg game: *Pierre and Paul are playing a game of hazard by flipping a fair coin. If the coin comes up tails the first time, Pierre has to pay Paul one dollar and the game is over. If the coin only comes up tails the second time, Paul wins two dollars; if it only comes up tails*

*the third time, he wins four dollars, and so on. What would be a fair
entry price for Paul to pay?*

How much would you offer? The fair price is the one that leaves open
whether the role of Pierre or Paul is better. (When a child cuts a piece of cake
in two, and a second child gets to choose one, the same principle of fairness
is in play.) According to the classical theory of rationality, the fair price is
determined by mathematical expectancy:

$$E = (1/2 \times 1 \text{ dollar}) + (1/4 \times 2 \text{ dollars}) + (1/8 \times 4 \text{ dollars})$$
$$+ \ldots + [(1/2)^n \times (2^{n-1} \text{dollars})] + \ldots = \infty$$

(10.2)

Translated into words, the probability of Paul winning \$1 is $p = 1/2$; of
winning two dollars, $p = 1/4$; of winning \$4, $p = 1/8$, and so on. Each of the
terms on the right side of the equation clearly corresponds to an expectation
of 1/2 dollars, and since the number of the terms is infinite, the expected
value is also endlessly large. In keeping with the theory that the expectation
is the fair price, we should wager all we own to play this game—and even
then we would be at an advantage, given that our assets are limited. Yet no
sensibly thinking person would be willing to pay more than a small sum,
perhaps \$5 to \$10, to play this game.

Why was the St. Petersburg paradox called a paradox? From today's point
of view, no such paradox seems to exist: There is no contradiction between
results that are derived from the same valid assumptions. From a classical
viewpoint, in contrast, the theory of probability was not a pure, content-free
theory but instead inseparable from its subject matter (Daston, 1988). This
subject matter was human rationality. The contradiction between theory and
rationality was therefore interpreted to be a paradox.

Daniel Bernoulli tried to solve this contradiction. Arguing that fairness
was not the only issue in the St. Petersburg problem, he suggested that
mathematical expectation should be replaced with the "moral" expectation
of a cautious businessman. He defined the latter as the product of the probability of an event and of what would later be called its utility. Bernoulli
reasoned that winning \$200 (in modern currency) is not necessarily double
the value of winning \$100 and that the wealthier a player is to begin with,
the more money he needs to win in order to be happy. Let's assume that the
relation between dollar (x) and utility U is logarithmic, $U(x) = log(x)$, and
that total assets A are currently \$50,000. The certain win W, which has the
same utility as participating in the St. Petersburg game, can be calculated
as follows:

$$U(A + W) = 1/2U(A + 1) + 1/4U(A + 2) + 1/8U(A + 4) + \ldots$$

(10.3)

The result of the calculation is approximately \$9. In other words, for some-
one with assets of \$50,000, the expected utility of the game is only \$9. This

value lies in the region of what someone using common sense would have agreed to pay for participating in the game.

With this solution to the St. Petersburg paradox, Daniel Bernoulli transformed the concept of expected value into the concept of expected utility, which continues to dominate the economic sciences today. Nicholas Bernoulli, who was a professor of Roman and canonical law at the University of Basel, disagreed with this solution and persisted in his view that fairness, which he saw as the foundation of legal contracts, was the model for human rationality. Daniel Bernoulli was instead inspired by the world of commerce and trade. Rationality for him was clever business sense, and it was certainly not wise from an economic standpoint to invest a high amount in the St. Petersburg game. In his new understanding of rational behavior, the prototype of rational human beings was no longer the impartial judge, but instead the businessman carefully weighing the pros and cons. The mathematical theory of human rationality had reached a major turning point.

The First Null Hypothesis Test

Mathematical probability has three sources: games of hazard, courts of law, and statistical tables. From these, the three main interpretations of the concept of probability are derived: propensity, subjective probability, and frequency. Propensity means the design of a die or a roulette wheel that determines the probability. The concept of subjective probability stems from legal questions, such as how a judge should assess the truthfulness of witnesses' statements when, for example, they are related or not related to the defendant. The interpretation of probability as long-term relative frequency is based on statistical information, such as birth and mortality tables. These tables were one of the first systematic databases to be created in the Western world and were also the basis for the first null hypothesis test.

John Arbuthnot (1710) posed an old question: Is there an active God? His method of finding an answer, however, was new and revolutionary. He searched for facts and an empirical test rather than belief and rhetoric. Arbuthnot observed that men lived more dangerously than women and that more young men than women died in accidents. If there were an active God who intended human beings to be monogamous, then he would create more boys than girls in order to compensate for this loss. Arbuthnot tested this hypothesis of divine providence against the null hypothesis of blind coincidence. To do so, he looked at the 82 years of birth statistics kept in London. He ascertained that more boys had been born in each of the 82 years and calculated the "expectancy" of this event (D) under the null hypothesis (H_0):

$$p(D \mid H_0) = (1/2)^{82} \qquad (10.4)$$

Because this probability was so extremely small, he excluded blind coincidence and saw the result as evidence for divine providence. Arbuthnot concluded:

> *Scholium.* From hence it follows, that Polygamy is contrary to the Law of Nature and Justice, and to the Propagation of the human Race; for where Males and Females are in equal number, if one Man takes Twenty Wifes, Nineteen Men must live in Celibacy, which is repugnant to the Design of Nature; nor is it probable that Twenty Women will be so well impregnated by one Man as by Twenty.

Arbuthnot's idea of testing a claim by using statistical data was revolutionary and far ahead of its time. First introduced in the late nineteenth century and early twentieth century, null hypothesis tests were made popular by the statistician and geneticist Sir Ronald Fisher. Arbuthnot's test illuminates the possibilities and limitations of a null hypothesis test (Arbuthnot did not use this term himself) better than later examples have. The test conveys the probability of a series of observations (more boys than girls in each of the 82 years), should the null hypothesis hold. It does not tell us the probability of the observations should the experimental hypothesis (in this case: divine providence) hold, because only the null is formulated in statistical terms. It is not specified what proportion of males/females the experimental hypothesis predicts. Divine providence always wins if the null hypothesis loses. Similarly, no alternative experimental hypothesis is formulated and tested. For example, an alternative hypothesis could purport that 3 percent of all female newborns are illegally abandoned or killed at birth and therefore do not appear in the statistics. If that were the case, Arbuthnot's test would wrongly attribute this effect to divine providence. The lack of precise experimental and alternative hypotheses is the largest snag in Arbuthnot's test and continues to be the problem with present-day uses of null hypothesis tests in the social sciences (see chapter 11).

Yet the significance of Arbuthnot's method does not lie in the special structure of null hypothesis tests, but in the groundbreaking idea of solving problems by using empirical data. This was a revolutionary approach then, although the revolution had to wait another two centuries; Arbuthnot's test went unheeded. Before frowning on that, we should remember that even today ideologies rather than empirical evidence often play a leading role in decisions on religious, pedagogical, medical, and political questions.

Who Discovered Bayes's Rule?

Testing a null hypothesis is not the only method of testing a hypothesis. *Bayes's rule* is one of the best-known alternatives. Thomas Bayes (1702–1761) was a Nonconformist minister who himself never published his famous treatise on the problem of "inverse probability"—the famous Bayes's rule that enables calculating the probability of a hypothesis in face of evidence.

R. A. Fisher (1935) was to later congratulate him on having withheld publication, believing that Bayes's rule was useless for testing scientific hypotheses and that Bayes himself, unlike his followers, had recognized this. Following the death of Bayes, Richard Price published Bayes's treatise in 1763.

In the simplest case where there are binary hypotheses H_1 and H_2 and a piece of data (evidence) D, Bayes's rule (in modern terminology) can be expressed as follows:

$$p(H_1 \mid D) = \frac{p(H_1)p(D \mid H_1)}{p(H_1)p(D \mid H_1) + p(H_2)p(D \mid H_2)} \tag{10.5}$$

In words, the a posteriori probability $p(H_1 \mid D)$ is based on the a priori probability $p(H_1)$ and the probabilities $p(D \mid H_1)$ and $p(D \mid H_2)$. For a contemporary example, take HIV screening for low-risk persons, such as those who do not take intravenous drugs. A positive test result (D) means that a blood sample tested positive in both the first test (ELISA) as well as the second (Western blot). Try to solve the following problem:

> About 1 in 10,000 men at low risk are infected with HIV. If a man is infected (H_1), the probability $p(D \mid H_1)$ that the test will be positive (D) is .999. If the man is not infected, the probability $p(D \mid H_2)$ that the test will be positive is .0001. A man tests positive. How high is the probability $p(H_1 \mid D)$ that he really is infected with the virus?

When these values are put into Bayes's rule, the result is $p(H_1 \mid D) = .5$. This means that only every second man who tests positive will in fact have the virus. Nonetheless, in a study of German counseling services, most professional AIDS counselors erroneously told their clients that it was absolutely or at least 99.9 percent sure that they were infected (Gigerenzer, Hoffrage, & Ebert, 1998). This illusion of certainty is also spread in the United States by so-called information brochures. For instance, in 2005, the Illinois Department of Health issued a leaflet "HIV counseling and testing" that answers the question what a positive test means. According to it, "a positive test result means antibodies to HIV were found. This means you are infected with the virus and pass HIV to others—even if you have no symptoms. You are infected for life." The consequences of this false information can be far-reaching, from job losses to suicide. No distinction between people at risk and those not at risk is made, and there is no trace of statistical thinking. These counselors and brochure writers urgently need better statistical training.

HIV screening can also illustrate the limits of routine null hypothesis testing. Consider the same problem from the perspective of testing a null. The H_0 would postulate that a person is not infected with HIV. Yet the person tests positive (D), and the question is posed whether the result is significant so that the null can be rejected. We know from the data provided above that the probability $p(D \mid H_0)$ that a positive test is obtained if the null hypothesis holds is only .0001. This is a significant probability. Therefore the null hypothesis is rejected with a high degree of confidence. As shown by Bayes's rule, however, the probability of an HIV infection when testing positive is .5. Why do the two methods come to such divergent conclusions? Null hypothesis testing only computes the probability of the data given the null but not the other relevant probabilities that Bayes's rule considers.

Yet like every statistical tool, Bayes's rule has its limits. In HIV or other screening tests, the base rate is fairly precisely known and can therefore serve as the a priori probability. When it comes to a scientific hypothesis, however, statistical information equivalent to the base rate is usually unavailable, and the a priori probability will necessarily be subjective. The potential arbitrariness of subjective probabilities was the target of R. A. Fisher's attack on using Bayes's rule for determining the probability of hypotheses. There are other limits that were pointed out in the earlier chapters of this book: If the number of variables (such as tests) becomes very large, computing Bayes's rule becomes intractable, and if the estimates from past data are unreliable, simple heuristics such as $1/N$ (chap. 1) can be faster and more accurate.

Let us return to Thomas Bayes. The historian of statistics Stephen M. Stigler (1999) once proposed a law about the origins of insights, which he named the *law of eponymy*. This law states that no scientific discovery is named after its original discoverer. Pythagoras's theorem was not discovered by Pythagoras, Pascal's triangle is not from Pascal, and the Gaussian distribution initially had nothing to do with Gauss. Bayes's rule is apparently no exception to the rule. In an intriguing detective story, Stigler calculates a probability of 3 to 1 that not Bayes, but Nicholas Saunderson first discovered the rule. Blind from birth, Saunderson taught optics and was incumbent of the prestigious Lucasian Chair of Mathematics in Cambridge, which Isaac Newton held before him. He died in 1739. However, Bayes cannot be accused of the less courteous (and false) interpretation of Stigler's law, which says that all scientific discoveries are named after the last person who did not cite their predecessor. As mentioned, Bayes never published his treatise. One small question remains: Who discovered Stigler's law?

The First Night in Paradise

The first day in paradise came to a close. Adam and Eve lay down to rest. They had seen the sun rise that morning and marveled as it made its course through the sky, illuminating all the beautiful trees, flowers, and birds. Later on, however, it grew cold as the sun disappeared beyond the horizon. Would it remain dark forever? Adam and Eve worriedly asked themselves what the chances were that the sun would rise again.

In retrospect, we might assume that Adam and Eve were sure that the sun would rise again. But given that they had only seen the sun rise once, what could they expect? The classical answer to this was given by the French mathematician Pierre Simon de Laplace in 1814.

If Adam and Eve had never seen the sun rise, they would hold both poten-tial events (rising again or remaining dark) as equally probable. To express this belief, they could put one white stone in a pouch to represent the sun ris-ing again and a black stone for it remaining dark. However, they had already seen the sun rise once and would therefore put another white stone into the pouch. The pouch thus contained one black and two white stones. This meant that the degree of their belief that the sun would rise again grew from one-half to two-thirds. On the following day, after the second sunrise, they added a third white stone. The probability of a sunrise had now increased from two-thirds to three-fourths. This is the logic behind Laplace's *rule of succession*, which indicates the probability $p(E \mid n)$ of an event E happening again after is has occurred n times:

$$p(E \mid n) = (n+1)/(n+2) \tag{10.6}$$

A 27-year-old has experienced approximately 10,000 sunrises in his or her lifetime. In this case, the degree of confidence that the sun will rise again on the next day is 10,001/10,002. Using Laplace's rule in this way has been criticized for making too much out of ignorance. Given that Laplace's rule is derived from Bayes's rule, this criticism also reveals problems with using the latter. Unlike HIV screening, where the base rate of infection in the population in question is known, Adam and Eve could not know the base rate of sunrises. They were therefore unable to know how many white and black stones they should put into the pouch on the first evening. If they were pessimists, they might have taken one white and ten black stones; if they were optimists, they might have reversed this number. Without any information to help estimate probabilities, one might simply assume equal probabilities for all possible outcomes. This rule of thumb is called the *principle of indifference*, which is an instance of the $1/N$ heuristic. Its advo-cates assert that the effects of initially assuming equal probabilities decline as the number of observations increases. For example, after 10 years, that is, over 3,560 sunrises, the calculated probability that it will rise tomorrow is virtually the same, independent of whether the first estimate was pes-simistic or optimistic.

Laplace had indeed assumed indifference on two points that surface when Bayes's rule is used. H_1 and H_2 stand for hypotheses that the sun will or will not rise each morning and D for the fact that Adam and Eve had seen a sunrise. The probability $p(H_1 \mid D)$ can therefore be calculated as follows:

$$p(H_1 \mid D) = \frac{p(H_1)p(D \mid H_1)}{p(H_1)p(D \mid H_1) + p(H_2)p(D \mid H_2)} \tag{10.7}$$

Recall, however, that Adam and Eve do not know the base rate. The rule of thumb, the principle of indifference, assumes that $p(H_1) = p(H_2) = 1/2$. That simplifies Bayes's rule to:

$$p(H_1|D) = \frac{(p(D|H_1)}{p(D|H_1)+p(D|H_2)}$$ (10.8)

By definition, the probability $p(D|H_1)$ is 1, but the probability $p(D|H_2)$ is unknown. Here the principle of indifference is used again: $p(D|H_2)=1/2$. The final result is:

$$p(H_1|D) = 2/3$$ (10.9)

The story of the first night in paradise illustrates that there may be a problem when using Bayes's rule in situations where little empirical data is available. As controversial as it may be, the principle of indifference is used even today, for example in paternity suits.

Alleging that he is the father of her child, a woman sues a man, who denies the claim. As Bayes's rule demonstrates, in order to determine the probability that a man is in fact the father of a child, an a priori probability or base rate is necessary. But what could this a priori probability be? Many laboratories use the principle of indifference and assume an a priori probability of 50 percent that the defendant is indeed the father (Gigerenzer 2002a). This procedure is contentious, since it presumes that the probability of the defendant being the father is equal to that of all other men put together. The question is how to weigh the two errors that a judge might make: exonerating a person who is guilty or finding an innocent person liable. This issue extends beyond paternity suits. The French mathematicians Dennis Poisson and Pierre Laplace took a conservative stance, where protecting society against criminals was more important than protecting individuals from mistaken convictions, in opposition to the early liberal reforms of the philosopher and politician Condorcet. Over the past few centuries to today, the answer to this question has continued to divide liberals and conservatives.

The Illusion of Certainty

The classical theory of probability prevailed against endeavors to reach absolute certainty with an epistemic interpretation of probability. This means that uncertainty was seen as originating in the ignorance of humans, not in nature itself. Ironically, the representatives of the classical theory of probability, from Pascal to Laplace, were determinists: They held the world itself to be absolutely determined. God or Laplace's secular superintelligence did not require any statistics, without which we humans would not survive. Albert Einstein shared this view: God does not gamble. An ontic interpretation of probability did not appear until the second half of the nineteenth century, when the founder of psychophysics, Gustav Theodor Fechner, and the philosopher Charles Sanders Peirce asserted that coincidence was inherent to Nature.

The evolution of statistical thinking, illustrated by the six classical problems, is in effect an evolution of skeptical thinking. As Pascal's wager demonstrated, the basis of skeptical thinking is the transition from striving for certainty to dealing rationally with an uncertain world. Benjamin Franklin once said, "In this world there is nothing certain but death and taxes." Yet more than two centuries later, this humorous but deep insight is still too uncomfortable to be accepted by all.

The search for illusive certainty is part of our emotional and cultural heritage, fulfilling human desire for security and authority. The New Age sections of contemporary bookstores are evidence that many people yearn for instant faith. Throughout the ages, people have constructed belief systems, such as religion, astrology and prophecies, which offer security and certainty as well as consolation, especially to those who have suffered great hardships. Certainty has since become a commodity. It is marketed across the world by insurance companies, investment consultants, and election workers but also by the medical and pharmaceutical industries.

In seventeenth-century Europe, a life insurance policy consisted of betting on the life expectancy of a prominent citizen. For example, the bet was whether the mayor of Paris would die within a particular time span; the person who wagered correctly had the chance of winning a small fortune (Daston 1987, 1988). As in the case of the chevalier de Méré, it was a game, not a moral obligation. Nowadays, insurance agents persuade us that life insurance is an essential safeguard and that we are morally obliged to wager money on our own lives, as it were, to provide for remaining family members.

The illusion of certainty can be used to reach political or economic goals. For example, as mad cow disease (BSE) spread across Europe, the German government held their country to be free of the disease. "German beef is safe"—this phrase was repeated nonstop by the president of the farmers' union, the minister of agriculture, and a whole troop of other functionaries. The German population was only too happy to hear this. Imports of British beef were banned, and consumers were advised to buy beef only from cattle that had been raised in Germany. The word was spread that negligence and flawed controls prevailed in other countries. However, when a large number of German cattle were finally tested for BSE, some also tested positive. The public was shocked: Two ministers who had previously proclaimed certainty had to resign, the price of beef dropped drastically, and other countries banned the import of German beef. In the end the government admitted that it had clung to the illusion that German cattle were not afflicted by the disease. In the meantime, the game of promising safety continued, only this time the actors had changed. Supermarkets and butchers hung posters up and distributed flyers ensuring their customers "guaranteed BSE-free beef." Some of them substantiated their claim with the fact that their "contented" cows were able to graze on organic pastures, while others purported that all of their cattle had been tested. Barely anyone mentioned that the BSE tests are often inaccurate.

When the media then reported on a cow that had tested negative but none-theless had BSE, the public was shocked anew. Once again an illusion of certainty had disappeared with a bang. The government and supermarkets had been more concerned with pacifying consumers than with presenting information about BSE.

The illusion of certainty is sometimes deliberately conjured up for a specific group of people. Jay Katz, law professor at Yale, once described a conversation with a surgeon friend of his in this way. Discussing the uncertainties involved in treating breast cancer, both of them agreed that no one knows what the ideal therapy is. Katz asked his friend how he counseled his female patients. The surgeon responded that he'd recently recommended an immediate mastectomy to a patient with breast cancer as the best method. Katz reproached his friend for the contradiction: How could he suddenly be so sure of the optimal therapy? Admitting that he barely knew the patient, the surgeon insisted, however, that if his female patients were told about the uncertainty regarding the best therapy, they would neither understand nor accept it. In his view, the female patients wanted the illusion of certainty and were given it.

Are modern technologies able to eradicate the last remains of uncertainty and finally provide certainty? This too is a widespread illusion. Modern HIV tests, for example, are some of the most accurate medical tests on the market. Nonetheless, as we have seen, because the base rate of low-risk persons with the infection is so low, only approximately every second person who tests positive has the virus. The false negative rate is only around 0.1 percent for HIV tests, yet the literature reports the case of an American construction worker who tested negative 35 times, even though he was infected with the virus. Medical tests are not absolutely certain, and neither is forensic evidence, such as fingerprints, DNA profiles, and other genetic tests (Gigerenzer, 2002a).

Empirical Thinking as a Way of Life

Skeptical thinking breaks away from the ideal of certain knowledge. It is based on an intellectual curiosity that is not willing to simply accept (or deny) convictions without assessing them on the basis of empirical evidence. This requires moving from anxiously striving for certainty to an informed and assured way of dealing with an uncertain world. Such an approach is relatively new, since in earlier times, empirical data were rarely available or collected for many areas of life. The mere existence of the term *evidence-based medicine* (imagine referring to *evidence-based physics*!) signals that there are large communities—here physicians—whose decisions are less guided by the available scientific evidence than by local customs and simple beliefs. In spite of the apparent flaws in John Arbuthnot's statistical test, it was an admirable step toward using evidence to test convictions.

In the eighteenth and nineteenth centuries, statistical information was usually only available to an elite minority and withheld from the public as a state secret. Political authorities were, however, aware of the significance of statistical information, such as population figures. Napoleon's passion for gathering statistics without delay from his *bureau de statistique* was legendary (Bourget, 1987). The readiness to make economic and demographic data available to the public, in contrast, is more recent; not until 1830 were statistics (at least in part) publicized. Since then, an "avalanche of printed numbers," to quote the philosopher Ian Hacking, has transformed the world into a teeming ocean of information fed by media, such as television and newspapers as well as the Internet. The increasing spread of statistical information in the nineteenth and twentieth centuries corresponded with and supported the rise of democracy in the Western world.

Statistical Thinking instead of Statistical Rituals

Statistical thinking is skeptical not only of the illusion of certainty, but also of the way statistics are dealt with. It is helpful to distinguish between two forms: statistical thinking and statistical rituals. Statistical thinking is self-reflexive; it consists of considering which method or model is most appropriate and in which circumstances. For example, Laplace's story of the first night in paradise makes it clear that using Bayes's rule is easier to justify when empirical information on the base rate and probabilities is at hand. When judges allow Bayes's rule to play a role in trials, it is usually only when empirical information is available. John Arbuthnot's proof of divine providence, in contrast, illustrates the problems and limits of null hypothesis tests.

Unlike in molecular biology, atomic physics, or other natural sciences, statistical rituals are widespread in the social sciences. When one and the same method is automatically used for every problem, we are looking at a statistic ritual. For example, path analyses are routinely calculated in some areas of educational psychology, despite statisticians' warnings (e.g., Freedman, 1987), factor analyses are standard in personality psychology, and the constant use of null hypothesis testing in experimental psychology recalls compulsive hand washing. Each field has its own statistical "superego." Researchers feel under pressure to apply the method used by everyone else and feel naked without it. Only a small percentage of academic psychologists, including those who teach statistics to psychologists, even understand what a significant result means or what can be concluded from it (see chap. 11). Like Arbuthnot, many erroneously believe that a significant result provides the probability that the null hypothesis is true or that the alternative hypothesis is false. However, unlike Bayes's rule, a null hypothesis test can never provide a probability for a hypothesis, but only for the data under the assumption that the null hypothesis is true. Alternative statistical methods, such as Neyman-Pearson hypothesis tests, Wald's sequential tests, Tukey's exploratory data analysis, or Bayes's rule are scarcely known, and there seems to be little interest in learning about them. R. A. Fisher, Jerzy Neyman, and other statisticians have repeatedly criticized the mindless application of one and the same statistical method, but those implicated have either not noticed or simply repressed the fact.

The evolution of statistical thinking may have solved problems, but it also created new ones. As the theory of probability developed, the multitude of concepts pertaining to chance and expectation were radically diminished. The term *probabilitas* originally referred to an opinion backed by authority. Neither this concept nor the other two close candidates, *luck* and *fate,* were embraced in the theory. Even today, the three interpretations of probability that initiated the theory often conflict with each other. Is probability a relative frequency in a reference class of events, such as in statistical tables? Or is it the degree of subjective confidence held by a rational human being? Or is it instead determined by design, like the construction of a gambling die? This question separated the frequentists, such as Richard von Mises and Jerzy Neyman, from the subjective Bayesians, such as Bruno de Finetti and Leonard Savage, and from representatives of propensities, such as Karl Popper. The answer to this question determines the subject matter to which the theory applies. For a subjectivist, this covers everything in the world that people have opinions on, as long as their opinions follow the laws of the theory. This includes probabilities for singular cases, even for events that have not yet been observed, such as the first full brain transplant. For a frequentist, the theory only applies to statements about apparently similar elements of a reference class for which a sufficient amount of statistical information is available. In this view, the theory is applicable to such situations as HIV screening, where enough data exist, but not to the night in paradise problem. For those who see probability as propensity (design), the theory applies to an even smaller domain, applying only to items whose causal structure or construction is known.

These various interpretations of the concept of probability can elicit different estimates of the risk in question. A few years ago I partook in a guided tour of the DASA (Daimler Benz Aerospace) factory producing the Ariane rockets that orbit satellites. Together with the tour guide, I looked at a large poster listing all 94 rockets (Ariane, Models 4 and 5) that had been launched and asked him about the risk of a launch failure. He replied that the security factor was around 99.6 percent. That seemed unnaturally high to me, since the poster showed eight stars representing eight accidents. I then asked how eight accidents out of 94 starts could equal a 99.6 percent security factor. The guide explained that the DASA did not count the launch failures but instead calculated the security factor based on the construction of the individual rocket parts. The failed launches also included human error. He added that the last failure, for example, was based on a misunderstanding between a worker who had forgotten a screw and his fellow worker on the next shift who mistakenly assumed that the first one had attached it. Hence the cited risk of launch failures was based on a propensity or design interpretation, not on the actual frequencies.

The Courage to Use One's Own Understanding

Statistical thinking is a product of the Enlightenment. The philosopher Kant began his essay "An answer to the question: What is enlightenment?" from 1784 as follows:

> Enlightenment is a release from self-imposed immaturity, immaturity meaning an inability to use one's understanding without depending on someone else's guidance. This immaturity is self-imposed when it is not caused by lack of understanding, but by lack of resolve and courage to use it without external guidance. Sapere Aude! "Have the courage to use your own understanding!"—that is the motto of enlightenment.

These are clear and deep thoughts. The key concept is *courage*. It is necessary because using one's own understanding can not only confer feelings of liberation and independence but also lead to punishment and pain. Kant himself learned this from firsthand experience. A few years after he wrote these sentences, authorities forbade him to write or teach on religious topics, fearing that his rationality could undermine the certainty of Christian dogma. More generally, overcoming immaturity can entail finding gaps or contradictions in reports, facts, and values in which one had always believed. Questioning certainties often means questioning social authority.

Learning to live with uncertainty poses an immense challenge for individuals and societies. A large part of our history was shaped by people who were absolutely convinced that their tribe, race, or religion was selected by God or Fate—and then assumed the right to fight dissenting ideas as well as the people who were "contaminated" by them. It was a long road to our contemporary forms of society that tolerate uncertainty and diversity. Nonetheless we are still far from being the courageous, informed human beings that Kant envisioned, an aspiration expressed in two simple Latin words: *Sapere aude*. Have the courage to think for yourself.

Chapter 11

Mindless Statistics

> No scientific worker has a fixed level of significance at which
> from year to year, and in all circumstances, he rejects hypotheses;
> he rather gives his mind to each particular case in the light of his
> evidence and his ideas.
>
> —Sir Ronald A. Fisher (1956)

I once visited a distinguished statistical textbook author, whose book went through many editions and whose name does not matter. His textbook represents the relative best in the social sciences. He was not a statistician; otherwise, his text would likely not have been used in a psychology class. In an earlier edition, he had included a chapter on Bayesian statistics and also mentioned (albeit in only one sentence) that there was a development in statistical theory from R. A. Fisher to Jerzy Neyman and Egon S. Pearson. To mention the existence of alternative statistical methods and the names associated with them is virtually unheard of in psychology. I asked the author why he removed the chapter on Bayes as well as the innocent sentence from all subsequent editions. "What made you present statistics as if it had only a single hammer, rather than a toolbox? Why did you mix Fisher's and Neyman-Pearson's theories into an inconsistent hybrid that every decent statistician would reject?"

To his credit, I should say that the author did not attempt to deny that he had produced the illusion that there is only one tool. But he let me know that he was not to blame. There were instead three culprits: his fellow researchers, the university administration, and his publisher. Most researchers, he argued, are not really interested in statistical thinking but only in how to get their papers published. The administration at his university promoted

This chapter is a revised version of G. Gigerenzer, "Mindless Statistics," *Journal of Socio-Economics* 33 (2004): 587–606.

researchers according to the number of their publications, which reinforced the researchers' attitude. And he passed on the responsibility to his publisher, who demanded a single-recipe cookbook. No controversies, please. His publisher had forced him to take out the chapter on Bayes as well as the sentence that named alternative theories, he explained. At the end of our conversation, I asked him what kind of statistical theory he himself believed in. "Deep in my heart," he confessed, "I am a Bayesian."

If the author was telling me the truth, he had sold his heart for multiple editions of a famous book whose message he did not believe in. He had sacrificed his intellectual integrity for success. Tens of thousands of students have read his text, believing that it reveals the method of science. Dozens of less informed textbook writers copied from his text, churning out a flood of offspring textbooks and not noticing the mess.

The Null Ritual

Textbooks and curricula in psychology almost never teach the statistical toolbox, which contains such tools as descriptive statistics, Tukey's exploratory methods, Bayesian statistics, Neyman-Pearson decision theory, and Wald's sequential analysis. Knowing the contents of a toolbox, of course, requires statistical thinking, that is, the art of choosing a proper tool for a given problem. Instead, one single procedure that I call the "null ritual" tends to be featured in texts and practiced by researchers. Its essence can be summarized in a few lines:

The null ritual

1. Set up a statistical null hypothesis of "no mean difference" or "zero correlation." Don't specify the predictions of your research hypothesis or of any alternative substantive hypotheses.
2. Use 5 percent as a convention for rejecting the null. If significant, accept your research hypothesis. Report the result as $p < 0.05$, $p < 0.01$, or $p < 0.001$ (whichever comes next to the obtained p-value).
3. Always perform this procedure.

The null ritual has sophisticated aspects I will not cover here, such as alpha adjustment and ANOVA procedures. But these do not change its essence. Often, textbooks also teach concepts alien to the ritual, such as statistical power and effect sizes, but these additions tend to disappear when examples are given. They just don't fit. More recently, the ritual has been labeled *null hypothesis significance testing*, for short, NHST or sometimes NHSTP (with *P* for "procedure"). It became institutionalized in the mid-1950s in curricula, editorials, and professional associations in psychology (Gigerenzer, 1987). The sixteenth edition of a highly influential textbook, Gerrig and Zimbardo's *Psychology and Life* (2002: 46), portrays the null ritual as statistics per se and calls it the "backbone of psychological research."

Its mechanical nature is sometimes presented like the rules of grammar. For instance, the 1974 *Publication Manual of the American Psychological Association* (APA) told authors what to capitalize, when to use a semicolon, and how to abbreviate states and territories. It also told authors how to interpret *p*-values: "Caution: Do not infer trends from data that fail by a small margin to meet the usual levels of significance. Such results are best interpreted as caused by chance and are best reported as such. Treat the result section like an income tax return. Take what's coming to you, but no more" (APA 1974: 19; this passage was deleted in the 3rd ed., 1983). Judgment is not invited. This reminds me of a maxim regarding the critical ratio, the predecessor of the significance level: "A critical ratio of three, or no Ph.D."

Anonymity is essential. The ritual is virtually always presented without names, as statistics per se. If names such as Fisher or Pearson are mentioned in textbooks in psychology, they are usually done so in connection with a minor detail, such as to thank E. S. Pearson for the permission to reprint a table. The major ideas are presented anonymously, as if they were given truths. Which text written for psychologists points out that null hypothesis testing was Fisher's idea? And that Neyman and Pearson argued against null hypothesis testing?

If names of statisticians surface, the reader is typically told that they are all of one mind. For instance, in response to a paper of mine (Gigerenzer, 1993b), the author of a statistical textbook, Chow (1998), acknowledged that different methods of statistical inference in fact exist. But a few lines later he (1998: xi) fell back into the "it's-all-the-same" fable: "To K. Pearson, R. Fisher, J. Neyman, and E. S. Pearson, NHSTP was what the empirical research was all about." Reader beware. Each of these eminent statisticians would have rejected the null ritual as bad statistics.

Fisher is mostly blamed for the null ritual. But toward the end of his life, Fisher (1955, 1956) rejected each of its three steps. First, "null" does not refer to a nil mean difference or zero correlation, but to any hypothesis to be "nullified." A correlation of 0.5, or a reduction of five cigarettes smoked per day, for instance, can be a null hypothesis. Second, as the epigraph illustrates, by 1956 Fisher thought that using a routine 5 percent level of significance indicated lack of statistical sophistication. No respectable researcher would use a constant level. Your chances of finding this quote in a statistical text in psychology are virtually nil. Third, for Fisher, null hypothesis testing was the most primitive type of statistical analyses and should be used only for problems about which we have *no or very little knowledge* (Gigerenzer et al., 1989: chap. 3). He proposed more appropriate methods for other cases.

Neyman and Pearson also would have rejected the null ritual but for different reasons. They rejected null hypothesis testing and favored competitive testing between two or more statistical hypotheses. In their theory, "hypotheses" is in the plural, enabling researchers to determine the Type-II error (which is not part of the null ritual and, consequently, not germane to NHSTP). The confusion between the null ritual and Fisher's theory, and sometimes even Neyman-Pearson theory, is the rule rather than the exception among psychologists.

Psychology seems to be one of the first disciplines where the null ritual became institutionalized as statistics per se, during the 1950s (Rucci and Tweney, 1980; Gigerenzer & Murray, 1987: chap. 1). Subsequently, it spread to many social, medical, and biological sciences, including economics (McCloskey & Ziliak, 1996), sociology (Morrison & Henkel, 1970), and ecology (Anderson, Burnham, & Thompson, 2000).

If psychologists are so smart, why are they so confused? Why is statistics carried out like compulsive hand washing? My answer is that the ritual requires confusion. To acknowledge that there is a statistical toolbox rather than one hammer would mean its end, as would realizing that the null ritual is practiced neither in the natural sciences nor in statistics proper. Its origin is in the minds of statistical textbook writers in psychology, education, and some other social sciences. It was created as an inconsistent hybrid of two competing theories: Fisher's null hypothesis testing and Neyman and Pearson's decision theory.

What Fisher and Neyman-Pearson Actually Proposed

In discussions about the pros and cons of significance testing in the social sciences, it is commonly overlooked (by both sides) that the ritual is not even part of statistics proper. So let us see what Fisher and Neyman-Pearson actually proposed. The logic of Fisher's (1955, 1956) null hypothesis testing can be summarized in three steps:

Fisher's null hypothesis testing

1. Set up a statistical null hypothesis. The null need not be a nil hypothesis (i.e., zero difference).
2. Report the exact level of significance (e.g., $p = 0.051$ or $p = 0.049$). Do not use a conventional 5 percent level and do not talk about accepting or rejecting hypotheses.
3. Use this procedure only if you know very little about the problem at hand.

Fisher's null hypothesis testing is, at each step, unlike the null ritual but also unlike Neyman-Pearson decision theory. It lacks a specified statistical alternative hypothesis. As a consequence, the concepts of statistical power, Type-II error rates, and theoretical effect sizes have no place in Fisher's framework—one needs a specified alternative for these concepts. The Polish mathematician Jerzy Neyman worked with Egon S. Pearson (the son of Karl Pearson) at University College in London and later, when the tensions between Fisher and himself grew too heated, moved to Berkeley, California. Neyman and Pearson criticized Fisher's null hypothesis testing for several reasons, including that no alternative hypothesis is specified. In its simplest version, Neyman-Pearson theory has two hypotheses and a binary decision criterion (Neyman, 1950, 1957).

Neyman-Pearson decision theory

1. Set up two statistical hypotheses, H_1 and H_2, and decide about α, β, and sample size before the experiment, based on subjective cost-benefit considerations. These define a rejection region for each hypothesis.
2. If the data fall into the rejection region of H_1, accept H_2; otherwise accept H_1. Note that accepting a hypothesis does not mean that you believe in it but only that you act as if it were true.
3. The usefulness of the procedure is limited among others to situations where you have a disjunction of hypotheses (e.g., either $\mu^1 = 8$ or $\mu^2 = 10$ is true) and where you can make meaningful cost-benefit trade-offs for choosing α and β.

A typical application of Neyman-Pearson testing is in quality control. Imagine manufacturers of metal plates that are used in medical instruments. They consider a mean diameter of 8 mm (H_1) as optimal and 10 mm (H_2) as dangerous to the patients and hence unacceptable. From past experience, they know that the random fluctuations of diameters are approximately normally distributed and that the standard deviations do not depend on the mean. This allows them to determine the sampling distributions of the mean for both hypotheses. They consider false alarms, that is, accepting H_2 while H_1 is true, to be the less serious error and misses of malfunctioning, that is, accepting H_1 while H_2 is true, to be more serious. Misses may cause harm to patients and to the firm's reputation. Therefore, they set the first error rate large and the second smaller, say $\alpha = 10\%$, and $\beta = 0.1\%$, respectively. They now calculate the required sample size n of plates that must be sampled every day to test the quality of the production. When accepting H_2, they act as if there were a malfunction and stop production, but this does not mean that they believe that H_2 is true. They know that they must expect a false alarm in 1 out of 10 days in which there is no malfunction (Gigerenzer et al., 1989: chap. 3).

Now it is clear that the null ritual is a hybrid of the two theories. The first step of the ritual, to set up only one statistical hypothesis (the null), stems from Fisher's theory, except that the null always means "chance," such as a zero difference. This first step is inconsistent with Neyman-Pearson theory; it does not specify an alternative statistical hypotheses, α, β, or the sample size. The second step, making a yes-no decision, is consistent with Neyman-Pearson theory, except that the level should not be fixed by convention but by thinking about α, β, and the sample size. Fisher (1955) and many statisticians after him, in contrast, argued that unlike in quality control, yes-no decisions have little role in science; rather, scientists should communicate the exact level of significance. The third step of the null ritual is unique in statistical theory. If Fisher and Neyman-Pearson agreed on anything, it was that statistics should never be used mechanically.

Fisher is best known as one of the inadvertent "fathers" of the null ritual. His influence has divided psychologists deeply, and interestingly, the rift runs between the great personalities in psychology, on the one hand, and a mass of anonymous researchers on the other. You would not have caught Jean

Piaget calculating a *t*-test. The seminal contributions by Frederick Bartlett, Wolfgang Köhler, and the Noble laureate I. P. Pavlov did not rely on *p*-values. Stanley S. Stevens, a founder of modern psychophysics, together with Edwin Boring, known as the dean of the history of psychology, blamed Fisher for a "meaningless ordeal of pedantic computations" (Stevens, 1960: 276). The clinical psychologist Paul Meehl (1978: 817) called routine null hypothesis testing "one of the worst things that ever happened in the history of psychology," and the behaviorist B. F. Skinner (1972: 319) blamed Fisher and his followers for having "taught statistics in lieu of scientific method." The mathematical psychologist R. Duncan Luce (1988: 582) called null hypothesis testing a "wrongheaded view about what constituted scientific progress," and the Nobel laureate Herbert A. Simon (1992: 159) simply stated that for his research, the "familiar tests of statistical significance are inappropriate."

It is telling that few researchers are aware that their own heroes rejected what they practice routinely. Awareness of the origins of the ritual and of its rejection could cause a virulent cognitive dissonance, in addition to dissonance with editors, reviewers, and dear colleagues. Suppression of conflicts and contradicting information is in the very nature of this social ritual.

Feelings of Guilt

Let me introduce Dr. Publish-Perish. He is the average researcher, a devoted consumer of statistical packages. His superego tells him that he ought to set the level of significance before an experiment is performed. A level of 1 percent would be impressive, wouldn't it? Yes, but...he fears that the *p*-value calculated from the data could turn out slightly higher. What if it were 1.1 percent? Then he would have to report a nonsignificant result. He does not want to take that risk. How about setting the level at a less impressive 5 percent? But what if the *p*-value turned out to be smaller than 1 percent or even 0.1 percent? He would then regret his decision deeply, because he would have to report this result as $p < 0.05$. He does not like that either. So he concludes that the only choice left is to cheat a little and disobey his superego. He waits until he has seen the data, rounds the *p*-value up to the next conventional level, and reports that the result is significant at $p < 0.001$, 0.01, or 0.05, whatever is next. That smells of deception, and his superego leaves him with feelings of guilt. But what should he do when honesty does not pay and nearly everyone else plays this little cheating game?

Dr. Publish-Perish does not know that his moral dilemma is caused by a mere confusion, introduced by textbook writers who failed to distinguish the three main interpretations of the level of significance.

I. Level of Significance = Mere Convention

Fisher wrote three books on statistics. For the social sciences, the most influential of them was the second one, *The Design of Experiments,* first published in 1935. Fisher's definition here of a level of significance differed from that in his later writings. In the book, Fisher (1935/1951: 13) suggested that the level of significance be thought of as a *convention*: "It is usual and convenient for experimenters to take 5% as a standard level of significance, in the sense that they are prepared to ignore all results which fail to reach this standard." His assertion that 5 percent (in some cases, 1 percent) is a convention to be adopted by all experimenters and in all experiments, while nonsignificant results are to be ignored, became part of the null ritual.

II. Level of Significance = Alpha

In Neyman-Pearson theory, the meaning of a level of significance, such as 2 percent, is the following: If H_1 is correct, and the experiment is repeated many times, the experimenter will wrongly reject H_1 in 2 percent of the cases. Rejecting H_1 if it is correct is called a Type-I error, and its probability is called alpha (α). One must specify the level of significance before the experiment in order to be able to interpret it as α. The same holds for beta (β), which is the rate of rejecting the alternative hypothesis H_2 if it is correct (Type-II error). Here we get the second classical interpretation of the level of significance: the error rate α, which is determined before the experiment, albeit not by mere convention, but by cost-benefit calculations that strike a balance between α, β, and sample size n. For instance, if $\alpha = \beta = 0.10$, then it does not matter whether the exact level of significance is 0.06 or 0.001. The exact level has no influence on α.

III. Level of Significance = Exact Level of Significance

Fisher had second thoughts about his proposal of a conventional level and stated these most clearly in the 1950s. In his last book, *Statistical Methods and Scientific Inference* (1956: 42, 100), Fisher rejected the use of a conventional level of significance and ridiculed this practice, together with the concepts of Type-I and Type-II errors, as "absurdly academic" and originating from "the phantasy of circles rather remote from scientific research." He was referring to mathematicians, specifically to Neyman. In science, Fisher argued, one does not repeat the same experiment again and again, as is assumed in Neyman and Pearson's interpretation of the level of significance as an error rate in the long run. What researchers should do instead, according to Fisher's second thoughts, is publish the *exact level of significance*, say, $p = 0.02$ (not $p < 0.05$). You communicate information; you do not make yes-no decisions.

The basic differences are this: For Fisher, the exact level of significance is a property of the data, that is, a relation between a body of data and a theory. For Neyman and Pearson, α is a property of the test, not of the data. In Fisher's *Design*, if the result is significant, you reject the null; otherwise you do not draw any conclusion. The decision is asymmetric. In Neyman-Pearson theory, the decision is symmetric. Fisher's level of significance and α are not the same thing. For Fisher, these differences were no peanuts. He branded Neyman's position as "childish" and "horrifying [for] the intellectual freedom of the west." Indeed, he (1955: 70) likened Neyman to

> Russians [who] are made familiar with the ideal that research in pure science can and should be geared to technological performance, in the comprehensive organized effort of a five-year plan for the nation...[While] in the U.S. also the great importance of organized technology has I think made it easy to confuse the process appropriate for drawing correct conclusions, with those aimed rather at, let us say, speeding production, or saving money.

It is probably not an accident that Neyman was born in Russia and, at the time of Fisher's comment, had moved to the United States.

Back to Dr. Publish-Perish and his moral conflict. His superego demands that he specify the level of significance before the experiment. We now understand that his superego's doctrine is part of the Neyman-Pearson theory. His ego personifies Fisher's theory of calculating the exact level of significance from the data, conflated with Fisher's earlier idea of making a yes-no decision based on a conventional level of significance. The conflict between his superego and his ego is the source of his guilt feelings, but he does not know that. He just has a vague feeling of shame for doing something wrong. Dr. Publish-Perish does not follow any of the three interpretations. Unknowingly, he tries to satisfy all of them and ends up presenting an exact level of significance as if it were an alpha level by rounding it up to one of the conventional levels of significance, $p < 0.05$, $p < 0.01$, or $p < 0.001$. The result is not α, nor an exact level of significance. It is the product of an unconscious conflict.

The conflict is institutionalized in the *Publication Manuals of the American Psychological Association*. The fifth edition of the *Manual* (2001: 162) finally added exact levels of significance to an ANOVA (analysis of variance) table but, at the same time, retained the $p < 0.05$ and $p < 0.01$ "asterisks" of the null ritual. The manual offers no explanation as to why both are necessary or what they mean (Fidler, 2002). Nor can Dr. Publish-Perish find information in it about the conflicting interpretations of "level of significance" and the origins of his feelings of guilt.

Collective Illusions

Rituals call for cognitive illusions. Their function is to make the final product, a significant result, appear highly informative, and thereby justify the ritual. Try to answer the following question:

> Suppose you have a treatment that you suspect may alter performance on a certain task. You compare the means of your control and experimental groups (say 20 subjects in each sample). Further, suppose you

use a simple independent means t-test and your result is significant (t = 2.7, d.f. = 18, p = 0.01). Please mark each of the statements below as "true" or "false." "False" means that the statement does not follow logically from the above premises. Also note that several or none of the statements may be correct.

1. You have absolutely disproved the null hypothesis (that is, there is no difference between the population means).
   ❑ True/False ❑
2. You have found the probability of the null hypothesis being true.
   ❑ True/False ❑
3. You have absolutely proved your experimental hypothesis (that there is a difference between the population means).
   ❑ True/False ❑
4. You can deduce the probability of the experimental hypothesis being true.
   ❑ True/False ❑
5. You know, if you decide to reject the null hypothesis, the probability that you are making the wrong decision.
   ❑ True/False ❑
6. You have a reliable experimental finding in the sense that if, hypothetically, the experiment were repeated a great number of times, you would obtain a significant result on 99 percent of occasions.
   ❑ True/False ❑

Which statements are in fact true? Recall that a p-value is the probability of the observed data (or of more extreme data points), given that the null hypothesis H_0 is true, defined in symbols as $p(D|H_0)$. This definition can be rephrased in a more technical form by introducing the statistical model underlying the analysis (Gigerenzer et al., 1989: chap. 3), although I will keep it simple.

Statements 1 and 3 are easily detected as being false, because a significance test can never disprove the null hypothesis or the (undefined) experimental hypothesis. They are instances of the *illusion of certainty* (Gigerenzer, 2002a).

Statements 2 and 4 are also false. The probability $p(D|H_0)$ is not the same as $p(H_0|D)$, and more generally, a significance test does not provide a probability for a hypothesis. The statistical toolbox, of course, contains tools that would allow estimating probabilities of hypotheses, such as Bayesian statistics. Statement 5 also refers to a probability of a hypothesis. This is because if one rejects the null hypothesis, the only possibility of making a wrong decision is if the null hypothesis is true. Thus, it makes essentially the same claim as Statement 2 does, and both are incorrect.

Statement 6 amounts to the replication fallacy (Gigerenzer, 2000). Here, p = 1% is taken to imply that such significant data would reappear in 99 percent of the repetitions. Statement 6 could be made only if one knew that the null hypothesis was true. In formal terms, $p(D|H_0)$ is confused with $1 - p(D)$.

To sum up, all six statements are incorrect. Note that all six err in the same direction of wishful thinking: They make a p-value look more informative than it is.

Haller and Krauss (2002) posed the above question to 30 statistics teachers, including professors of psychology, lecturers, and teaching assistants, 39 professors and lecturers of psychology (not teaching statistics), and 44 psychology students. Teachers and students were from the psychology departments at six German universities. Each statistics teacher taught null hypothesis testing, and each student had successfully passed one or more statistics courses in which it was taught. Figure 11.1 shows the results.

None of the students noticed that all of the statements were wrong; every student endorsed one or more of the illusions about the meaning of a p-value. Perhaps these students lacked the right genes for statistical thinking? Or they did not pay attention to their teachers and were simply lucky in passing the exams? The results, however, indicate a different explanation. The students inherited the illusions from their teachers: 90 percent of the professors and lecturers believed one or more of the six statements to be correct. Most surprisingly, 80 percent of the statistics teachers shared illusions with their students. Note that one does not need to be a brilliant mathematician to answer the question "What does a significant result mean?" One only needs to understand that a p-value is the probability of the data (or more extreme

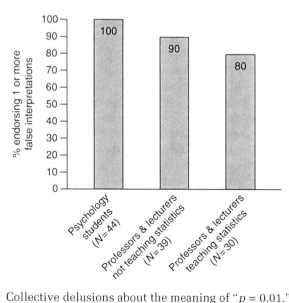

Figure 11.1: Collective delusions about the meaning of "$p = 0.01$." The percentages refer to the participants in each group who endorsed one or more of the six false statements (see Gigerenzer, Krauss, & Vitouch, 2004; Haller and Krauss, 2002).

data), given that the H_0 is true. The most frequent illusion was Statement 5, endorsed by about 70 percent of all three groups. In an earlier study with academic psychologists in the United Kingdom (Oakes, 1986) as many as 86 percent thought that this statement was true. The replication fallacy (Statement 6) was the second most frequent illusion, believed to be true by about half of the teachers and 37 percent of those who taught statistics. The corresponding figure for the U.K. psychologists was 60 percent. About 60 percent of the students and one-third of each of the teacher groups believed that one can deduce the probability that the experimental hypothesis is true from the p-value (Statement 4). In Oakes's study, two-thirds of British academic psychologists believed this. On average, students endorsed 2.5 illusions; their professors and lecturers, 2.0 illusions; and those who taught significance testing, 1.9 illusions (Gigerenzer, Krauss, & Vitouch, 2004; Haller & Krauss, 2002). All in all, the German professors and lecturers did somewhat better than the British academic psychologists studied earlier by Oakes (1986), yet the number of illusions they held remains breathtaking. Falk and Greenbaum (1995) added the right alternative ("none of the statements is correct") and also made Israeli students read Bakan's (1966) classical article, which warns of these illusions. Nevertheless, 87 percent of the students opted for one or several illusions. A global fantasy seems to travel by cultural transmission from teacher to student.

If students "inherited" the illusions from their teachers, where did the teachers acquire them? The answer is right there in the first textbooks introducing psychologists to null hypothesis testing more than 50 years ago. Guilford's *Fundamental Statistics in Psychology and Education,* first published in 1942, was probably the most widely read textbook in the 1940s and 1950s. Guilford suggested that hypothesis testing would reveal the probability that the null hypothesis is true. "If the result comes out one way, the hypothesis is probably correct, if it comes out another way, the hypothesis is probably wrong" (Guilford, 1942: 156). Guilford's logic wavered back and forth between correct and incorrect statements, and ambiguous ones that can be read like Rorschach inkblots. He used such phrases as "we obtained directly the probabilities that the null hypothesis was plausible" and "the probability of extreme deviations from chance" interchangeably for the level of significance. Guilford is no exception. He marked the beginning of a genre of statistical texts that vacillate between the researchers' desire for probabilities of hypotheses and what significance testing can actually provide. For instance, within three pages of text, Nunally (1975: 194–196; italics in the original) used all of the following statements to explain what a significant result such as 5 percent actually means:

- "the probability that an observed difference is real"
- "the *improbability* of observed results being due to error"
- "the *statistical confidence*...with odds of 95 out of 100 that the observed difference will hold up in investigations"
- "the danger of accepting a statistical result as real when it is actually due only to error"

- the degree to which experimental results are taken "seriously"
- the degree of "faith [that] can be placed in the reality of the finding"
- "the investigator can have 95 percent confidence that the sample mean actually differs from the population mean"
- "if the probability is low, the null hypothesis is improbable"
- "all of these are different ways to say the same thing"

The poor students who try to digest these explanations! They likely misattribute the author's confusion to their own lack of statistical intelligence. This state of bewilderment will last as long as the ritual continues to exist. Today's students still encounter oracular statements in the most-widely read texts: "Inferential statistics indicate the probability that the particular sample of scores obtained are actually related to whatever you are attempting to measure or whether they could have occurred by chance" (Gerrig and Zimbardo, 2002: 44).

Early authors promoting the error that the level of significance specified the probability of hypothesis include Anastasi (1958: 11), Ferguson (1959: 133), and Lindquist (1940: 14). But the belief has persisted over decades: for instance, in Miller and Buckhout (1973; statistical appendix by Brown: 523), and in the examples collected by Bakan (1966), Pollard and Richardson (1987), Gigerenzer (1993b), Mulaik, Raju, and Harshman (1997), and Nickerson (2000). I sometimes hear that if the associated illusions were eliminated, the null ritual would emerge as a meaningful method. As I mentioned before, in contrast, I believe that some degree of illusion is necessary to keep the null ritual alive, and the empirical evidence supports this conjecture (e.g., Lecoutre, Poitevineau, & Lecoutre, 2003; Tversky & Kahneman, 1971). Without illusions, the ritual would be easily recognized for what it is.

An Editor with Guts

Everyone seems to have an answer to this question: Who is to blame for the null ritual? Always someone else. A smart graduate student told me that he did not want problems with his thesis advisor. When he finally got his Ph.D. and a postdoc, his concern was to get a real job. Soon he was an assistant professor at a respected university, but he still felt he could not afford statistical thinking because he needed to publish quickly to get tenure. The editors required the ritual, he apologized, but after tenure, everything would be different and he would be a free man. Years later, he found himself tenured but still in the same environment. And he had been asked to teach a statistics course, featuring the null ritual. He did. As long as the editors of the major journals punish statistical thinking, he concluded, nothing will change.

Blaming editors is not entirely unfounded. For instance, the former editor of the *Journal of Experimental Psychology,* Melton (1962), insisted on the null ritual in his editorial and also made it clear that he wants to see $p < 0.01$, not just $p < 0.05$. In his editorial, he produced the usual illusions, asserting that the lower the p-value, the higher the confidence that the alternative hypothesis is true and the higher the probability that a replication will find a significant result. Nothing beyond p-values was mentioned; precise hypotheses, good descriptive statistics, confidence intervals, effect sizes, and power did not appear in the editor's definition of good research. A small p-value was the hallmark of excellent experimentation, a convenient yardstick for whether or not to accept a paper at a time when the number of journals, articles, and psychologists had skyrocketed.

There was resistance. The Skinnerians founded a new journal, the *Journal of the Experimental Analysis of Behavior*, in order to be able to publish their kind of experiments (Skinner, 1984: 138). Similarly, one reason for launching the *Journal of Mathematical Psychology* was to escape the editors' pressure to routinely perform null hypothesis testing. One of its founders, R. D. Luce (1988: 582), called this practice a "mindless hypothesis testing in lieu of doing good research: measuring effects, constructing substantive theories of some depth, and developing probability models and statistical procedures suited to these theories."

Should we blame the editors? The story of Geoffrey Loftus, editor of *Memory and Cognition*, however, suggests that the truth is not as simple as that. In 1991, Loftus reviewed *The Empire of Chance* (Gigerenzer et al., 1989), in which we presented one of the first analyses of how psychologists jumbled ideas of Fisher and Neyman-Pearson into one hybrid logic. When Loftus became editor-elect of *Memory and Cognition*, he made it clear in his editorial that he did not want authors to submit papers in which p, t, or F-values had been mindlessly calculated and reported (Loftus, 1993). Rather, his guideline was: "By default, data should be conveyed as a figure depicting sample means *with associated standard errors and/or, where appropriate, standard deviations*" (ibid.; emphasis in the original). His policy encouraged researchers to use proper descriptive statistics and freed them from the pressure to test null hypotheses and make yes-no decisions whose relevance are obscure. I admire Loftus for the courage to take such a step.

When I met Loftus during his editorship, I asked him how his crusade was going. Loftus bitterly complained about the many researchers who stubbornly refused the opportunity and insisted on their p-values and yes-no decisions. How much success did he have over the years?

Loftus was preceded as editor by Margaret Jean Intons-Petersen, who commenced in 1990. In her incoming editorial, she mentioned the use of descriptive statistics, including variability estimates, but emphasized the usual significance tests. During her term, 53 percent of the articles relied exclusively on the null ritual (Finch et al., 2004). Under Loftus, who served as the editor from 1994 to 1997, this proportion decreased to 32 percent. During the term of Loftus's successor, Morton Ann Gernsbacher (1998), who did not comment on statistical procedures or on Loftus's recommendations in her editorial, the proportion rose again to about half, reaching a new high of 55 percent in 2000.

The far majority of the remaining articles also relied on the null ritual but provided some additional information, such as figures with means, standard errors, standard deviations, or confidence intervals. Loftus's recommendation to provide this information without performing the null ritual was followed in only 6 percent of the articles during his editorship and in only one(!) case in the years before and after (Finch et al., 2004). Before Loftus, only 8 percent of the articles provided figures with error bars and/ or reported confidence intervals, and among these, in every second case it was left unclear what the bars represented—standard errors, standard deviations, confidence intervals? Loftus brought this proportion up to 45 percent and that of unclear error bars down (Finch et al., 2004). But under his successor, the proportion decreased again, to 27 percent, and that of the unclear bars rose.

Loftus reported that many researchers exhibited deep anxiety at the prospect of abandoning their *p*-values, confused standard errors with standard deviations, and had no idea how to compute a confidence interval based on their ANOVA packages. Looking back, he estimated that he requested approximately 300 confidence intervals and probably computed about 100 himself. Did Loftus's experiment have the desired impact? During his editorship, he succeeded in reducing reliance on the null ritual; afterward, the effect declined. Whether his example has a long-term impact is an open question. Loftus was ahead of his time, and I can only hope that his admirable experiment will eventually inspire other editors.

At issue here is the importance of good descriptive and exploratory statistics rather than mechanical hypothesis testing with yes-no answers. Good descriptive statistics (as opposed to figures without error bars, or unclear error bars, and routine aggregate instead of individual analysis, for example) is necessary and mostly sufficient. Note that in scientific problems, the relevance of optimization procedures, such as Neyman-Pearson decision theory is notoriously unclear. For instance, unlike in quality control, experimental subjects are rarely randomly sampled from a specified population. Thus, it is unclear for which population the inference from a sample should be made, and "optimal" yes-no decisions are of little relevance. The attempt to give an "optimal" answer to the wrong question has been called "Type-III error." The statistician John Tukey (e.g., 1969) argued for a change in perspective: An appropriate answer to the right problem is better than an optimal answer to the wrong problem (Perlman & Wu, 1999). Neither Fisher's null hypothesis testing nor Neyman–Pearson decision theory can answer most scientific problems. The issue of optimizing versus satisficing is equally relevant for research on bounded rationality and fast and frugal heuristics (chaps. 1–3).

The Superego, the Ego, and the Id

Why do intelligent people engage in statistical rituals rather than in statistical thinking? Every person of average intelligence can understand that $p(D|H)$ is not the same as $p(H|D)$. That this insight fades away when it comes to hypothesis testing suggests that the cause is not intellectual, but social and emotional. Here is a hypothesis (Acree, 1978; Gigerenzer, 1993b): The conflict between statisticians, both suppressed by and inherent in the textbooks, has become internalized in the minds of researchers. The statistical ritual is a form of conflict resolution, like compulsive hand washing, which makes it resistant to arguments. To illustrate this thesis, I use the Freudian unconscious conflicts as an analogy (figure 11.2).

The Neyman-Pearson theory serves as the superego of Dr. Publish-Perish. It demands in advance that alternative hypotheses, alpha, and power to calculate the sample size necessary be specified precisely, following the frequentist doctrine of repeated random sampling (Neyman, 1957). The superego forbids the interpretation of levels of significance as the degree of confidence that a particular hypothesis is true or false. Hypothesis testing is about what to do; that is, one acts as if a hypothesis were true or false, without necessarily believing that it is true or false.

The Fisherian theory of null hypothesis testing functions as the ego. The ego gets things done in the laboratory and papers published. Levels of significance are computed after the experiment, the power of the test is ignored, and the sample size is determined by a rule of thumb. The ego does not state its research hypothesis in a precise way but at best in form of a directional prediction, yet does not hesitate to claim support for it by rejecting a null hypothesis. The ego makes abundant epistemic statements about its confidence in particular hypotheses. But it is left with feelings of guilt and shame for having violated the rules. The Bayesian view forms the id. Its goal is a statement about the probabilities of hypotheses, which is censored by both the purist superego and the pragmatic ego. However, these probabilities are exactly what the id wants, after all. It gets its way by blocking the intellect

Superego	Neyman-Pearson	Two or more statistical hypotheses; alpha and beta determined before the experiment; compute sample size; no statements about the truth of hypotheses
Ego	Fisher	Null hypothesis only; significance level computed after the experiment; beta ignored; sample size by rule of thumb; gets paper published but left with feeling of guilt
Id	Bayes	Desire for probabilities of hypotheses

Figure 11.2: A Freudian analogy for the unconscious conflict between statistical ideas in the minds of researchers.

from understanding that $p(D|H)$ is not the same as $p(H|D)$. This enables wishful thinking.

The Freudian analogy brings the anxiety and the feelings of guilt into the foreground. It seems as if the raging personal and intellectual conflicts between Fisher and Neyman-Pearson, and between these frequentists and the Bayesians, were projected into an "intrapsychic" conflict in the minds of researchers. In Freudian theory, ritual is a way of resolving unconscious conflict, but at considerable costs.

Meehl's Conjecture

Paul Meehl, a brilliant clinical psychologist with a broad interest in the philosophy of science, was one of those who blamed Fisher for the decline of statistical thinking in psychology. "Sir Ronald has befuddled us, mesmerized us, and led us down the primrose path. I believe the almost universal reliance on merely refuting the null hypothesis...is a terrible mistake, is basically unsound, poor scientific strategy, and one of the worst things that ever happened in the history of psychology" (Meehl, 1978: 817). Meehl is a bit harsh on blaming Fisher rather than the null ritual; recall that Fisher also proposed other statistical tools, and in the 1950s, he thought of null hypothesis testing as adequate only for situations in which we know nothing or little. Meehl made a challenging prediction concerning null hypothesis tests in nonexperimental settings, where random assignment to treatment and control group is not possible, due to ethical or practical constraints. It (Meehl 1978) can be summarized as follows:

Meehl's conjecture

In nonexperimental settings with large sample sizes, the probability of rejecting the null hypothesis of nil group differences in favor of a directional alternative is about 0.50.

Isn't that good news? We guess that X is larger than Y—and we get it right half of the time. For instance, if we make up the story that Protestants have a higher memory span than Catholics, slower reaction times, smaller shoe size, and higher testosterone levels, each of these hypotheses has about a 50 percent chance of being accepted by a null hypothesis test. If we do not commit to the direction and just guess that X and Y are different, we get it right virtually 100 percent of the time. Meehl reasoned that in the real world—as opposed to experimental settings—the null hypothesis ("nil" as defined by the null ritual, not by Fisher) is always wrong. Some difference exists between any natural groups. Therefore, with sufficient statistical power, one will almost always find a significant result. If one randomly guesses the direction of the difference, it follows that one will be correct in about 50 percent of the cases (with an unspecified alternative hypothesis, one will be correct in about 100 percent of them).

Niels Waller (2004) set out to test Meehl's conjecture empirically. He had access to the data of more than 81,000 individuals who had completed the 567 items of the Minnesota Multiphase Personality Inventory–Revised (MMPI-2). The MMPI-2 asks people about a broad range of contents, including health, personal habits, attitudes toward sex, and extreme manifestations of psychopathology. Imagine a gender theorist who has concocted a new theory that predicts directional gender differences, that is, women will score higher on some item than men, or vice versa. Can we predict the probability of rejecting the null hypothesis in favor of the new theory? According to Meehl's conjecture, it is about 50 percent. In Waller's simulation, the computer picked the first of the 511 items of the MMPI-2 (excluding 56 for their known ability to discriminate between the sexes), determined randomly the direction of the alternative hypothesis, and computed whether the difference was significant in the predicted direction. This procedure was repeated with all 511 items. The result: 46 percent of the predictions were confirmed, often with very impressive p-values. Many of the item mean differences were 50–100 times larger than the associated standard errors!

These empirical results support Meehl's conjecture, consistent with earlier findings by Bakan (1966) and Meehl himself. A bit of statistical thinking can make the logic of the conjecture transparent to an undergraduate. Yet one can find experienced researchers who proudly report that they have studied several hundreds or even thousands of subjects and found a highly significant mean difference in the predicted direction, say $p < 0.0001$. How big this effect is, however, is not reported in some of these articles. The combination of large sample size and low p-values is of little value in itself.

The general problem addressed by Meehl is the inattention to effect sizes in the null ritual. Effect sizes have been discussed by Cohen (1988) and Rosenthal and Rubin (1982). The Task Force on Statistical Inference (TFSI) of the American Psychological Association (Wilkinson and TFSI, 1999) recommended reporting effect sizes (theoretical ones as in Neyman-Pearson theory, or empirical ones) as essential. The fifth edition of the *Publication Manual of the American Psychological Association* (2001) followed up this recommendation, although only half-heartedly. In the examples given, effect sizes are either not included or not explained and interpreted (Fidler, 2002).

Without a theoretical effect size, the statistical power of a test cannot be computed. In 1962, Jacob Cohen reported that the experiments published in a major psychology journal had, on average, only a fifty-fifty chance of detecting a medium-sized effect if there was one. That is, the statistical power was as low as 50 percent. This result was widely cited, but did it change researchers' practice? Sedlmeier and Gigerenzer (1989) checked the studies in the same journal, 24 years later, a time period that should allow for change. Yet only 2 out of 64 articles mentioned power, and it was never estimated. Unnoticed, the average power had actually decreased (researchers now used alpha adjustment, which shrinks power). Thus, if there had been an effect of a medium size, the researchers would have had a better chance of finding it by throwing a coin rather than conducting their time-consuming, elaborate, and expensive experiments. In the years 2000–2002, among some 220 empirical articles, there were finally 9 researchers who computed the power of their tests (Gigerenzer, Krauss, & Vitouch, 2004). Forty years after Cohen, the first sign of change appeared. The fourth edition of the *Publication Manual of the American Psychological Association* (1994) was the first to recommend that researchers take power seriously, and the fifth edition (2001) repeated this advice. Yet despite providing an abundance of examples for how to report *p*-values, the manual still does not include any examples of reporting power (Fidler, 2002).

Feynman's Conjecture

The routine reliance on the null ritual discourages not only statistical thinking, but theoretical thinking as well. One does not need to specify one's hypothesis or a challenging alternative hypothesis. There is no premium on "bold" hypotheses, in the sense of Karl Popper or Bayesian model comparison (MacKay, 1995). In many experimental papers in social and cognitive psychology, there is no theory within shooting distance, only surrogates, such as redescription of the results (Gigerenzer, 2000: chap. 14). The sole requirement is to reject a null that is identified with "chance." Statistical theories, such as Neyman-Pearson theory and Wald's theory, in contrast, begin with two or more statistical hypotheses.

In the absence of theory, the temptation is to look first at the data and then see what is significant. The physicist Richard Feynman (1998: 80–81) has taken notice of this misuse of hypothesis testing. I summarize his argument.

Feynman's conjecture

To report a significant result and reject the null in favor of an alternative hypothesis is meaningless unless the alternative hypothesis has been stated before the data was obtained.

When he was a graduate student at Princeton, Feynman got into an argument with a researcher in the psychology department. The researcher had designed an experiment, in which rats ran in a T-maze. The rats did not behave as predicted. Yet the researcher noticed something else, that the rats seem to alternate, first right, then left, then right again, and so on. He asked Feynman to calculate the probability under the null hypothesis (chance) that this pattern would be obtained. On this occasion, Feynman (ibid.) learned about the 5 percent level:

And it's a general principle of psychologists that in these tests they arrange so that the odds that the things that happen happen by chance is small, in fact, less than one in twenty.... And then he ran to me,

and he said, "Calculate the probability for me that they should alternate, so that I can see if it is less than one in twenty." I said, "It probably is less than one in twenty, but it doesn't count." He said, "Why?"
I said, "Because it doesn't make any sense to calculate after the event.
You see, you found the peculiarity, and so you selected the peculiar
case."...If he wants to test this hypothesis, one in twenty, he cannot
do it from the same data that gave him the clue. He must do another
experiment all over again and then see if they alternate. He did, and
it didn't work."

Feynman's conjecture is again and again violated by routine significance
testing, where one looks at the data to see what is significant. Statistical
packages allow every difference, interaction, or correlation against chance
to be tested. They automatically deliver ratings of "significance" in terms of
stars, double stars, and triple stars, encouraging the bad after-the-fact habit.
The general problem Feynman addressed is known as overfitting. Fitting a
model to data that is already obtained is not sound hypothesis testing, even
if the resulting explained variance, or R^2, is impressive. The reason is that
one does not know how much noise one has fitted, and the more adjustable
parameters one has, the more noise one can fit. Psychologists habitually fit
rather than predict and rarely test a model on new data, such as by cross-
validation (Roberts and Pashler, 2000). Fitting per se has the same problems
as story telling after the fact, which leads to a "hindsight bias." The true
test of a model is to fix its parameters on one sample and to test it in a new
sample. Then it turns out that predictions based on simple heuristics can
be more accurate than routine multiple regressions (chaps. 1–3). Less can
be more. The routine use of linear multiple regression exemplifies another
mindless use of statistics.

The Dawn of Statistical Thinking

Rituals seem to be indispensable for the self-definition of social groups
and for transitions in life, and there is nothing wrong with them. However,
they should be the subject rather than the procedure of social sciences.
Elements of social rituals include (i) the repetition of the same action, (ii)
a focus on special numbers or colors, (iii) fears about serious sanctions for
rule violations, and (iv) wishful thinking and delusions that virtually eliminate critical thinking (Dulaney and Fiske, 1994). The null ritual has each
of these four characteristics: incremental repetition of the same procedure;
the magical 5 percent number; fear of sanctions by editors or advisors; and
wishful thinking about the outcome, the p-value, which blocks researchers'
intelligence.

We know but often forget that the problem of inductive inference has no
single solution. There is no uniformly most powerful test, that is, no method
that is best for every problem. Statistical theory has provided us with a toolbox of effective instruments, which require judgment as to when it is right to

use them. When textbooks and curricula begin to teach the toolbox, students will automatically learn to make judgments. And they will realize that in many applications, a skillful and transparent descriptive data analysis is sufficient and preferable to the application of statistical routines chosen for their complexity and opacity. Judgment is part of the art of statistics.

To stop the ritual, we also need more guts and nerve. It takes some measure of courage to cease playing along in this embarrassing game. This may cause friction with editors and colleagues, but in the end it will help them enter the dawn of statistical thinking.

Chapter 12

Children Can Solve Bayesian Problems

There is an apparent paradox concerning the human ability to reason according to the laws of probability. On the one hand, according to the classical work by Piaget and Inhelder (1951/1975), by age 12 or so, children understand the laws of combinatorics, the law of large numbers, the irreversibility of chance processes, and other characteristics of probability. Recent studies have qualified this finding and demonstrated that, depending on the task, even younger children show signs of probabilistic reasoning (e.g., Falk & Wilkening, 1998; Schlottmann & Anderson, 1994). Piaget and Inhelder's work stands in the epistemological tradition of the Enlightenment's view of probability, according to which the laws of probability and the laws of human reasoning are two sides of the same coin. In Laplace's (1814/1951: 196) famous phrase, the theory of probability is "only common sense reduced to calculus."

In apparent contradiction to these results, research in cognitive and social psychology since the 1970s has been interpreted as demonstrating that many adults fail to reason according to the laws of probability (e.g., Gilovich, Griffin, & Kahneman, 2002). In the cognitive illusions program, the very same laws that the Enlightenment probabilists and their modern followers, including Piaget, thought to match intuitive reasoning—such as the law of large numbers and set inclusion—were seen as difficult for human intuition. More recently, many of the original negative findings have been qualified and revised (e.g., Juslin, Winman, & Olsson, 2000; Kahneman & Fredrick, 2002; Koehler, 1996a; Lopes, 1991). Nevertheless, a question arises. Why should Geneva children reason according to the laws of probability when Stanford undergraduates seem to be have problems doing so? This apparent paradox of early competence versus late failure has puzzled several scholars (e.g., Schlottmann, 2001).

This chapter is a revised version of L. Zhu and G. Gigerenzer, "Children Can Solve Bayesian Problems: The Role of Representation in Mental Computation," *Cognition* 98 (2006): 287–308.

In this chapter, we deal with a form of probabilistic reasoning that is considered difficult, namely, Bayesian reasoning. Do children reason the Bayesian way? To the best of our knowledge, there is no single study on children's Bayesian intuitions. There has been research with bees, bumblebees, birds, and other animals, concluding that animals are fairly good Bayesians (e.g., Real, 1991), whereas research with adult humans often came to the opposite conclusion. We argue that the question "Do children reason the Bayesian way?" can be answered only when it is posed conditional to the external representation of numerical information.

Bayesian Reasoning

Piaget and Inhelder (1951/1975) discuss the ideas of various mathematicians, mostly frequentists, such as von Mises and Reichenbach, but Bayes's rule is never mentioned. Here we deal with an elementary form of Bayesian reasoning, which has been the focus of almost all studies in adults (see Krauss, Martignon, & Hoffrage, 1999, for an exception). The elementary situation consists of a binary hypothesis (e.g., disease or no disease) and binary data (test positive or negative). The task is to evaluate the chances of the hypothesis given the data (e.g., of disease given a positive test). The use in this chapter of the term *Bayesian reasoning* refers to reasoning in regard to this elementary situation.

For binary hypotheses (H and not-H) and data D, Bayes's rule is:

$$p(H \mid D) = \frac{p(H)p(D \mid H)}{p(H)p(D \mid H) + p(\text{not-}H)p(D \mid \text{not-}H)} \tag{12.1}$$

In words, Bayes's rule specifies how to derive the posterior probability $p(H \mid D)$ of a hypothesis with the provided data. This probability can be derived from the base rate (or prior probability) $p(H)$ in light of new data. The impact of the data is specified by the conditional probabilities $p(D \mid H)$ and $p(D \mid \text{not-}H)$.

The Impact of Representation on Bayesian Reasoning

Conditional probabilities, as in equation 12.1, are a recent way to represent uncertainties, dating back to the invention of the mathematical theory of reasonableness in the mid-seventeenth century. There are different ways of representing uncertainties. One representation is in terms of natural frequencies, which correspond to the result of observing outcomes in natural environments, that is, *counting without normalizing*. This has been the format in which humans—and animals—have encountered information in their environments during most of their history.

The difference between a representation in terms of conditional probabilities and natural frequencies is illustrated by one of the problems ("Red Nose") given to the children in this study.

Red Nose problem: Conditional probabilities

Pingping goes to a small village to ask for directions. In this village, the probability that the person he meets will lie is 10 percent. If a person lies, the probability that he or she has a red nose is 80 percent. If a person doesn't lie, the probability that he or she also has a red nose is 10 percent. Imagine that Pingping meets someone in the village with a red nose. What is the probability that the person will lie?

Red Nose problem: Natural frequencies

Pingping goes to a small village to ask for directions. In this village, 10 out of every 100 people will lie. Of the 10 people who lie, 8 have a red nose. Of the remaining 90 people who don't lie, 9 also have a red nose. Imagine that Pingping meets a group of people in the village with red noses. How many of these people will lie? _____ out of _____.

When the information is in conditional probabilities, the solution can be obtained by inserting the probabilities into Bayes's rule, as defined by equation 12.1. The result is a probability of 47 percent that the person will lie. With natural frequencies, Bayesian computations become simpler (Kleiter, 1994):

$$p(H \mid D) = \frac{d}{d+f} \tag{12.2}$$

Natural frequencies are illustrated by the tree in figure 12.1. There are a cases (e.g., people), of which b cases show H (e.g., that they are liars) and c cases do not. Among the H cases, there are d cases that show D (e.g., a cue such as red nose) and e cases that do not; among the not-H cases, f show D and g do not. Thus, the answer is: 8 out of 17 people with a red nose will lie, which corresponds to a probability of 47 percent.

The reason for the computational simplification is that natural frequencies still contain information about base rates, whereas conditional probabilities are obtained by taking the base rate information out of the natural frequencies (i.e., normalization). As a result, when one transforms the natural frequencies in equation 12.2 into probabilities, the base rates have to be put back into equation 12.1 by multiplying the conditional probabilities by the base rates. This can be seen by comparing the structures of equations 12.1 and 12.2, which are exactly the same.

Note that the natural frequencies correspond to the way a child would learn from direct observation, whereas conditional probabilities are derived by normalizing natural frequencies. It is important to keep in mind that not all frequencies are natural frequencies. For instance, relative frequencies

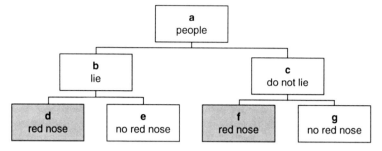

Figure 12.1: Illustration of a natural frequency tree. The total observed frequency *a* is split into *b* (e.g., the number of people who lie) and *c* (the number of people who do not lie). The frequency *b* out of *a* is the base rate (e.g., of lying). The frequency *b* is, in turn, split into *d* (e.g., the number of people with red noses among those who lie) and *e* (the number of people without red noses among those who lie). The frequency *d* out of *b* is the hit rate (or sensitivity). Similarly, the frequency *c* is split into *f* (e.g., the number of people with red noses among those who do not lie) and *g* (the number of people without red noses among those who do not lie). The frequency *f* out of *c* is the false-positive rate. Bayes's rule amounts to $d/(d + f)$; that is, only the two natural frequencies in the bolded boxes need to be attended to. The base rate can be ignored because it is contained in these natural frequencies.

do not lead to computational simplification (Gigerenzer & Hoffrage, 1995: prediction 4 and experiment 2). Some researchers, however, have confused natural frequencies with *any* kind of frequencies. For instance, Johnson-Laird et al. (1981: 81) stated that, "in fact, data in the form of frequencies by no means guarantee good Bayesian reasoning" and referred to a study in which *normalized, but not natural frequencies* were provided. Similarly, Evans et al. (2000) tested normalized frequencies, found no difference from conditional probabilities, concluded that frequencies per se do not explain the facilitation of Bayesian reasoning, and presented this result as evidence against Gigerenzer and Hoffrage's (1995, 1999) thesis. Yet the argument is that representations do part of the computations, not that frequencies per se would, for some unknown reason, facilitate Bayesian computations (see Brase, 2002; Hoffrage et al., 2002).

Multiple Cognitive Strategies

How do children and adults try to solve Bayesian-type tasks, such as the Red Nose problem? Previous research on children's cognitive strategies in different tasks suggests that there is often not a single strategy (such as an adding rule), but rather a toolbox of strategies available (e.g., Siegler, 1999, 2000). Similarly, research on Bayesian tasks has shown that adults use about five different strategies and that the prevalence of these strategies varies with the format of information (Gigerenzer & Hoffrage, 2007). The possible existence of multiple strategies in children has methodological consequences. First, we will analyze strategies of children at the individual level, rather than at the level of aggregates of individuals. Second, given the observation in previous research with adults that individuals sometimes switch strategies from problem to problem rather than consistently use only one strategy, we will also analyze an individual's strategy for each problem rather than aggregate across all problems. In other words, the unit of analysis is an individual-task combination. Finally, the existence of multiple strategies requires testing the data of each individual-task combination against multiple hypotheses (i.e., the candidate strategies) rather than a single null hypothesis.

The frequency distributions of cognitive strategies can change systematically over time. Strategies that are frequent in early age often drop out over time, and new strategies join and may become dominant. For instance, Siegler (1999) described the developmental change in strategies that preschoolers use for addition, such as 3 + 5, and Gigerenzer and Richter (1990) analyzed the developmental change in strategies used to estimate the area of rectangular shapes. The common observation is that strategy development does not proceed from using one strategy at one stage to using a different strategy at a second stage, and so on. Rather, developmental change seems to follow Siegler's (1999) overlapping waves model, in which multiple strategies coexist at each point; what changes is their onset and prevalence. The methodological consequence of this observation is again to analyze strategies at the individual (and task) level and to describe the rise and fall of strategies throughout development in terms of the frequency distribution of each strategy.

Questions

This chapter addresses three questions:

1. Does children's ability to solve Bayesian problems depend on the information presentation? Specifically, do natural frequencies help children to reason the Bayesian way? If so, at what age?
2. What are the cognitive strategies children use to solve Bayesian problems? How do they differ from the strategies adults use?
3. What is the developmental pattern of change in strategies?

We performed two studies with a similar design. Because both studies had the same structure, the results are reported together.

Method

Participants, Age, and Design

In both studies, the children were from ordinary elementary schools in Beijing. The adults were MBA students from the School of Management,

Beijing University of Aeronautics and Astronautics. In study 1, the mean age of the fourth graders was 9;9 (range from 9;4 to 10;3), the mean age of the fifth graders was 10;8 (range from 10;1 to 11;4), and the mean age of the sixth graders was 11;9 (range from 11;3 to 12;6). The mean age of the adults was 29 (range from 25 to 35). The number of participants was 16, 15, 14, 23, and 23, for the fourth, fifth, and sixth graders, and the two adult groups, respectively. In study 1, children were tested with natural frequencies alone, whereas one group of adults was tested on conditional probabilities and the other on natural frequencies.

In study 2, the mean age of the fourth graders was 9;7 (range from 9;2 to 10;1), the mean age of the fifth graders was 10;7 (range from 10;1 to 11;3), and the mean age of the sixth graders was 11;6 (range from 11;2 to 12;2). The mean age of the adults was 20 (range from 19 to 23). The number of participants was 30 in each of the four groups for the natural frequency representation. In addition, we tested children and adults on the probability version, with 10 children in each of the three age groups and a total of 30 adults. We used a smaller number of children for the probability condition because we feared that establishing the probability baseline might frustrate them if the task was too difficult.

Reasoning Problems

We constructed 10 Bayesian problems whose content was suited to children. One of these is the Red Nose problem described above; the others are given in the appendix to this chapter. Study 1 used 7 and study 2 all 10 problems. As the Red Nose problem shows, probabilities were always expressed as percentages.

Procedure

Children were tested in small groups of three to six persons. The adults were tested in larger groups in a classroom. In study 2, children were randomly assigned to either conditional probability or natural frequency representation, and thus the factor representation was varied between participants. The instruction was the same for all age groups: "Please solve the following problems. Each problem includes several numbers and a question. Please write down how you got the answer or mark the numbers you used to get the answer."

Criteria for Identifying Bayesian Responses

When the Bayesian answer is 8 out of 17 (or a probability of 47 percent), should a child's answer "9 out of 17" (or a probability of 53 percent) count as a Bayesian response? To avoid classifying an answer as a Bayesian response although the underlying strategy was in fact not a Bayesian strategy, we used a strict outcome criterion (similar to Gigerenzer & Hoffrage, 1995): An

178 RATIONALITY FOR MORTALS

individual's response had to be numerically identical to the Bayesian solution. By that we mean that children and adults had to report the exact frequency or probability; otherwise it was not coded as a Bayesian response. This was the case, for instance, with the answer "9 out of 17" in the Red Nose problem, although the absolute difference from "8 out of 17" may be considered an insignificantly small deviation in a significance test. The strict criterion diminishes the probability that a mere guess is mistakenly classified as a Bayesian response (see below).

In addition, participants were encouraged to circle the numbers they had used. For instance, one child wrote "21 + 28 = 49, 21/49 = 3/7," circled the "21" and the "28," and answered "3 out of 7" (for problem 5, see appendix). The circled numbers were used as a double check: If the circled numbers were inconsistent with Bayesian reasoning, then the response was not counted as a Bayesian response. We did not find such cases, however; children's numerical answers and the numbers they circled were consistent.

The opposite error, not classifying Bayesian reasoning as a Bayesian response, might occur when a person reasons the Bayesian way but makes an error in the calculation, for instance, when the information is in probabilities that involve substantial calculations. Therefore, if a person showed Bayesian reasoning in terms of process—for instance, when writing down the equation $.10 \times .80/(.10 \times .80 + .90 \times .10)$ for the Red Nose problem—but subsequently made a calculation error or did not calculate the result, we classified this as a Bayesian solution. The reason is that we are investigating people's Bayesian reasoning, not their calculation skills. These cases occurred only with probability formats and only in adults (in 12 out of a total of 230 Bayesian responses).

Results

Can Children Reason the Bayesian Way with Conditional Probabilities?

The results with probability format were straightforward (figure 12.2). Adults were able to solve 47 percent of the problems (and 57 percent in study 1, where children were not tested with a probability format). None of the fourth graders, none of the fifth graders, and none of the sixth graders could solve any of the problems when the information was in probabilities. Their strategies seemed to be random: They picked one of the percentages, or added or subtracted two or three percentages, and sometimes answered that the probability was 160 percent or a similarly impossible value. The children seemed to have no clue how to solve the problems when the information was in terms of probabilities. We take this result as a baseline for the possible effect of natural frequencies.

The inability of children to solve these problems should be evaluated against the fact that these children were not familiar with the mathematical

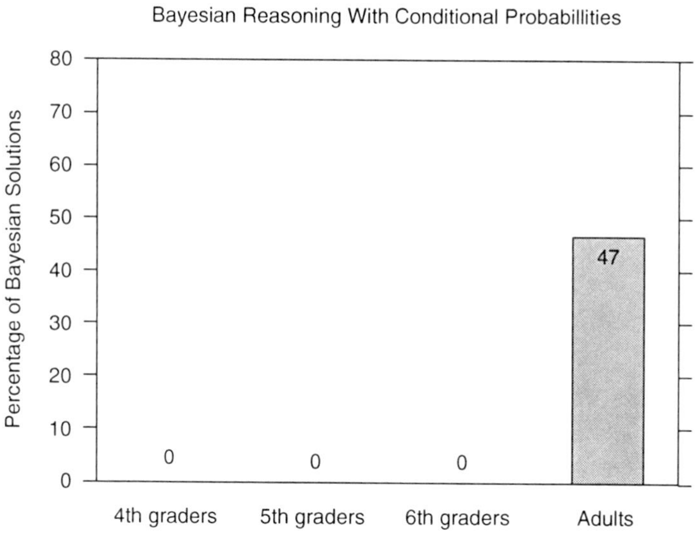

Bayesian Reasoning With Conditional Probabillities

Figure 12.2: Percentage of Bayesian solutions with conditional probabilities. Based on 60 participants (10 in each of the children groups and 30 adults) and 10 problems, there were a total of 600 individual problems. None of the children could solve any of the problems.

concepts of probability and percentage. Percentages were, at the time of the study, not taught in Chinese primary schools before the middle of sixth grade (the sixth graders in this study were tested before they were exposed to percentages). The results in figure 12.2 were consistent with the expectations of the children's teachers, who predicted that the children would not be able to solve these problems, given that they had never been exposed to them. Were the teachers' expectations still true when probabilities were replaced by natural frequencies?

Can Natural Frequencies Improve Bayesian Reasoning in Children?

Fourth graders were able to solve 17 percent and 19 percent of the problems in study 1 and 2, respectively, when the information was in natural frequencies (figure 12.3). For the fifth graders, this number increased to 30 percent and 42 percent. By sixth grade, children solved 70 percent and 48 percent of the problems. Adults reached a performance of 75 percent and 77 percent in study 1 and 2, respectively. Averaged across both studies and weighted by the sample sizes, the results are 19 percent, 39 percent, 54 percent, and 76 percent Bayesian solutions for the fourth, fifth, and six graders and the adults, respectively. When one compares across representations, the sixth graders' performance with natural frequencies matched and surpassed the performance of adults with probabilities (figure 12.2).

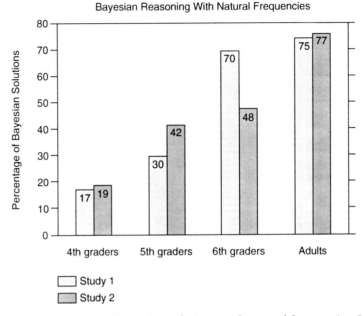

Figure 12.3: Percentage of Bayesian solutions with natural frequencies. In study 1, there were 16, 15, 14, and 23 participants in the four age groups, respectively. In study 2, there were 30 participants in each group. The total number of individual problems (natural frequency representations) was 476 in study 1 and 1,200 in study 2.

Table 12.1 shows that the Bayesian responses were not uniformly distributed across participants, but showed marked individual differences. Among the fourth graders, a large proportion could not solve a single one of the problems. Most others succeeded with one or two of the problems. These could be signs of an occasional flash of Bayesian reasoning in this age group. Most remarkably, in study 2, one child solved all 10 problems and three solved 8 or 9 of the problems. These extraordinary children reasoned systematically better—with natural frequencies—than did a number of the adult MBA students.

The picture for the fifth graders is different. The proportion of Bayesian responses was twice as high (figure 12.3) and the interindividual variability increased (table 12.1). In study 1, 5 out of the 15 children gave the Bayesian response most of the time, whereas 6 children showed no sign of Bayesian reasoning—the same number as among the fourth graders. In study 2, 7 out of 30 children found the Bayesian solution for every problem, whereas 13 could not solve a single problem.

For the sixth graders, there were essentially two groups left. The majority of children now reasoned the Bayesian way for most or all of the problems. At the same time, almost one-third of the sixth graders still showed no sign of Bayesian intuition and could solve none of the problems.

Table 12.1: Distribution of the number of Bayesian responses

Grade	Number of Bayesian responses: Study 1								n	Total
	0	1	2	3	4	5	6	7		
Fourth	6	2	7	1	0	0	0	0	16	19
Fifth	6	2	1	1	2	2	1	0	15	31
Sixth	3	0	0	1	0	0	4	6	14	69
Adults	4	1	0	0	1	0	3	14	23	121

Grade	Number of Bayesian responses: Study 2											n	Total
	0	1	2	3	4	5	6	7	8	9	10		
Fourth	18	5	0	0	0	1	1	1	2	1	1	30	58
Fifth	13	1	0	2	1	0	2	0	2	2	7	30	127
Sixth	11	1	2	0	0	0	0	1	8	2	5	30	144
Adults	5	0	1	0	0	0	2	0	0	4	8	30	230

n = number of participants in each group; Total = number of Bayesian responses in each group. For each participant, the total number of Bayesian responses could vary between 0 and 7 in study 1 (top panel) and between 0 and 10 in study 2 (bottom panel). For instance, in study 1, six children in fourth grade and four adults could not solve any of the problems.

To summarize: At an age where conditional probabilities pose immense difficulties, natural frequencies can foster Bayesian reasoning in children. Sixth graders' performance with natural frequencies matched the performance of adults with probabilities. But the general increase in performance was accompanied by striking individual differences. Whereas more than half of the sixth graders solved most or all problems, most of the others could not solve a single one.

How do children (and adults) who do not reason the Bayesian way attempt to solve the problems? Do they merely guess or do they use systematic, non-Bayesian strategies?

Non-Bayesian Intuitions

In the absence of previous research with children, we started with the three most frequent non-Bayesian strategies in adults as hypotheses (Gigerenzer & Hoffrage, 1995). The *joint occurrence* strategy is related to the positive-testing strategy (Klayman & Ha, 1987), where people only look for the frequency of confirming evidence, such as how often both symptom and disease occur together. For this and other non-Bayesian strategies, we used the same criteria as for identifying Bayesian reasoning. In the Red Nose problem, the joint occurrence strategy predicts that children will use the number of people who have a red nose and lie (here: 8 out of 100). However, the children in our two studies never followed this strategy. Instead, we observed cases consistent with the two other strategies adults use, *conservatism* and *representative thinking,* along with two strategies that had not been reported in earlier studies. The logic of the resulting four strategies is shown in figure 12.4, using the Red Nose problem.

If a child centers on only one aspect of the problem, then this aspect is either the event to be predicted (e.g., people who lie) or the evidence available (e.g., red nose). If the child centers on the event, the following strategy results (*a* and *b* refer to figure 12.1):

$$Conservatism: b/a \qquad (12.3)$$

The underlying intuition is to stick with one's prior beliefs and disregard new evidence. This strategy has been labeled "conservatism" (Edwards, 1968) and "base-rate only" (Gigerenzer & Hoffrage, 1995). It amounts to the opposite of base-rate neglect. In the Red Nose problem, conservatism generates the answer "10 out of 100" rather than "8 out of 17." It typically underestimates the Bayesian probability or frequency. In studies with natural frequencies, a small proportion of adult laypeople (Gigerenzer & Hoffrage, 1995) and physicians making diagnostic inferences (Hoffrage & Gigerenzer, 1998) have been reported to rely on conservatism.

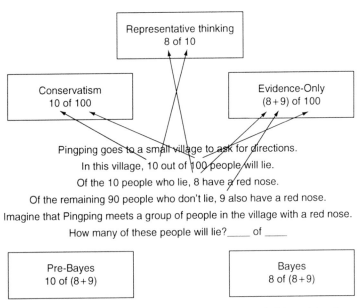

Figure 12.4: Non-Bayesian and Bayesian strategies in children. For three of the strategies, arrows show what information children pay attention to (to avoid illegibility, arrows are omitted for two strategies). The formula underneath the name shows how the numbers are combined. For instance, the strategy called *conservatism* leads to the answer that "10 out of 100 people will lie."

If the child centers only on the evidence, then a different strategy results:

$$Evidence\text{-}Only: (d+f)/a \qquad\qquad (12.4)$$

The intuition underlying this strategy is the opposite of conservatism: People jump at the new evidence and disregard prior beliefs. Evidence-only disregards the base rate of the target event and focuses only on how often the evidence or signal $(d + f)$ occurred among all cases (a). In the Red Nose problem, evidence-only generates the answer "17 out of 100." This strategy was not reported by Gigerenzer and Hoffrage (1995). The third strategy has been observed frequently in adults and uses a different denominator than the two centering strategies:

$$Representative\ thinking: d/b \qquad\qquad (12.5)$$

The intuition underlying this strategy is to see how often the evidence (e.g., red nose) occurs when the event (lying) is there. This strategy has been variously called "representative thinking" (Dawes, 1986), or "Fisherian" (Gigerenzer & Hoffrage, 1995). The reason for the latter is because it corresponds to a widely used method of hypothesis testing, known as significance testing. In Fisher's theory of significance testing, an inference from data D to a null hypothesis H_0 is based solely on $p(D|H_0)$, which is known as the exact level of significance. As figure 6.1 illustrates, the proportion d of b is equivalent to $p(D|H)$. Unlike Bayes's rule, significance testing ignores both base rates and false-positive rates. Representative thinking produces the confusion of the Bayesian posterior probability with the hit rate and has been reported to describe some physicians' and lawyers' intuitions when the information is presented in conditional probabilities (Dawes, 1986; Koehler, 1996b). In the Red Nose problem, this strategy generates the response "8 out of 10" rather than the Bayesian answer "8 out of 17."

Only one strategy had the same denominator as Bayes's rule:

$$Pre\text{-}Bayes: b/(d+f) \qquad\qquad (12.6)$$

To the best of our knowledge, this strategy has not been reported in the literature before. We call it pre-Bayes because it gets the denominator right and the numerator approximates the numerator in Bayes's rule for high hit rates. Children who use this strategy focus on the number b of target events (such as cases of lying) rather than on the number d of cases where a cue (red nose) is present among the target events. In the Red Nose problem, this strategy generates the answer "10 out of 17" instead of the correct answer "8 out of 17." As this example illustrates, picking b instead of d can lead to estimates close to answers based on Bayesian reasoning.

Some children wrote down clearly how they arrived at their answer, and here we also have process information for the non-Bayesian strategies. For instance, for problem 2 (salty cookies), one child wrote "20/100 = 1/5" and

Table 12.2: Distribution of the number of children's responses following each of four strategies in study 1

Grade	Pre-Bayes							Total
	1	2	3	4	5	6	7	
Fourth	4	3	0	0	0	0	0	10
Fifth	2	1	1	0	2	0	1	24
Sixth	6	0	0	0	0	0	0	6
Adults	0	0	0	0	0	0	0	0

Grade	Conservatism							Total
	1	2	3	4	5	6	7	
Fourth	5	5	0	0	0	1	0	21
Fifth	2	0	0	0	1	0	1	14
Sixth	0	0	0	0	0	0	0	0
Adults	1	0	0	0	0	1	0	7

Grade	Evidence-only							Total
	1	2	3	4	5	6	7	
Fourth	2	3	0	0	0	0	0	8
Fifth	0	0	1	1	1	0	0	12
Sixth	0	0	0	0	0	0	0	0
Adults	0	0	0	0	0	0	0	0

Grade	Representative thinking							Total
	1	2	3	4	5	6	7	
Fourth	6	3	0	0	0	0	0	12
Fifth	0	0	0	0	0	0	0	0
Sixth	0	0	0	0	0	0	0	0
Adults	1	0	0	0	0	0	0	1

The sample size is $n=16$, 15, 14, and 23 in fourth, fifth, and sixth graders, and adults, respectively.

then responded "1 out of 5" (conservatism); another child wrote "$14+24=38$, $38:100=38/100$" and then answered "38 out of 100" (evidence-only); and a third child wrote "$14+24=38$, $20:38=20/38=10/19$," and then answered "10 out of 19" (pre-Bayes).

Tables 12.2 and 12.3 show how often children and adults followed each of the four strategies. For instance, in study 1, three fourth graders followed pre-Bayes in two out of seven problems, and one fifth grader did so consistently in all seven problems.

But how can we know whether these response patterns are the product of systematic strategies rather than of mere guessing by picking numbers randomly? Specifically, we need to ask for each candidate strategy whether there were more correct responses in total than would have been expected

Table 12.3: Distribution of the number of children's responses following each of four strategies in study 2

Grade	Pre-Bayes										Total
	1	2	3	4	5	6	7	8	9	10	
Fourth	4	2	0	0	0	1	0	0	0	0	14
Fifth	0	1	0	1	0	0	2	0	0	0	20
Sixth	4	3	1	0	0	1	1	5	0	0	66
Adults	2	0	1	0	0	0	1	0	0	1	22

Grade	Conservatism										Total
	1	2	3	4	5	6	7	8	9	10	
Fourth	4	1	2	1	0	0	0	0	0	0	16
Fifth	1	0	0	0	0	0	0	0	0	0	1
Sixth	1	1	0	0	0	0	0	0	0	1	13
Adults	1	0	0	0	1	0	0	0	0	0	6

Grade	Evidence-only										Total
	1	2	3	4	5	6	7	8	9	10	
Fourth	0	1	0	0	0	0	0	0	0	0	2
Fifth	0	0	0	0	0	0	0	0	0	0	0
Sixth	0	0	1	0	1	1	0	0	0	2	34
Adults	0	0	0	0	0	0	0	0	0	0	0

Grade	Representative thinking										Total
	1	2	3	4	5	6	7	8	9	10	
Fourth	1	0	2	0	0	0	0	0	0	0	7
Fifth	0	0	1	0	0	0	0	0	0	0	3
Sixth	0	0	0	0	0	0	0	0	0	0	0
Adults	0	0	0	0	0	0	0	0	0	0	0

The sample size is $n = 30$ in each group.

if the children had guessed and whether some children followed the strategy systematically. It is not easy to define the set of options from which children could randomly pick. We suggest doing this on the basis of two observations: (i) children consistently picked either two or three, but not more of the total of five numbers specified in each problem (e.g., two for conservatism and representative thinking, three for pre-Bayes and evidence-only), and (ii) when children picked three numbers, they added—rather than subtracted—two of them. This results in 20 ways to pick two out of five numbers and in 60 ways to pick three. These 80 random choices reduce to 40 because of the logical constraint that the second number in the response "____ out of ____" cannot be smaller than the first, a constraint that children consistently followed.[1] For simplicity, we define the chance hypothesis by a uniform distribution; that is, random picking means that each of these 40 patterns has the same probability.

The first question is whether the total number of patterns consistent with each of the four candidate strategies is actually larger than what can be expected by chance. The total number of children's Bayesian responses is 119 (out of 315) in study 1 and 329 (out of 900) in study 2. Thus, we have 196 and 571 unaccounted responses, which total 767. Assuming that these children picked randomly, one expects $767/40 = 19.2$ picks that look like one of the four strategies, whereas the actual numbers were 140, 65, 56, and 22, for pre-Bayes, conservatism, evidence-only, and representative thinking, respectively (tables 12.2 and 12.3). That is, patterns implied by the first three strategies occur much more frequently than expected by the chance model, whereas the same analysis shows no support for representative thinking.

This aggregate analysis, however, does not consider the possibility of systematic individual differences. Are there children who follow one strategy consistently? Consider first pre-Bayes (tables 12.2 and 12.3). For study 1, a binomial test ($p = 1/40$; $n = 7$) shows that the probability of producing three (or more) times the predicted pattern by chance is $p = .0005$. Thus, three or more answers are unlikely to occur by chance. For the two fifth graders who followed the predicted pattern five out of seven times, the corresponding probability is in the order of one in a billion, and that of the fifth grader who always followed the prediction of pre-Bayes is even smaller. For study 2, a binomial test ($p = 1/40$; $n = 10$) indicates that similar systematic patterns of individual differences exist. Eleven children, for instance, followed pre-Bayes four or more times; in each case, the probability of this result under the chance hypothesis is $p = .00007$. The corresponding probability for the five sixth graders whose response pattern is consistent with the pre-Bayes pattern in 8 out of 10 problems is smaller than one in a billion. Thus, we can conclude that there is evidence that the responses consistent with pre-Bayes are not random but systematic. This strategy is most pronounced in grades five and six.

By the same analysis, one can detect a comparatively small number of children who systematically follow conservatism, with two following this strategy in every problem. The same holds for the evidence-only strategy. In contrast, there is again relatively little support for representative thinking in study 1. In study 2, there are three children whose responses are consistent with this strategy three times. The probability of this result under

---

1. One can generate 5×4 ordered pairs from five numbers, and one of each pair (a, b) and (b, a) is eliminated by the logical constraint. This coincides with the number of nonordered pairs (where the order of a and b is irrelevant), which amounts to 10. Similarly, one can generate 10 nonordered triples out of five numbers. Each triple (a, b, c) of numbers picked can result in six judgments, "a out of $b + c$," "b out of $a + c$," "c out of $a + b$," "$a + b$ out of c," "$a + c$ out of b," and "$b + c$ out of a." Since there are 10 triples, this amounts to 60 judgments. The logical constraints reduce these by half.

the random picking hypothesis is $p=.0005$ in every case. Nevertheless, we conclude that this candidate strategy does not have the magnitude of support that the other three strategies have; there is no single child who follows it most or all of the time. The support for representative thinking is therefore open and requires further backing from independent studies.

In summary, when information is represented in terms of natural frequencies, Bayesian reasoning, as well as three non-Bayesian strategies, can be documented in children. One of them, pre-Bayes, is close to Bayesian reasoning. The others can lead to systematic and large deviations because they center on only one aspect of the problem.

Is There a Developmental Change in Strategies?

The main developmental change documented is the fast increase of Bayesian responses from approximately ages 10 to 12 (figure 12.3) when the information is in natural frequencies. A second major change concerned the rate of "guessing" (responses that were neither Bayesian nor one of the non-Bayesian strategies) and of "no answer." Guessing decreased from 50 percent in fourth graders to 41 percent, 12.6 percent, and 16.1 percent in fifth graders, sixth graders, and adults, respectively. The percentage of participants who gave no answer decreased from 9.5 percent in fourth graders to 1.7 percent, 4 percent, and 0 percent, respectively.

Is there also a developmental trajectory in the non-Bayesian strategies? There seems to be a developmental change akin to Siegler's overlapping waves model, with what appear to be four waves:

Wave 1: *Guessing.* In this mental state of confusion, children and adults find neither the Bayesian answer nor a consistent strategy. The responses to the problems are based on arbitrarily picking a few numbers or no answer. The first wave strongly decreases from an initial 50 percent in fourth grader, but never completely disappears and remains present in adult life.

Wave 2: *Centering.* Children center on one of the two aspects of the problem: the event or the evidence. This wave consists of strategies that have not yet found the proper denominator: conservatism and evidence-only. The developmental trajectory of the second wave is less clear than that of the first. The second wave is weaker than the first at all ages and seems to have a slowly decreasing trajectory. It also extends into adult life.

Wave 3: *Pre-Bayes.* The third wave consists of a first approximation of Bayesian reasoning, where children no longer center on one aspect of the problem. They have found the proper denominator but not yet the numerator. The temporal overlap between the second and third wave seems substantial. Pre-Bayes peaks in the older children and can be seen as a forerunner of Bayesian reasoning.

Wave 4: *Bayesian reasoning.* The fourth and last wave is Bayesian reasoning. Here, the pattern is again very clear. Bayesian reasoning increases monotonically with age and reaches its mode in adults.

We would like to emphasize that this sequence of waves should be seen as a hypothesis, for the data on which it is based is limited. Data on both younger and older children are required for further test.

Conclusion

This chapter provides an ecological perspective on the development of reasoning: The external representation does part of the internal computation. The major result is that children can systematically reason the Bayesian way if the information is provided in natural frequencies rather than in conditional probabilities. This does not exclude the possibility that other representations also foster insight, specifically if they mimic the structure of natural frequencies and lead to the same computational facilitation (e.g., Gigerenzer & Hoffrage, 2007; Girotto & Gonzales, 2001). More generally, any numerical information can be represented in various forms, as Roman and Arabic numbers illustrate, but these are not neutral forms for the same content because they actually facilitate certain computations and insights and hinder others (Martignon et al., 2003). As the physicist Richard Feynman (1967: 53) remarked, different representations of the same mathematical formula can evoke varied mental pictures and lead to new solutions.

Aside from doing part of the computation, representations influence thinking in another way. Representations can constrain the possible set of mental strategies and thereby the resulting judgments. For instance, with Bayesian problems in the form of conditional probabilities, base rates need to be attended to, such as the base rate b/a of liars in figure 12.1. With natural frequencies, in contrast, base rates need not be attended to; the ratio b/a can be ignored. The reason is that base-rate information is contained in natural frequencies, whereas conditional probabilities (and relative frequencies) are normalized with respect to the base rates. Thus, when moving from natural frequencies to other representations, one needs to learn to pay attention to base rates.

Natural frequency representations can provide explanations for other phenomena besides Bayesian reasoning. Consider an error commonly made by children (Carpenter et al., 1978). When asked to find the sum of one-half and one-third, the answer is often two-fifth. This is called the freshman error of adding numerators and adding denominators (Silver, 1986). Natural frequency representations can offer an account for this error. If one assumes that natural frequencies, such as "1 out of 2" and "1 out of 3," are developmentally primary and that relative frequencies (or fractions), such as one-half and one-third, are only understood later in development, the error can be deduced. The reason is that one can add "numerators" and "denominators" of natural frequencies. For instance, in the Red Nose problem, "8 out of 10" people who lie have a red nose, and "9 out of 90" people who do not lie also have a red nose. You can add these to total "17 out of 100" people who have a red nose. This operation is correct in an environment with natural frequencies. In contrast, a relative frequency 8/10 is the same as 4/5, and adding the numerators and denominators of 4/5 and 9/90 will result in an error. Our explanation for the freshman error is that children or adults apply the principles of natural frequencies to fractions or relative frequencies.

Natural frequencies facilitate Bayesian reasoning because they work by simple enumeration without normalization (compare equations 12.1 and 12.2). The power of enumeration extends beyond the problems studied in this chapter. Infants are sensitive to changes in the numerosity of a collection of visual objects (Antell & Keating, 1983; Starkey & Cooper, 1980); at six months, they seem to form arithmetical expectations when an object is added or taken away from a small collection (Wynn, 1992). Fractions are hard to understand, whereas collections seem to be easy (Brase, Cosmides, & Tooby, 1998), as illustrated by the almost universal use of fingers as a representational system (Butterworth, 1999), and brain imaging studies suggest that key number areas are closely connected to the finger circuit (Dehaene et al., 1999). Krauss and Wang (2003) studied the notorious Monty Hall problem, which most adults fail to solve, and showed that correct answers can be facilitated by changing the single-event question ("should I switch or not switch doors") into a frequency question ("in how many cases will switching win?"), and Krauss and Atmaca (2004) showed similar facilitation for children and adolescents aged 11 to 19.

Can the present results be generalized to children in other cultures with other educational backgrounds? In a replicate study with German children, Lücking (2004) investigated fifth, sixth, and seventh graders. She chose children who were one year older because, just like the Chinese teachers, the German teachers and experts she consulted did not believe that children could solve these problems—whatever the external representation might be. Furthermore, given the higher mathematical performance and motivation of Chinese children compared to German children (Stern et al., 2001), Lücking expected that German children would not be able to solve the problems as early as Chinese children. However, the performance of the German fifth and sixth graders was indistinguishable from that of the Chinese. Lücking also tested the conjecture by Girotto and Gonzalez (2001) that "single-step questions" (as used in the present study) would result in substantially lower numbers of correct solutions than "two-step questions" (where first the value of the denominator in equation 12.2 and then that of the numerator is asked) but found no evidence. Nor did additional questions that amplified the set relations between frequencies increase performance.

In this chapter, we asked: Can fourth, fifth, and sixth graders solve Bayesian problems when the information is in conditional probabilities? The answer is no. Can Bayesian reasoning be elicited when the representation is switched to natural frequencies? The answer is yes. By sixth grade, the effect of representation was as strong as or stronger than the average effect on university students, 16 percent versus 46 percent (15 problems: Gigerenzer & Hoffrage, 1995); on physicians, 10 percent versus 46 percent (four problems:

Hoffrage & Gigerenzer, 1998); and on members of the National Academy of Neuropsychology, 9 percent versus 63 percent (one problem: Labarge, McCaffrey, & Brown, 2003). But this general increase was accompanied by systematic individual differences. More than half of the sixth graders solved most or all problems, whereas one-third could not solve a single one. An analysis of the children's responses provides evidence for the use of three non-Bayesian strategies. These follow an overlapping wave model of development and continue to be observed in the minds of adults. More so than adults' probabilistic reasoning, children's reasoning depends on a proper representation of information.

Let us return at the end to the beginning, to the Enlightenment's vision that human intuition and the laws of probability are just two sides of the same coin and to the contrasting view of much of recent cognitive psychology. What does children's performance tell us about this apparent paradox? It offers a way to resolve the contradiction. The solution may lie in the representation, that is, in the way one presents information to children and adults. When one chooses a representation that comes natural to the human mind and reduces computation, the Enlightenment's view is not too far removed from the evidence. Confronted with conditional probabilities, in contrast, children are helpless, as are many adults. These results have implications for teaching statistical reasoning (Sedlmeier, 1999). Learning to play with representations should be part of mathematics education. Solving a problem involves finding a proper representation.

Appendix: Reasoning Problems

The first 7 problems were used in study 1; all 10 problems were used in study 2. Problem 1 (Red Nose) is given in the text, both in natural frequencies and in probabilities. Problems 2 through 10 are given below in terms of natural frequencies. The probability version can be deduced from it and is therefore omitted here.

2. There is a large package of sweet or salty cookies with various kinds of shapes. In the package, 20 out of every 100 cookies are salty. Of the 20 salty cookies, 14 are round. Of the remaining 80 sweet cookies, 24 are also round. Imagine you take out a pile of round cookies. How many of them are salty cookies? _____ out of _____

3. The principal of a school announced and explained a new school rule to all the students gathering together on the playground. Then the principal said: "Those who understand what I mean, please put up your hands": 70 out of every 100 students understood. Of these 70 who understood, 63 put up their hands. Of the remaining 30 who didn't understand, 9 put up their hands. Imagine a group of students who put up their hands. How many of them understood the principal? _____ out of _____

4. 20 out of every 100 children in a school have bad teeth. Of these 20 children who have bad teeth, 10 love to eat sweet food. Of the remaining 80 children who don't have bad teeth, 24 also like to eat sweet food. Here is a group of children from this school who love to eat sweet food. How many of them may have bad teeth? _____ out of _____

5. To protect their children's eyes, mothers always urge children not to watch too much TV. Suppose you want to test this belief and get the following information: 30 out of every 100 children become near-sighted. Of these 30 near-sighted children, 21 of them watch too much TV. Of those 70 children with normal sight, 28 of them watch too much TV. Suppose you meet a group of children who watch too much TV. How many of them may become near-sighted? _____ out of _____

6. In Dongdong's town, 10 out of every 100 children are overweight. Of the 10 overweight children, 3 of them have overweight mothers. Of the remaining 90 children who have normal weight, 18 of them still have overweight mothers. Suppose you meet a group of overweight mothers in the town. How many of them have overweight children? _____ out of _____

7. A group of children are playing games with cards. Those who get a card with a picture of a cat on the inner side win a piece of candy. Out of every 100 cards, 30 have a cat picture on one side. Of the 30 cards with a cat picture, 12 of them are red on the other side. Of the remaining 70 cards that have no cat pictures, 35 of them are still red on the other side. Imagine Dingding takes out a group of red cards. How many of them have a cat picture on the other side? _____ out of _____

8. In a cold winter in a town, 40 out of every 100 people hurt their hands by the cold. Of the 40 people who hurt their hands, 36 wear gloves in the open air. Of the remaining 60 people with normal hands, 30 also wear gloves. Suppose you meet a group of people who wear gloves in the town. How many of them hurt their hands? _____ out of _____

9. In a hospital, 60 out of every 100 patients get a cold. Of the 60 patients who get a cold, 42 have a headache. Of the remaining 40 patients with other diseases, 12 also have a headache. Suppose you meet a group of patients who have a headache in a hospital. How many of them get a cold? _____ out of _____

10. On a campus, 90 out of every 100 young people you meet are college students of this university. Of the 90 college students, 45 wear glasses. Of the remaining 10 young people that are not students of the university, 3 also wear glasses. Suppose you meet a group of young people who wear glasses on the campus. How many of them are students at this university? _____ out of _____

Chapter 13

In the Year 2054

Innumeracy Defeated

It is the year 2054. The Great Hall at the Sorbonne is packed with flowers and guests to celebrate the final victory over an intellectual disability that has plagued humankind for centuries: statistical innumeracy, the inability to think with numbers that represent risks and uncertainties. The celebration coincides with a triple anniversary: the 400th anniversary of the mathematical theory of probability, the 200th of George Boole's *The Laws of Thought,* and the 100th of the publication of Leonard Savage's *Foundations of Statistics.* The meeting is presided jointly by the president of the European Union and the president of the World Health Organization. On a curved podium, four of the most distinguished scholars in the social statistical sciences have taken their seats. The topic of this afternoon's panel discussion is "Statistical Innumeracy Is History." It is chaired by Professor Emile Ecu, an economist at the Sorbonne.

CHAIR: Madame le President, Monsieur le President, dear panel, guests, and audience. We have exactly 30 minutes to reconstruct what is arguably the greatest success of the social sciences in the twenty-first century, the defeat of innumeracy. The twentieth century had eradicated illiteracy, that is, the inability to read and write, at least in France. The challenge to our century was innumeracy. Its costs have been a tremendous financial burden to modern economies, as had been those of illiteracy before. This year, the war against innumeracy has been declared won by the World Health Organization in our panelists' home countries. Let me ask our distinguished panel how this victory came about?

POLITICAL SCIENTIST (BERLIN):   It all began with a programmatic statement by the first female chancellor of Germany, Angela Merkel, a physicist by training. In 2007, she said that statistical thinking would be indispensable in a world that grows more and more complex and that it should already

This chapter is a revised version of G. Gigerenzer, "In the Year 2054: Innumeracy Defeated," in *Frequency Processing and Cognition,* ed. P. Sedlmeier and T. Betsch (Oxford: Oxford University Press, 2002), 55–66.

be taught in kindergartens and primary schools. That set the stage for a new curriculum on risk and uncertainty beginning in first grade, which created a new generation of educated citizens who could finally understand the risks in a modern technological world.

STATISTICIAN (BEIJING):   The first was Mao, not Merkel—in the 1940s he wrote that his comrades should have a head for figures and know the basic statistics. The process was somewhat delayed by the cultural revolution, but...

PSYCHOLOGIST (STANFORD):   No, it all began with the father of modern science fiction, Herbert George Wells, best known, perhaps, as the author of *The Time Machine*. In the early twentieth century, Wells predicted that "statistical thinking will one day be as necessary for efficient citizenship as the ability to read and write." His message inspired the influential work that led to the eradication of innumeracy. Here, we have a wonderful case in which literature eventually incited a revolution.

STATISTICIAN: Wells didn't incite a revolution, whereas Mao did. What you quoted was the epigraph in a twentieth-century bestseller, *How to Lie with Statistics,* and was probably a fake. Making up quotations was consistent with the title of the book. Always check your sources!

CHAIR: Are you saying that the crusade against innumeracy was started by a fake?

STATISTICIAN: No, this is not...

HISTORIAN OF SCIENCE (PARIS):   It wasn't modern literature that initiated the crusade against innumeracy. It all started exactly 400 years ago with one of the greatest of all intellectual revolutions, the probabilistic revolution. At this time a notion of rationality was developed that eventually replaced the old ideal of certainty with a new, modest conception of rational belief that acknowledged uncertainty. Between July and October of 1654, the French mathematicians Blaise Pascal and Pierre Fermat solved problems of gambling and developed the calculus of probability. This revolution was not just an intellectual one, it was also a moral one, the...

CHAIR: What's moral about gambling?

HISTORIAN OF SCIENCE: Not gambling, probability. Take Pascal's wager. Before then, people believed in God because they were absolutely certain that He existed. For Pascal, God existed only as a probability, and the decision to believe or not to believe in Him should be the outcome of a rational calculation of possible costs and benefits—not of blind faith or stubborn atheism.

CHAIR: I always had a hunch that God was an economist. She must have loved this Pascal. I believe it was he who said, "The heart has its reasons of which reason knows nothing."

PSYCHOLOGIST: Let's get back down to earth. Whatever the moral implications of the calculus of probability, it was soon discovered that ordinary minds didn't understand probabilities, most of the time. This phenomenon was called statistical innumeracy.

HISTORIAN OF SCIENCE: No, no, no. On the contrary, Pierre Laplace and, even earlier, the Enlightenment mathematicians believed that probability theory was just common sense reduced to a calculus and that educated persons—*les hommes éclairé*—have this common sense. And so thought the British mathematician George Boole in 1854, when he set out to derive the laws of probability and logic from the psychological laws of thought. It was known that people were occasionally confused by probabilities; Laplace himself described the "gambler's fallacy" and other errors. But these mistakes were thought to result from emotion and wishful thinking intervening with rational processes. The two major rules of probability were firmly believed to be descriptions of actual human reasoning: the law of large numbers by Jacob Bernoulli and the rule of inverse probabilities by Thomas Bayes. Statistical innumeracy came rather late...

CHAIR: I wonder about that strange sequence of numbers: 1654, 1854, 1954 with Savage's book, and again 2054. Yet one date is missing. Did anything of great importance for statistics happen in 1754?

HISTORIAN OF SCIENCE: Hmm...Bayes did not publish his treatise but had thought about it for years. He died in 1761, so it could well be that he discovered his famous theorem in 1754.

STATISTICIAN: Numerology gone rampant.

PSYCHOLOGIST: Can we move on? The mathematician John Allen Paulos coined the term *innumeracy* in his 1988 bestseller of the same name. The book begins with the story of a TV weathercaster who announced that there was a 50 percent chance of rain for Saturday and a 50 percent chance for Sunday and then concluded that there was a 100 percent chance of rain that weekend.

HISTORIAN OF SCIENCE: Paulos did not coin the term; he just forgot to cite earlier work. Douglas Hofstadter, author of the cult book *Gödel, Escher, Bach*, which wove music, logic, biology, and *Alice in Wonderland* into a song of praise for cognitive science, had already written about *number numbness* in 1982. For him, innumeracy was the inability to deal with large numbers, a matter of life and death in a modern technological society.

PSYCHOLOGIST: In any case, around 1970, psychologists such as Daniel Kahneman and Amos Tversky began to design experiments to demonstrate that people cannot reason well with probabilities. They did not talk about innumeracy but instead about "cognitive illusions." But it's the same thing: the base-rate fallacy, the conjunction fallacy, the...

HISTORIAN OF SCIENCE: The conjunction fallacy had actually been described by Bärbel Inhelder and Jean Piaget in their 1958 book on the early growth of logic in the child; they had just used a different term, namely "set inclusion" rather than "conjunction." It's the same phenomenon. The base-rate fallacy was discovered two years later by the French mathematician Henry Rouanet...

CHAIR: I thought that historians had already given up priority questions in the last century. What's the point of priority if there is no patent, copyright, or other source of income at stake?

PSYCHOLOGIST: OK, in the 1970s, ample evidence for a state of mind eventually labeled innumeracy had been created.

CHAIR: Why was innumeracy diagnosed so late, around 1970? Why was it not noticed before that time? I have heard that our statistician and our political scientist have different answers to this question.

POLITICAL SCIENTIST: May I go first? In the 1960s, the Western world was confronted with a flood of seemingly irrational behavior, from the assassinations of John F. Kennedy and Martin Luther King Jr. in the United States to the violent student revolutions of 1968 in countries all over the world. These events shattered the ideal of reasonable discourse and brought human irrationality to the foreground. It inspired psychologists to look for irrationality everywhere. Something similar had happened after the French Revolution, the bloody aftermath of which destroyed the idea that common sense would follow the calculus of reason and that probability theory would describe human thinking...

CHAIR: Yes, I agree, degrees of belief are too disorderly to be a proper subject matter for the theory of probability, as opposed to orderly frequencies of stable sociological phenomena, like murder, prostitution...

POLITICAL SCIENTIST: Fine, but my thesis is that the constant degree of innumeracy that had always existed was amplified by the political events of the 1960s, as it had been before by those of the French Revolution. Psychologists of the 1970s just took advantage of the political climate and presented the results everyone wanted to hear. They claimed that human disasters of any kind, including racial prejudice and "hot" social behavior, could be explained by "cold" cognitive illusions. Consistent with my hypothesis, errors in statistical reasoning were no big deal in psychology before the political events of the 1960s. The topics of psychology are a reflection of the political climate in which psychologists happen to work. This is why political science explains psychology.

(Giggling in the audience)

STATISTICIAN: I think that looking for political causes of innumeracy, or even the awareness of it, is a bit too far-fetched. Neither the assassinations in the United States nor the political turmoil of the cultural revolution in China, if I may add another event of the 1960s, produced innumeracy. It did not come from outside influences; it came from within the decision community itself. Listen carefully: whether you like it or not, innumeracy was, to some degree, created by decision theorists like Leonard Savage...

(Unrest in the audience)

STATISTICIAN: ...with their ultra-liberal, one might even say, expansionist policy of extending the laws of probability to everything between heaven and earth. These neo-Bayesians were not satisfied that probabilities mean observable frequencies; no, they claimed that one can and should attach a probability to everything. This expansionist move created massive confusion in ordinary minds. Please recall what kind of statements confused people. These were statements involving probabilities for everything imaginable, specifically single-event probabilities! Savage popularized single-event probabilities, and Ward Edwards and others brought the message to the social sciences. For our historian of science, I add that Savage built on von Neumann and Morgenstern's work in the 1940s, so you don't have to lecture us on that.

(Unrest in the audience finds relief in laughter)

STATISTICIAN: Since about 1830, probability has been interpreted as a relative frequency in a reference class, or as a physical propensity, and this gave the laws of probability a well-defined, although modest, realm of application. Unlike many of his followers, Savage was aware of the oddity of his proposal.

CHAIR: You mean extending the laws of probability to messy mental products, such as degrees of belief?

STATISTICIAN: Exactly. In his 1954 book, Savage began his chapter on personal probability by saying he considered it more probable that a Republican president would be elected in 1996 than that it would snow in Chicago sometime in the month of May 1994. He then added that many people, after careful consideration, are convinced that such subjective probabilities mean precisely nothing or, at best, nothing precisely.

CHAIR: Right!

PSYCHOLOGIST: We actually had a Democratic, not a Republican president in 1996, and there was no snow in Chicago in May 1994. So Savage was wrong…

POLITICAL SCIENTIST: No, he wasn't. A probability statement about a single event can never be wrong, except when the probabilities are 0 or 1.

HISTORIAN OF SCIENCE: Look, our statistician's thesis is that the extension of the laws of probability to degrees of belief, including beliefs about singular events, confused people and provided fertile ground for demonstrating reasoning fallacies. In other words, without this extension, there would not have been that magnitude of innumeracy. What she means is that most reasoning fallacies were demonstrated with probabilities of single events rather than with frequencies.

POLITICAL SCIENTIST: Don't be blind to the political dimension! How was it that before 1968 almost all psychologists agreed that man is a good intuitive statistician—pardon the sexist language of the times—and only a few years later, from the 1970s on, the same people embraced the opposite message? That change was not supported by fact but grew out of a new political climate in which irrationality got the applause, and if one looked long enough…

CHAIR: Here is the disagreement: Our political scientist argues that the interest in statistical innumeracy was born out of the political events of the 1960s. In contrast, our statistician conjectures that innumeracy had been partly created by Savage's extension of the laws of probability beyond frequencies, specifically to singular events. Ordinary people, she assumes, are frequentists deep in their hearts.

HISTORIAN OF SCIENCE: Neither of these two interpretations—political turmoil or overextension of the meaning of mathematical probability—was ever discussed in the 1970s. The explanation usually presented was that people simply suffer from cognitive illusions in the same way that they suffer from visual illusions. Our statistician's hypothesis should not be misread in the sense that innumeracy was not real; that would be a misunderstanding. Newspapers, weather reports, and medical textbooks began to use single-event probabilities, and citizens and students alike were confused, often without even noticing it. That was all real. Eventually, there were even court trials over the meaning of a single-event probability. In one case, the prosecution had offered a defendant a plea bargain, but his lawyer told him that he had a 95 percent chance of acquittal based on an insanity plea. Therefore, the defendant rejected the plea bargain, stood trial, and was sentenced to 20 years in prison for first-degree murder. So he sued his attorney for having given him an unrealistic probability. Courts had to deal with the question, 'Can a single-event probability be wrong?' If it cannot, then what does it mean?

STATISTICIAN: The same confusion emerged in everyday life when institutions started to communicate all kinds of uncertainties in probabilities. In 1965, the U.S. National Weather Service began to express forecasts in single-event probabilities...

HISTORIAN OF SCIENCE: That quantophrenia never occurred in France!

STATISTICIAN: ...such as that there is a 30 percent chance of rain tomorrow. Most thought they knew what was meant. However, some understood that it would rain in 30 percent of the area, others that it would rain 30 percent of the time, and others that it would rain on 30 percent of the days where the prediction was made. A single-event probability leaves, by definition, the reference class open: area, hours, days, or something else. But people, then and now, think in terms of concrete cases and fill in a class.

PSYCHOLOGIST: In one legal study, a group of probation officers was asked "What is the probability that Mr. Smith will commit a violent act if he is discharged?" whereas another was asked, "Think of 100 men like Mr. Smith. How many of them will commit a violent act if they are discharged?" When the average estimate of the probability of harm was .30, the frequency estimate was only 20 of 100.

CHAIR: Why is that?

PSYCHOLOGIST: For the same reason as with probabilities of rain. Asking for a single-event probability leaves the reference class open. The probation officers themselves needed to fill in one: Does the probability refer to the situation that Mr. Smith is on weekend release 100 times, or that 100 people like Mr. Smith are on weekend release once, or something else? These are different questions.

STATISTICIAN: The important step toward a cure for innumeracy was the insight that the problem may not simply reside inside the mind, as suggested by the cognitive illusions view, but in the external representation of the information. You can't do much about a miswired brain, but you can rewire the information presentation. Single-event probabilities tend to confuse; frequency statements can turn confusion into insight. Yet single-event probabilities were not the only culprits. It soon became clear that there was an entire gang of confusing representations, such as conditional probabilities and relative risks.

HISTORIAN OF SCIENCE: I agree that uncovering the effect of external representations on statistical thinking started the ball rolling against innumeracy. Once it was realized that the problem was not just a lack of training in the laws of statistics, innumeracy could be tackled much more efficiently and easily. And it turned out that the representations that clouded people's minds were the ones generally used in teaching, medicine, the media, courts of law...

PSYCHOLOGIST: But finding representations of risk that the mind could easily digest was initially met with little enthusiasm. In 1982, two American scholars, Christensen-Szalanski and Beach, had introduced natural sampling, which resulted in natural frequencies and fostered insight in Bayesian problems. Coming under attack by those who did not want to see cognitive illusions disappear, they did not develop the idea further. This was the time when psychological articles that reported irrationality were cited much more often than those that reported rational behavior.

Not until the 1990s did the importance and usefulness of natural frequencies become accepted, after being pushed by German psychologists who resisted the game of irrationality.

HISTORIAN OF SCIENCE: The move away from internal explanations—cognitive illusions—to external ones that create insight turned the question of innumeracy into an ecological, perhaps even an evolutionary, one.

CHAIR: Bayes and evolution?

PSYCHOLOGIST: The argument was that animals and humans have spent most of their evolution in an environment of natural sampling—before the development of probability theory or statistical surveys. Natural frequencies are the result of natural sampling. For instance, take a physician in an illiterate society who is confronted with a new disease. The physician has observed 20 cases of a symptom with the disease and 40 cases of the symptom without the disease. When a new case with the symptom comes in, she can easily compute the Bayesian posterior probability of this patient having the disease: 20/(20 + 40), which is one-third. That's how Bayesian inference was done before mathematical probabilities were introduced in 1654.

CHAIR: Oh, now I understand the paradox that animals were reported to be good Bayesians but humans were not. It's the representation, not the species. Animals encode natural frequencies, and we poor humans were given conditional probabilities...

PSYCHOLOGIST: Right. And modern doctors can learn to understand probabilities in the same way as those in a society without books and surveys.

CHAIR: Was this the point where the World Health Organization took over and finally began to systematically educate physicians on understanding risks?

HISTORIAN OF SCIENCE: No, this psychological research first had its impact in the British and North American courts, possibly because of their adversarial procedure. Defense attorneys realized that typically the prosecution alone benefited from probability-based confusions. For many decades, experts had testified in the form of single-event probabilities—for instance, "The probability that this DNA match occurred by chance is 1 in 100,000." Jurors were made to think that the defendant belonged behind bars. But when experts testified in frequencies instead, the case against the defendant appeared much weaker: "Out of every 100,000 people, 1 will show a match." Mathematically, that's the same, but, psychologically, it made jurors think about how many suspects there might be. In a city with 1 million adults, there should be 10 who match.

CHAIR: I see. But what took defense teams so long to realize this?

HISTORIAN OF SCIENCE: Even before 2000, there were a few attempts to introduce transparent risk communication into court proceedings. Based on the laboratory research on natural frequencies, the O. J. Simpson defense team asked Judge Ito to bar the prosecution's DNA expert, Professor Bruce Weir, from testifying in terms of conditional probabilities and likelihood ratios, which are ratios of conditional probabilities. The defense requested frequencies instead. Judge Ito and the prosecution agreed, but the prosecution expert used likelihood ratios anyway! That was in the "good" old days when statistical experts didn't care about the psychology of jurors and judges.

POLITICAL SCIENTIST: That's when the International Feminist Association entered the stage...

STATISTICIAN: Because Simpson had beaten his wife?

POLITICAL SCIENTIST: Ha, ha, very funny. No, it happened in 2020. The Feminist Association had a larger goal...

HISTORIAN OF SCIENCE: Sorry to contradict, but the Transparency International Testimony Act was a few years earlier. After some local rulings by judges in England and the U.S. disallowing statements involving conditional probabilities or single-event probabilities in testimony, the International Federation of Law ruled that court testimony had to be communicated in terms of natural frequencies rather than probabilities or likelihood ratios. That was in 2016, three decades after DNA fingerprinting was introduced into U.S. criminal investigations. Probability statements about singular events and other confusing representations were no longer admissible; transparent representations were required. The act helped to bring insight into the court proceedings and eliminate confusion.

PSYCHOLOGIST: I am not a legal scholar, but isn't there typically more evidence than just a DNA match?

HISTORIAN OF SCIENCE: Yes, there is, but jurors and judges need to understand DNA evidence independent of additional evidence, such as eyewitness accounts. And since we have had complete DNA databases in all European and North American countries for the last twenty years, police officers tend to sit in front of their computers and search in databases rather than go out and search at the scene of a crime.

POLITICAL SCIENTIST: I am not persuaded that this law started the war against innumeracy. It is correct that for years, the International Feminist Association had not noticed the harm done to women through misleading representations of risk. But that eventually changed. In the mid-1990s, the U.K. media reported a study showing that women who take oral contraceptives increase their risk of thromboembolism by 100 percent. Frightened British women stopped taking the pill, which led to unwanted pregnancies and some 10,000 abortions above the normal. These poor women had never been learned to ask, 100 percent of what? The study had found that out of every 14,000 women not taking the pill, one suffered a thromboembolism, and among the same number taking the pill, there were two. The risk increased from one to two. If the headline had presented the absolute risk increase of 1 in 14,000 rather than the relative risk increase of 100 percent, it would have provoked yawns at the most. Years later, when new pill scares hit the headlines, women were as unprepared as before. Eventually, the Feminist Association realized that there was a massive societal problem and, piece by piece, uncovered the general pattern with which women were misled. For instance, women were told that mammography screening reduced breast cancer mortality by 25 percent. Many women mistakenly concluded that, out of 1,000 women, 250 were saved from breast cancer. In fact, it's only 1 out of 1,000.

CHAIR: How can 25 percent be the same as 0.1 percent?

PSYCHOLOGIST: For the same reason as in the pill scare...

POLITICAL SCIENTIST: The Feminist Association was also concerned that the potential harm of screening was poorly communicated to women, including the possibility of unnecessary operations after false positive testing and breast cancers induced by the X rays. Many brochures explained benefits in terms of relative risk reduction, that is, big numbers, and potential harms in terms of absolute risks, that is, small numbers. The International Feminist Association finally sued medical associations and industries around the world for deliberately producing the wrong impression that screening would be highly beneficial and without any significant harms, thus misleading women in a way that violated their right to complete and transparent information. Misleading representations of risk made informed consent impossible.

HISTORIAN OF SCIENCE: That was a smart move on the part of the Feminist Association. The national health associations and industries were sentenced to pay 7 billion euros in damages. That forced the World Health Organization into action.

POLITICAL SCIENTIST: The big surprise was yet to come. The public was prepared to believe that such representations as conditional probabilities and relative risks make patients innumerate, but it turned out that physicians were affected as well. With that, informed consent definitely became a fantasy.

STATISTICIAN: But much time passed before the WHO finally took action. There was a battle over whether the WHO should admit to or even treat innumeracy in physicians. Those in favor had all the evidence on their side: In study after study, 80 to 90 percent of physicians did not understand how to estimate the probability of a disease being present after a positive screening test. Those in favor also had the therapeutic tools to counteract innumeracy. Their opponents feared that conceding that most physicians do not understand medical evidence would undermine authority and public trust. Eventually, innumeracy was declared a general mental aberration like the attention deficit syndrome and entered into the DSM-VIII; thus it did not look like a doctor's disorder alone, which in fact it wasn't.

HISTORIAN OF SCIENCE: I also believe that the WHO turned the tables, not with the DSM-VIII, but by changing the medical curricula in universities. The decisive step was taken with its Anti-Mental-Pollution Act, which made transparency the rule in communicating risks, eliminating forms of communication that had 'polluted' minds. Medical students learned how to express risks as absolute risks rather than relative risk reductions and in natural frequencies rather than conditional probabilities; they learned how to specify reference classes; and so on. At the same time, school curricula focused on training statistical thinking beginning in primary school, and students learned how to play with representations. My own kids loved being able to confuse their parents with percentages; this was much more fun than algebra and geometry.

CHAIR: Don't overlook the economic consequences. The Anti-Mental-Pollution Act and the fact that the WHO added innumeracy to their catalogue made millions of dollars available for research and implementation programs. My estimate is that about $10 billion alone were poured into education in professional schools and high schools.

HISTORIAN OF SCIENCE: But how can we be sure that a country is innumeracy-free now?

STATISTICIAN: The most recent Program for International Student Assessment (PISA) study focused exclusively on statistical thinking and defined innumeracy operationally in terms of performance on a test. The test items measured the ability to use representations to which the human mind is adapted, such as figures and natural frequencies. They also measured understanding uncertainties in the real world rather than using hypothetical situations. The study enabled each country's performance to be measured by the same standard; when 95 percent of 15-year-olds passed the test, the country was declared free of innumeracy.

POLITICAL SCIENTIST: What's with the rest of the population? The older people, those with chronic math anxiety, those who read poetry while others discuss baseball statistics?

STATISTICIAN: In my country, we reached the PISA performance level for the first time this year. The professional schools in law, medicine, and business already reached that level a decade ago.

POLITICAL SCIENTIST: But still, what's with the older fellows like you and me?

CHAIR: Time is up. And I still don't understand how 25 percent can be the same as 0.1 percent.

Note by Professor Emile Ecu (Chair): I have been informed that psychology is a discipline with a short-term memory. That is, work older than 20 years is no longer read and out of collective memory. This most unfortunate state of affairs does not exist in economics, sociology, or in the history of science. Thus, I have added some references for psychologists.

To begin with, the events 400 years ago that led to the mathematical theory of probability and to the rise and fall of the classical interpretation of probability have been analyzed by Lorraine Daston, *Classical Probability in the Enlightenment* (1988), and Ian Hacking, *The Emergence of Probability* (1975). Two hundred years ago, George Boole's *An Investigation of the Laws of Thought on Which Are Founded the Mathematical Theories of Logic and Probabilities* (1854/1958) was published, a seminal work in which the laws of logic and probability are derived from the laws of thought. One hundred years ago, Leonard J. Savage published *The Foundations of Statistics* (1954), a seminal book that promoted a subjective view of probability and the revival of personal probabilities during the second half of the twentieth century.

BIBLIOGRAPHY

Acree, M. C. (1978). *Theories of statistical inference in psychological research: A historicocritical study* (University Microfilms No. H790 H7000). Ann Arbor, MI: University Microfilms International.

Akaike, H. (1973). Information theory and an extension of the maximum likelihood principle. In B. N. Petrov & F. Csáki (eds.), *2nd International Symposium on Information Theory, Tsahkadsor, Armenia, USSR, September 2–8, 1971* (pp. 267–281). Budapest: Akadémiai Kiadó.

Ambady, N., & Rosenthal, R. (1993). Half a minute: Predicting teacher evaluations from thin slices of nonverbal behavior and physical attractiveness. *Journal of Personality and Social Psychology, 64,* 431–441.

American Psychological Association (APA). (1974). *Publication Manual of the American Psychological Association* (2nd ed.; 3rd ed., 1983; 4th ed., 1994; 5th ed., 2001). Baltimore: Garamond/Pridemark.

Anastasi, A. (1958). *Differential psychology* (3rd ed.). New York: Macmillan.

Anderson, D. R., Burnham, K. P., & Thompson, W. L. (2000). Null hypothesis testing: Problems, prevalence, and an alternative. *Journal of Wildlife Management, 64,* 912–923.

Anderson, J. R. (1990). *The adaptive character of thought.* Hillsdale, NJ: Erlbaum.

Antell, S. E., & Keating, D. P. (1983). Perception of numerical invariance in neonates. *Child Development, 54,* 695–701.

Arbuthnot, J. (1710). An argument for Divine Providence, taken from the constant regularity observ'd in the births of both sexes. *Philosophical Transactions of the Royal Society, 27,* 186–190.

Arkes, H. R., & Ayton, P. (1999). The sunk cost and Concorde effects: Are humans less rational than lower animals? *Psychological Bulletin, 125,* 591–600.

Arrow, K. J. (2004). Is bounded rationality unboundedly rational? Some ruminations. In M. Augier & J. G. March (eds.), *Models of a man: Essays in memory of Herbert A. Simon* (pp. 47–55). Cambridge, MA: MIT Press.

Babler, T. G., & Dannemiller, J. L. (1993). Role of image acceleration in judging landing location of free-falling projectiles. *Journal of Experimental Psychology: Human Perception and Performance, 19,* 15–31.

Bakan, D. (1966). The test of significance in psychological research. *Psychological Bulletin, 66,* 423–437.

Balda, R. P., & Kamil, A. C. (1992). Long-term spatial memory in Clark's nutcracker (*Nucifruga columbiana*). *Animal Behavior, 44,* 761–769.

Basolo, A. L., & Trainor, B. C. (2002). The confirmation of a female preference for a composite male trait in green swordtails. *Animal Behavior, 63,* 469–474.

Baum, K. A., Grant, W. E. (2001). Hummingbird foraging behavior in different patch types: Simulation of alternative strategies. *Ecological Modeling, 137,* 201–209.

Bayes, T. (1763). An essay towards solving a problem in the doctrine of chances. *Philosophical Transactions of the Royal Society of London, 53,* 370–418.

Benhamou, S. (1992). Efficiency of area-concentrated searching behaviour in a continuous patchy environment. *Journal of Theoretical Biology, 159,* 67–81.

Berg, N., & Gigerenzer, G. (2006). Peacemaking among inconsistent rationalities? In C. Engel & L. Daston (eds.), *Is there value in inconsistency?* (pp. 421–433). Baden-Baden: Nomos.

Bergert, F. B., & Nosofsky, R. M. (2007). A response-time approach to comparing generalized rational and take-the-best models of decision making. *Journal of Experimental Psychology: Learning, Memory, and Cognition, 33,* 107–129.

Bernoulli, D. (1954). Exposition of a new theory on the measurement of risk. *Econometrica, 22,* 23–36. (Original work published 1738)

Bishop, M. A. (2000). In praise of epistemic irresponsibility: How lazy and ignorant can you be? *Synthese, 122,* 179–208.

Bonduriansky, R. (2003). Layered sexual selection: a comparative analysis of sexual behaviour within an assemblage of piophilid flies. *Canadian Journal of Zoology, 81,* 479–491.

Bookstaber, R., & Langsam, J. (1985). On the optimality of coarse behavior rules. *Journal of Theoretical Biology, 116,* 161–193.

Boole, G. (1958). *An investigation of the laws of thought on which are founded the mathematical theories of logic and probabilities.* New York: Dover. (Original work published 1854)

Bourguet, M.-N. (1987). Décrire, compter, calculer: The debate over statistics during the Napoleonic period. In L. Krüger, L. Daston, & M. Heidelberger (eds.), *The probabilistic revolution: Vol. 1. Ideas in history* (pp. 305–316). Cambridge, MA: MIT Press.

Brandstätter, E., Gigerenzer, G., & Hertwig, R. (2006). The priority heuristic: A process model of risky choice. *Psychological Review, 113,* 409–432.

Brase, G. L. (2002). Ecological and evolutionary validity: Comment on Johnson-Laird, Legrenzi, Girotto, Legrenzi, & Caverni's (1999) mental model theory of extensional reasoning. *Psychological Review, 109,* 722–728.

Brase, G. L., Cosmides, L., & Tooby, J. (1998). Individuation, counting, and statistical inference: The role of frequency and whole-object representations in judgment under uncertainty. *Journal of Experimental Psychology: General, 127,* 3–21.

Breiman, L., Friedman, J. H., Olshen, R. A., & Stone, C. J. (1984). *Classification and regression trees.* Belmont, CA: Wadsworth International Group.

Brighton, H. (2006). Robust inference with simple cognitive models. In C. Lebiere & R. Wray (eds.), *Between a rock and a hard place: Cognitive science principles meet AI-hard problems; Papers from the AAAI Spring Symposium.* (AAAI Tech. Rep. No. SS-06–03, pp. 17–22). Menlo Park, CA: AAAI Press.

Brighton, H., & Gigerenzer, G. (2008). Bayesian brains and cognitive mechanisms: Harmony or dissonance? In N. Chater & M. Oaksford (eds.), *The probabilistic mind: Prospects for Bayesian cognitive science* (pp. 189–208). New York: Oxford University Press.

Bröder, A. (2000). Assessing the empirical validity of the "Take-the-Best" heuristic as a model of human probabilistic inference. *Journal of Experimental Psychology: Learning, Memory, and Cognition, 26,* 1332–1346.

———. (2002). Take the Best, Dawes' Rule, and compensatory decision strategies: A regression-based classification method. *Quality & Quantity, 36,* 219–238.

———. (2003). Decision making with the "adaptive toolbox": Influence of environmental structure, intelligence, and working memory load. *Journal of Experimental Psychology: Learning, Memory, and Cognition, 29,* 611–625.

Bröder, A., & Schiffer, S. (2003a). Bayesian strategy assessment in multiattribute decision making. *Journal of Behavioral Decision Making, 16,* 193–213.

———. (2003b). Take the Best versus simultaneous feature matching: Probabilistic inferences from memory and effects of representation format. *Journal of Experimental Psychology: General, 132,* 277–293.

Brunswik, E. (1934). *Wahrnehmung und Gegenstandswelt: Grundlegung einer Psychologie vom Gegenstand her* [Perception and the world of objects: The foundations of a psychology in terms of objects]. Leipzig: Deutike.

———. (1955). Representative design and probabilistic theory in a functional psychology. *Psychological Review, 62,* 193–217.

Burke, D., & Fulham, B. J. (2003). An evolved spatial memory bias in a nectar-feeding bird? *Animal Behavior, 66,* 95–701.

Busemeyer, J. R., & Rapoport, A. (1988). Psychological models of deferred decision making. *Journal of Mathematical Psychology, 32,* 91–134.

Busemeyer, J. R., & Townsend, J. T. (1993). Decision field theory: A dynamic-cognitive approach to decision making in an uncertain environment. *Psychological Review, 100,* 432–459.

Butterworth, B. (1999). *What counts: How every brain is hardwired for math.* New York: Free Press.

Calkins, J. D., & Burley, N. T. (2003). Mate choice for multiple ornaments in the California quail, *Callipepla californica. Animal Behavior, 65,* 69–81.

Camazine, S., Deneubourg, J.-L., Franks, N. R., Sneyd, J., Theraulaz, G., & Bonabeau, E. (2001). *Self-organization in biological systems.* Princeton, NJ: Princeton University Press.

Camerer, C. F. (1995). Individual decision making. In J. H. Kagel & A. E. Roth (eds.), *The handbook of experimental economics* (pp. 587–703). Princeton, NJ: Princeton University Press.

Camerer, C. F. (1998). Bounded rationality in individual decision making. *Experimental Economics, 1,* 163–183.

Candolin, U. (2003). The use of multiple cues in mate choice. *Biological Review, 78,* 575–595.

Carpenter, T., Coburn, T. G., Reys, R. E., & Wilson, J. W. (1978). *Results from the first mathematics assessment of the National Assessment of Educational Progress.* Reston, VA: National Council of Teachers of Mathematics.

Casscells, W., Schoenberger, A., & Grayboys, T. (1978). Interpretation by physicians of clinical laboratory results. *New England Journal of Medicine, 299,* 999–1000.

Catalano, R. A., Kessell, E. R., McConnell, W., & Pirkle, E. (2004). Psychiatric emergencies after the terrorist attacks of September 11, 2001. *Psychiatric Services, 55,* 163–166.

Charnov, E. L. (1976). Optimal foraging, the marginal value theorem. *Theoretical Population Biology, 9,* 129–136.

Christensen-Szalanski, J. J. J., & Beach, L. R. (1982). Experience and the base-rate fallacy. *Organizational Behavior and Human Performance, 29,* 270–278.

Chow, S. L. (1998). Précis of "Statistical significance: Rationale, validity, and utility." *Behavioral and Brain Sciences, 21,* 169–239.

Cohen, J. (1962). The statistical power of abnormal-social psychological research: A review. *Journal of Abnormal and Social Psychology, 65,* 145–153.

Cohen, L. J. (1981). Can human irrationality be experimentally demonstrated? *Behavioral and Brain Sciences, 4,* 317–370.

———. (1988). *Statistical power analysis for the behavioral sciences* (2nd ed.). Hillsdale, NJ: Lawrence Erlbaum.

Comune di Prato. (n.d.). Retrieved December 4, 2003, from http://www.comune.prato.it/associa/cai/htm/bolmeteo.htm/.

Conlisk, J. (1996). Why bounded rationality? *Journal of Economic Literature, 34,* 669–700.

Cooper, G. (1990). The computational complexity of probabilistic inference using Bayesian belief networks. *Artificial Intelligence, 42,* 393–405.

Cosmides, L. (1989). The logic of social exchange: Has natural selection shaped how humans reason? Studies with the Wason selection task. *Cognition, 31,* 187–276.

Cosmides, L., & Tooby, J. (1992). Cognitive adaptions for social exchange. In J. H. Barkow, L. Cosmides, & J. Tooby (eds.), *The adapted mind: Evolutionary psychology and the generation of culture* (pp. 163–228). New York: Oxford University Press.

———. (1996). Are humans good intuitive statisticians after all? Rethinking some conclusions from the literature on judgment under uncertainty. *Cognition, 58,* 1–73.

Cronbach, L. J. (1957). The two disciplines of scientific psychology. *American Psychologist, 12,* 671–684.

Czerlinski, J., Gigerenzer, G., & Goldstein, D. G. (1999). How good are simple heuristics? In G. Gigerenzer, P. M. Todd, & the ABC Research Group, *Simple heuristics that make us smart* (pp. 97–118). New York: Oxford University Press.

Dagum, P., & Luby, M. (1993). Approximating probabilistic inference in Bayesian belief networks is NP-hard. *Artificial Intelligence, 60,* 141–153.

Danziger, K. (1990). *Constructing the subject: Historical origins of psychological research.* Cambridge, UK: Cambridge University Press.

Darwin, C. (1969). *The autobiography of Charles Darwin, 1809–1882.* New York: Norton. (Original work published 1887)

Daston, L. J. (1987). The domestication of risk: Mathematical probability and insurance, 1650–1830. In L. Krüger, L. Daston, & M. Heidelberger (eds.), *The probabilistic revolution: Vol. 1. Ideas in history* (pp. 237–260). Cambridge, MA: MIT Press.

———. (1988). *Classical probability in the Enlightenment.* Princeton, NJ: Princeton University Press.

Daston, L. J., & Park, K. (1998). *Wonders and the order of nature, 1150–1750.* New York: Zone Books.

Davies, N. B., & Houston, A. I. (1981). Owners and satellites: The economics of territory defence in the pied wagtail, *Motacilla alba. Journal of Animal Ecology, 50,* 157–180.

Davis, J. N., Todd, P. M., & Bullock, S. (1999). Environment quality predicts parental provisioning decisions. *Proceedings of the Royal Society B: Biological Sciences, 266,* 1791–1797.

Dawes, R. M. (1979). The robust beauty of improper linear models in decision making. *American Psychologist, 34,* 571–582.

———. (1986). Representative thinking in clinical judgment. *Clinical Psychology Review, 6,* 425–441.

Dawes, R. M., & Corrigan, B. (1974). Linear models in decision making. *Psychological Bulletin, 81,* 95–106.

Dawes, R. M., & Mulford, M. (1996). The false consensus effect and overconfidence: Flaws in judgment, or flaws in how we study judgment? *Organizational Behavior and Human Decision Processes, 65,* 201–211.

Dawkins, R. (1989). *The selfish gene* (2nd ed.). Oxford, UK: Oxford University Press. (Original work published 1976)

Dehaene, S., Spelke, E., Pinel, P., Stanescu, R., & Tsivkin, S. (1999). Sources of mathematical thinking: Behavioral and brain-imaging evidence. *Science, 284,* 970–974.

DeMiguel, V., Garlappi, L., & Uppal, R. (June 22, 2006). *1/N.* Unpublished manuscript, EFA 2006 Zurich Meetings. Available through the Social Science Resource Network (SSRN) Web site at http://ssrn.com/abstract=911512.

de Montmort, P. R. (1713). *Essai d'analyse sur les jeux de hasard* (2nd ed.). Paris: Jacques Quillau.

Detrain, C., & Deneubourg, J.-L. (2002). Complexity of environment and parsimony of decision rules in insect societies. *Biological Bulletin, 202,* 268–274.

Deutsch, J. A., & Ramachandran, V. S. (1990). Binocular depth reversals despite familiarity cues: An artifact? *Science, 25,* 56.

Dhami, M. K. (2003). Psychological models of professional decision making. *Psychological Science, 14,* 175–180.

Dhami, M. K., & Ayton, P. (2001). Bailing and jailing the fast and frugal way. *Journal of Behavioral Decision Making, 14,* 141–168.

Dhami, M. K., & Harries, C. (2001). Fast and frugal versus regression models in human judgement. *Thinking & Reasoning, 7*, 5–27.

Dhami, M., Hertwig, R., & Hoffrage, U. (2004). The role of representative design in an ecological approach to cognition. *Psychological Bulletin, 130*, 959–988.

Dieckmann, A., & Todd, P. M. (2004). Simple ways to construct search orders. In K. Forbus, D. Gentner, & T. Regier (eds.), *Proceedings of the 26th Annual Conference of the Cognitive Science Society* (pp. 309–314). Mahwah, NJ: Erlbaum.

Driessen, G., & Bernstein, C. (1999). Patch departure mechanisms and optimal host exploitation in an insect parasitoid. *Journal of Animal Ecology, 68*, 445–459.

Dugatkin, L. A. (1992). Sexual selection and imitation: Females copy the mate choice of others. *American Naturalist, 139*, 1384–1389.

———. (1996). Interface between culturally based preferences and genetic preferences: Female mate choice in *Poecilia reticulata, Proceedings of the National Academy of Sciences of the United States of America, 93*, 2770–2773.

Dulaney, S., & Fiske, A. P. (1994). Cultural rituals and obsessive-compulsive disorder: Is there a common psychological mechanism? *Ethos, 22*, 243–283.

Edwards, A. G. K., Elwyn, G. J., Covey, J., Mathews, E., & Pill, R. (2001). Presenting risk information—A review of the effects of "framing" and other manipulations on patient outcomes. *Journal of Health Communication, 6*, 61–82.

Edwards, A. G. K., Elwyn, G. J., & Mulley, A. (2002). Explaining risks: Turning numerical data into meaningful pictures. *British Medical Journal, 324*, 827–830.

Edwards, W. (1968). Conservatism in human information processing. In B. Kleinmuntz (ed.), *Formal representation of human judgment* (pp. 17–52). New York: Wiley.

Einhorn, H. J., & Hogarth, R. M. (1975). Unit weighting schemes for decision making. *Organizational Behavior and Human Performance, 13*, 171–192.

Elman, J. L. (1993). Learning and development in neural networks: The importance of starting small. *Cognition, 48*, 71–99.

Elmore, J., & Gigerenzer, G. (2005). Benign breast disease—The risks of communicating risk. *New England Journal of Medicine, 353*, 297–299.

Elwyn, G., Edwards, A., Eccles, M., & Rovner, D. (2001). Decision analysis in patient care. *The Lancet, 358*, 571–574.

Enquist, M., Leimar, O., Ljungberg, T., Mallner, Y., & Sgerdahl, N. (1990). A test of the sequential assessment game: Fighting in the cichlid fish *Nannacara anomala. Animal Behavior, 10*, 1–14.

Erev, I., & Roth, A. E. (2001). Simple reinforcement learning models and reciprocation in the prisoner's dilemma game. In G. Gigerenzer & R. Selten (eds.), *Bounded rationality: The adaptive toolbox* (pp. 215–231). Cambridge, MA: MIT Press.

Erev, I., Wallsten, T. S., & Budescu, D. V. (1994). Simultaneous over- and underconfidence: The role of error in judgment processes. *Psychological Review, 101*, 519–527.

Estes, W. K. (1959). The statistical approach to learning theory. In S. Koch (ed.), *Psychology: A study of science* (vol. 2, pp. 380–491). New York: McGraw-Hill.

Evans, J. St. B. T., Handley, S. J., Perham, N., Over, D. E., & Thompson, V. A. (2000). Frequency versus probability formats in statistical word problems. *Cognition, 77,* 197–213.

Fahey, T., Griffiths, S., & Peters, T. J. (1995). Evidence based purchasing: Understanding results of clinical trials and systematic reviews. *British Medical Journal, 311,* 1056–1059.

Fairhurst, S., Gallistel, C. R., & Gibbon, J. (2003). Temporal landmarks: Proximity prevails. *Animal Cognition, 6,* 113–120.

Falk, R., & Greenbaum, C. W. (1995). Significance tests die hard. *Theory and Psychology, 5,* 75–98.

Falk, R., & Wilkening, F. (1998). Children's construction of fair chances: Adjusting probabilities. *Developmental Psychology, 34,* 1340–1357.

Fawcett, T. W. (2003). *Multiple cues and variation in mate-choice behaviour.* Unpublished doctoral dissertation, University of Cambridge.

Fawcett, T. W., & Johnstone, R. A. (2003). Optimal assessment of multiple cues. *Proceedings of the Royal Society B: Biological Sciences, 270,* 1637–1643.

Ferguson, L. (1959). *Statistical analysis in psychology and education.* New York: McGraw-Hill.

Feynman, R. P. (1967). *The character of physical law.* Cambridge, MA: MIT Press.

———. (1998). *The meaning of it all: Thoughts of a citizen-scientist.* Reading, MA: Perseus.

Fidler, F. (2002). The fifth edition of the APA Publication Manual: Why its statistics recommendations are so controversial. *Educational and Psychological Measurement, 62,* 749–770.

Fiedler, K. (1988). The dependence of the conjunction fallacy on subtle linguistic factors. *Psychological Research, 50,* 123–129.

Fiedler, K., & Juslin, P. (Eds.). (2006). *Information sampling and adaptive cognition.* New York: Cambridge University Press.

Fiedler, K., Walther, E., & Nickel, S. (1999). Covariation-based attribution: On the ability to assess multiple covariates of an effect. *Personality & Social Psychology Bulletin, 25,* 607–622.

Fillenbaum, S. (1977). Mind your p's and q's: The role of content and context in some uses of and, or, and if. *Psychology of Learning and Motivation, 11,* 41–100.

Finch, S., Cumming, G., Williams, J., Palmer, L., Griffith, E., & Alders, C., et al. (2004). Reform of statistical inference in psychology: The case of memory and cognition. *Behavior Research Methods, Instruments and Computers, 36,* 312–324.

Fischer, J. E., Steiner, F., Zucol, F., Berger, C., Martignon, L., & Bossart, W., et al. (2002). Use of simple heuristics to target macrolide prescription in children with community-acquired pneumonia. *Archives of Pediatrics & Adolescent Medicine, 156,* 1005–1008.

Fischhoff, B., & MacGregor, D. (1982). Subjective confidence in forecasts. *Journal of Forecasting, 1,* 155–172.

Fisher, R. A. (1935). *The design of experiments* (1st ed.; 5th ed., 1951; 7th ed., 1960; 8th ed., 1966). Edinburgh: Oliver and Boyd.

Fisher, R. A. (1955). Statistical methods and scientific induction. *Journal of the Royal Statistical Society, Series B, 17,* 69–78.

———. (1956). *Statistical methods and scientific inference.* Edinburgh: Oliver and Boyd.

Floor, C. (1992). *Kans op regen. Zenit.* Retrieved December 1, 2003, from http://www.knmi.nl/, the Royal Dutch Meteorological Institute Web site.

Ford, J. K., Schmitt, N., Schechtman, S. L., Hults, B. H., & Doherty, M. L. (1989). Process tracing methods: Contributions, problems, and neglected research questions. *Organizational Behavior and Human Decision Processes, 43,* 75–117.

Forster, M., & Sober, E. (1994). How to tell when simpler, more unified, and less *ad hoc* theories will provide more accurate predictions. *British Journal of the Philosophy of Science, 45,* 1–35.

Fortin, D. (2003). Searching behavior and use of sampling information by free-ranging bison (*Bos bison*). *Behavioral Ecology and Sociobiology, 54,* 194–203.

Freedman, D. A. (1987). As others see us: A case study in path analysis. *Journal of Educational Statistics, 12,* 101–128.

Frey, B. S., & Eichenberger, R. (1996). Marriage paradoxes. *Rationality and Society, 8,* 187–206.

Friedman, M. (1953). *Essays in positive economics.* Chicago: University of Chicago Press.

Gallistel, C. R. (1990). *The organization of learning.* Cambridge, MA: MIT Press.

Garcia y Robertson, R., & Garcia, J. (1985). X-rays and learned taste aversions: Historical and psychological ramifications. In T. G. Burish, S. M. Levy, & B. E. Meyerowitz (eds.), *Cancer, nutrition, and eating behavior: A biobehavioral perspective* (pp. 11–41). Hillsdale, NJ: Erlbaum.

Geman, S. E., Bienenstock, E., & Doursat, R. (1992). Neural networks and the bias/variance dilemma. *Neural Computation, 4,* 1–58.

Gernsbacher, M. A. (1998). Editorial comment. *Memory and Cognition, 26,* 1.

Gerrig, R. J., & Zimbardo, P. G. (2002). *Psychology and life* (16th ed.). Boston: Allyn and Bacon.

Gibson, R. M. (1996). Female choice in sage grouse: The roles of attraction and active comparison. *Behavioral Ecology and Sociobiology, 39,* 55–59.

Gigerenzer, G. (1984). External validity of laboratory experiments: The frequency-validity relationship. *American Journal of Psychology, 97,* 185–195.

———. (1987). Probabilistic thinking and the fight against subjectivity. In L. Krüger, G. Gigerenzer, & M. S. Morgan (eds.), *The probabilistic revolution: Vol. 2. Ideas in the sciences* (pp. 11–33). Cambridge, MA: MIT Press.

———. (1991). From tools to theories: A heuristic of discovery in cognitive psychology. *Psychological Review, 98,* 254–267.

———. (1993a). The bounded rationality of probabilistic mental models. In K. I. Manktelow & D. E. Over (eds.), *Rationality: Psychological and philosophical perspectives* (pp. 284–313). London: Routledge.

Gigerenzer, G. (1993b). The Superego, the Ego, and the Id in statistical reasoning. In G. Keren & C. Lewis (eds.), *A handbook for data analysis in the behavioral sciences: Methodological issues* (pp. 313–339). Hillsdale, NJ: Erlbaum.

———. (1996). On narrow norms and vague heuristics: A reply to Kahneman and Tversky (1996). *Psychological Review, 103,* 592–596.

———. (2000). *Adaptive thinking: Rationality in the real world.* New York: Oxford University Press.

———. (2001). Content-blind norms, no norms, or good norms? A reply to Vranas. *Cognition, 81,* 93–103.

———. (2002a). *Calculated risks: How to know when numbers deceive you.* New York: Simon & Schuster. (UK version: *Reckoning with risk: Learning to live with uncertainty,* Penguin)

———. (2002b). In the year 2054: Innumeracy defeated. In P. Sedlmeier & T. Betsch (eds.), *Frequency processing and cognition* (pp. 55–66). New York: Oxford University Press.

———. (2003). The adaptive toolbox and lifespan development: Common questions? In U. M. Staudinger & U. E. R. Lindenberger (eds.), *Interactive minds: Life-span perspectives on the social foundation of cognition* (pp. 319–346). Cambridge: Cambridge University Press.

———. (2004a). Dread risk, September 11, and fatal traffic accidents. *Psychological Science, 15,* 286–287.

———. (2004b). Fast and frugal heuristics: The tools of bounded rationality. In D. J. Koehler & N. Harvey (eds.), *Blackwell handbook of judgment and decision making* (pp. 62–88). Oxford, UK: Blackwell.

———. (2004c). Striking a blow for sanity in theories of rationality. In M. Augier & J. G. March (eds.), *Models of a man: Essays in memory of Herbert A. Simon* (pp. 389–409). Cambridge, MA: MIT Press.

———. (2004d). Die Evolution des statistischen Denkens [The evolution of statistical thinking]. *Unterrichtswissenschaft, 32,* 4–22.

———. (2004e). Mindless statistics. *Journal of Socio-Economics, 33,* 587–606.

———. (2005). I think, therefore I err. *Social Research, 72,* 195–218.

———. (2006a). Bounded and rational. In R. J. Stainton (ed.), *Contemporary debates in cognitive science* (pp. 115–133). Oxford, UK: Blackwell.

———. (2006b). Out of the frying pan into the fire: Behavioral reactions to terrorist attacks. *Risk Analysis, 26,* 347–351.

———. (2006c). What's in a sample? A manual for building cognitive theories. In K. Fiedler & P. Juslin (eds.), *Information sampling and adaptive cognition* (pp. 239–260). New York: Cambridge University Press.

———. (2007). *Gut feelings: The intelligence of the unconscious.* New York: Viking.

———. (2008). Moral intuition = Fast and frugal heuristics? In W. Sinnott-Armstrong (ed.), *Moral psychology: Vol 2. The cognitive science of morality: Intuition and diversity* (pp. 1–26). Cambridge, MA: MIT Press.

Gigerenzer, G., & Edwards, A. G. K. (2003). Simple tools for understanding risks: From innumeracy to insight. *British Medical Journal, 327,* 741–744.

Gigerenzer, G., & Engel, C. (2006). *Heuristics and the law.* Cambridge, MA: MIT Press.

Gigerenzer, G., & Goldstein, D. G. (1996). Reasoning the fast and frugal way: Models of bounded rationality. *Psychological Review, 103*, 650–669.

——. (1999). Betting on one good reason: The Take The Best heuristic. In G. Gigerenzer, P. M. Todd, & the ABC Research Group, *Simple heuristics that make us smart* (pp. 75–95). New York: Oxford University Press.

Gigerenzer, G., Hertwig, R., van den Broek, E., Fasolo, B., & Katsikopoulos, K. V. (2005). "A 30% chance of rain tomorrow": How does the public understand probabilistic weather forecasts? *Risk Analysis, 25*, 623–629.

Gigerenzer, G., & Hoffrage, U. (1995). How to improve Bayesian reasoning without instruction: Frequency formats. *Psychological Review, 102*, 684–704.

——. (1999). Overcoming difficulties in Bayesian reasoning: A reply to Lewis & Keren and Mellers & McGraw. *Psychological Review, 106*, 425–430.

——. (2007). The role of representation in Bayesian reasoning: Correcting common misconceptions. *Behavioral and Brain Sciences, 30*, 264–267.

Gigerenzer, G., Hoffrage, U., & Ebert, A. (1998). AIDS counselling for low-risk clients. *AIDS Care, 10*, 197–211.

Gigerenzer, G., Hoffrage, U., & Kleinbölting, H. (1991). Probabilistic mental models: A Brunswikian theory of confidence. *Psychological Review, 98*, 506–528.

Gigerenzer, G., & Hug, K. (1992). Domain-specific reasoning: Social contracts, cheating, and perspective change. *Cognition, 43*, 127–171.

Gigerenzer, G., Krauss, S., & Vitouch, O. (2004). The null ritual: What you always wanted to know about null hypothesis testing but were afraid to ask. In D. Kaplan (ed.), *Handbook on quantitative methods in the social sciences* (pp. 391–408). Thousand Oaks, CA: Sage.

Gigerenzer, G., & Murray, D. J. (1987). *Cognition as intuitive statistics*. Hillsdale, NJ: Erlbaum.

Gigerenzer, G., & Richter, H. R. (1990). Context effects and their interaction with development: Area judgments. *Cognitive Development, 5*, 235–264.

Gigerenzer, G., & Selten, R. (2001a). Rethinking rationality. In G. Gigerenzer & R. Selten (eds.), *Bounded rationality: The adaptive toolbox* (pp. 1–12). Cambridge, MA: MIT Press.

——. (Eds.). (2001b). *Bounded rationality: The adaptive toolbox*. Cambridge, MA: MIT Press.

Gigerenzer, G., Swijtink, Z., Porter, T., Daston, L., Beatty, J., & Krüger, L. (1989). *The empire of chance: How probability changed science and everyday life*. Cambridge: Cambridge University Press.

Gigerenzer, G., Todd, P. M., & the ABC Research Group. (1999). *Simple heuristics that make us smart*. New York: Oxford University Press.

Gigone, D., & Hastie, R. (1997). The impact of information on small group choice. *Journal of Personality and Social Psychology, 72*, 132–140.

Gilovich, T., Griffin, D., & Kahneman, D. (2002). *Heuristics and biases: The psychology of intuitive judgment*. Cambridge: Cambridge University Press.

Girotto, V., & Gonzalez, M. (2001). Solving probabilistic and statistical problems: A matter of information structure and question form. *Cognition, 78*, 247–276.

Gode, D. K., & Sunder, S. (1993). Allocative efficiency of markets with zero-intelligence traders: Market as a partial substitute for individual rationality. *Journal of Political Economy, 101,* 119–137.

Goldstein, D. G., & Gigerenzer, G. (1999). The recognition heuristic: How ignorance makes us smart. In G. Gigerenzer, P. M. Todd, & the ABC Research Group, *Simple heuristics that make us smart* (pp. 37–58). New York: Oxford University Press.

———. (2002). Models of ecological rationality: The recognition heuristic. *Psychological Review, 109,* 75–90.

Goldstein, D. G., Gigerenzer, G., Hogarth, R. M., Kacelnik, A., Kareev, Y., & Klein, G., et al. (2001). Group report: Why and when do simple heuristics work? In G. Gigerenzer & R. Selten (eds.), *Bounded rationality: The adaptive toolbox* (pp. 173–190). Cambridge, MA: MIT Press.

Gould, J. L., & Gould, C. G. (1988). *The honey bee.* New York: Scientific American Library.

Gould, S. J. (1992). *Bully for brontosaurus: Further reflections in natural history.* New York: Penguin Books.

Gould S. J., & Lewontin, R. C. (1979). The spandrels of San Marco and the Panglossian paradigm: A critique of the adaptationist programme. *Proceedings of the Royal Society of London B, 205,* 581–598.

Goulson, D. (2000). Why do pollinators visit proportionally fewer flowers in large patches? *Oikos, 91,* 485–492.

Green, L., & Mehr, D. R. (1997). What alters physicians' decisions to admit to the coronary care unit? *Journal of Family Practice, 45,* 219–226.

Green, R. F. (1984). Stopping rules for optimal foragers. *American Naturalist, 123,* 30–43.

Gregory, R. L. (1974). *Concepts and mechanisms of perception.* New York: Scribner.

Grice, H. P. (1989). *Studies in the way of words.* Cambridge, MA: Harvard University Press.

Griffin, D., & Tversky, A. (1992). The weighing of evidence and the determinants of confidence. *Cognitive Psychology, 24,* 411–435.

Griliches, Z. (1974). Errors in variables and other unobservables. *Econometrica, 42,* 971–998.

Gruber, H. E., & Vonèche, J. J. (1977). *The essential Piaget.* New York: Basic Books.

Guilford, J. P. (1942). *Fundamental statistics in psychology and education* (3rd ed., 1956; 6th ed., 1978). (with B. Fruchter, ed.). New York: McGraw-Hill.

Hacking, I. (1975). *The emergence of probability.* Cambridge: Cambridge University Press.

———. (1990). *The taming of chance.* Cambridge: Cambridge University Press.

Haller, H., & Krauss, S. (2002). Misinterpretations of significance: A problem students share with their teachers? *Methods of Psychological Research Online* (http://www.mpr-online.de), *7,* 1–20.

Hammond, K. R. (1966). *The psychology of Egon Brunswik.* New York: Holt, Rinehart & Winston.

Hankinson, S. J., & Morris, M. R. (2003). Avoiding a compromise between sexual selection and species recognition: Female swordtail fish assess multiple species-specific cues. *Behavioral Ecology, 14,* 282–287.

Hartmann, L. C., Schaid, D. J., Woods, J. E., Crotty, T. P., Myers, J. L., & Arnold, P. G., et al. (1999). Efficacy of bilateral prophylactic mastectomy in women with a family history of breast cancer. *New England Journal of Medicine, 340,* 77–84.

Hasson, O. (1991). Sexual displays as amplifiers: Practical examples with an emphasis on feather decorations. *Behavioral Ecology, 2,* 189–197.

Hebets, E. A. (2005). Attention-altering signal interactions in the multimodal courtship display of the wolf spider *Schizocosa uetzi. Behavioral Ecology, 16,* 75–82.

Heller, R. F., & Dobson, A. J. (2000). Disease impact number and population impact number: Population perspectives to measures of risk and benefit. *British Medical Journal, 321,* 950–953.

Hertwig, R., & Gigerenzer, G. (1999). The "conjunction fallacy" revisited: How intelligent inferences look like reasoning errors. *Journal of Behavioral Decision Making, 12,* 275–305.

Hertwig, R., Hoffrage, U., & Martignon, L. (1999). Quick estimation: Letting the environment do the work. In G. Gigerenzer, P. M. Todd, & the ABC Research Group, *Simple heuristics that make us smart* (pp. 209–234). New York: Oxford University Press.

Hertwig, R., Pachur, T., & Kurzenhäuser, S. (2005). Judgments of risk frequencies: Tests of possible cognitive mechanisms. *Journal of Experimental Psychology: Learning, Memory, and Cognition, 31,* 621–642.

Hertwig, R., & Todd, P. M. (2003). More is not always better: The benefits of cognitive limits. In D. Hardman & L. Macchi (eds.), *The psychology of reasoning and decision making: A handbook* (pp. 213–231). Chichester, UK: Wiley.

Hill, J. A., Enstrom, D. A., Ketterson, E. D., Nolan, V., & Ziegenfus, C. (1999). Mate choice based on static versus dynamic secondary sexual traits in the dark-eyed junco. *Behavioral Ecology, 10,* 91–96.

Hoffrage, U. (1995). *Zur Angemessenheit subjektiver Sicherheits-Urteile: Eine Exploration der Theorie der probabilistischen mentalen Modelle* [The adequacy of subjective confidence judgments: Studies concerning the theory of probabilistic mental models]. Unpublished doctoral dissertation, University of Salzburg, Austria.

Hoffrage, U., & Gigerenzer, G. (1998). Using natural frequencies to improve diagnostic inferences. *Academic Medicine, 73,* 538–540.

Hoffrage, U., Gigerenzer, G., Krauss, S., & Martignon, L. (2002). Representation facilitates reasoning: What natural frequencies are and what they are not. *Cognition, 84,* 343–352.

Hoffrage, U., Hertwig, R., & Gigerenzer, G. (2000). Hindsight bias: A by-product of knowledge updating? *Journal of Experimental Psychology: Learning, Memory, and Cognition, 26,* 566–581.

Hoffrage, U., Lindsey, S., Hertwig, R., & Gigerenzer, G. (2000). Communicating statistical information. *Science, 290,* 2261–2262.

Hofstadter, D. (1979). *Gödel, Escher, Bach: An eternal golden braid.* New York: Basic Books.

Hogarth, R. M., & Karelaia, N. (2005). Ignoring information in binary choice with continuous variables: When is less "more"? *Journal of Mathematical Psychology, 49,* 115–124.

———. (2006). "Take-the-best" and other simple strategies: Why and when they work "well" with binary cues. *Theory and Decision, 61,* 205–249.

Holton, G. (1988). *Thematic origins of scientific thought* (2nd ed.). Cambridge, MA: Harvard University Press.

Houston, A., Kacelnik, A., & McNamara, J. M. (1982). Some learning rules for acquiring information. In D. J. McFarland (ed.), *Functional ontogeny* (pp. 140–191). London: Pitman.

Hutchinson, J. M. C., & Gigerenzer, G. (2005). Simple heuristics and rules of thumb: Where psychologists and behavioural biologists might meet. *Behavioural Processes, 69,* 97–124.

Hutchinson, J. M. C., & Halupka, K. (2004). Mate choice when males are in patches: Optimal strategies and good rules of thumb. *Journal of Theoretical Biology, 231,* 129–151.

Inhelder, B., & Piaget, J. (1958). *Growth of logical thinking: From childhood to adolescence.* New York: Basic Books.

———. (1964). *The early growth of logic in the child* (E. A. Lunzer, trans.). New York: Norton Library. (Original work published 1959)

Intons-Peterson, M. J. (1990). Editorial. *Memory and Cognition, 18,* 1–2.

Iwasa, Y., Higashi, M., & Yamamura, N. (1981). Prey distribution as a factor determining the choice of optimal foraging strategy. *American Naturalist, 117,* 710–723.

Iyengar, S. S., & Lepper, M. R. (2000). When choice is demotivating: Can one desire too much of a good thing? *Journal of Personality and Social Psychology, 79,* 995–1006.

Jain, B. P., McQuay, H., & Moore, A. (1998). Number needed to treat and relative risk reduction. *Annals of Internal Medicine, 128,* 72–73.

Janetos, A. C. (1980). Strategies of female mate choice: A theoretical analysis. *Behavioral Ecology and Sociobiology, 7,* 107–112.

Janetos, A. C., & Cole, B. J. (1981). Imperfectly optimal animals. *Behavioral Ecology and Sociobiology, 9,* 203–209.

Janis, I., & Mann, L. (1977). *Decision making: A psychological analysis of conflict, choice, and commitment.* New York: Free Press.

Jennions, M. D., & Petrie, M. (1997). Variation in mate choice and mating preferences: A review of causes and consequences. *Biological Review, 72,* 283–327.

Johnson, E. J., Hershey, J., Meszaros, J., & Kunreuther, H. (1993). Framing, probability distortions, and insurance decisions. *Journal of Risk and Uncertainty, 7,* 35–51.

Johnson, E. J., Meyer, R. J., & Ghose, S. (1989). When choice models fail: Compensatory models in negatively correlated environments. *Journal of Marketing Research, 26,* 255–270.

Johnson, J. G., & Raab, M. (2003). Take the first: Option generation and resulting choices. *Organizational Behavior and Human Decision Processes, 91,* 215–229.

Johnson-Laird, P. N., Legrenzi, P., Girotto, V., Legrenzi, M. S., & Caverni J.-P. (1999). Naïve probability: A mental model theory of extensional reasoning. *Psychological Review, 106,* 62–88.

Jolls, C., Sunstein, C. R., & Thaler, R. H. (1998). A behavioral approach to law and economics. *Stanford Law Review, 50,* 1471–1550.

Jorland, G. (1987). The Saint Petersburg Paradox, 1713–1937. In L. Krüger, G. Gigerenzer, & M. S. Morgan (eds.), *The probabilistic revolution: Vol. 1. Ideas in history* (pp. 157–190). Cambridge, MA: MIT Press.

Juslin, P., Fiedler, K., & Chater, N. (2006). Less is more in covariation detection—Or is it? In K. Fiedler & P. Juslin (eds.), *Information sampling and adaptive cognition* (pp. 92–123). New York: Cambridge University Press.

Juslin, P., Winman, A., & Olsson, H. (2000). Naive empiricism and dogmatism in confidence research: A critical examination of the hard-easy effect. *Psychological Review, 107,* 384–396.

Kahneman, D., & Frederick, S. (2002). Representativeness revisited: Attribute substitution in intuitive judgment. In T. Gilovich, D. Griffin, & D. Kahnemann (eds.), *Heuristics and biases: The psychology of intuitive judgment* (pp. 49–81). New York: Cambridge University Press.

Kahneman, D., Slovic, P., & Tversky, A. (Eds.). (1982). *Judgment under uncertainty: Heuristics and biases.* Cambridge: Cambridge University Press.

Kahneman, D., & Tversky, A. (1979). Prospect theory: An analysis of decision under risk. *Econometrica, 47,* 263–291.

———. (1982). On the study of statistical intuitions. *Cognition, 11,* 123–141.

———. (1984). Choices, values, and frames. *American Psychologist, 39,* 341–350.

———. (1996). On the reality of cognitive illusions. *Psychological Review, 103,* 582–591.

Kant, I. (1784). Beantwortung der Frage: Was ist Aufklärung? [An answer to the question: What is enlightenment?]. *Berlinische Monatsschrift, Dezember-Heft,* 481–494.

Kanwisher, N. (1989). Cognitive heuristics and American security policy. *Journal of Conflict Resolution, 33,* 652–675.

Kareev, Y. (2000). Seven (indeed, plus or minus two) and the detection of correlations. *Psychological Review, 107,* 397–402.

———. (2006). Good sampling, distorted views: The perception of variability. In K. Fiedler & P. Juslin (eds.), *Information sampling and adaptive cognition* (pp. 33–52). New York: Cambridge University Press.

Karsai, I., & Pénzes, Z. (2000). Optimality of cell arrangement and rules of thumb of cell initiation in *Polistes dominulus:* A modeling approach. *Behavioral Ecology, 11,* 387–395.

Kaufman, B. E. (1999). Emotional arousal as a source of bounded rationality. *Journal of Economic Behaviour and Organization, 38,* 135–144.

Keeney, R. L., & Raiffa, H. (1993). *Decisions with multiple objectives.* Cambridge: Cambridge University Press.

Kelley, H. H. (1967) Attribution theory in social psychology. In D. Levine (ed.), *Nebraska symposium on motivation* (vol. 15, pp. 192–238). Lincoln: University of Nebraska Press.

Kelly, G. A. (1955). *The psychology of personal constructs.* New York: Norton.

Kendall, M. G. (1943). *The advanced theory of statistics* (vol. 1). New York: Lippincott.

Kirk, E., & Fraedrich, K. (n.d.). *Prognose der Niederschlagswahrscheinlichkeit: Modelle und Verifikation* [Precipitation probability forecasting: Models and verification]. Retrieved December 9, 2003, from Meteorological Institute, University of Hamburg, Germany: http://puma.dkrz.de/ theomet/prognosen/paper.html/.

Klayman, J., & Ha, Y. (1987). Confirmation, disconfirmation, and information in hypothesis testing. *Psychological Review, 94,* 211–228.

Kleffner, D. A., & Ramachandran, V. S. (1992). On the perception of shape from shading. *Perception & Psychophysics, 52,* 18–36.

Kleiter, G. D. (1994). Natural sampling: Rationality without base rates. In G. H. Fischer & D. Laming (eds.), *Contributions to mathematical psychology, psychometrics, and methodology* (pp. 375–388). New York: Springer.

KNMI [Royal Dutch Meteorological Institute]. (2002). *Het weer nader verklaard: Neerslagkans* [The weather explained: Precipitation chances]. Retrieved May 5, 2003, from the KNMI Web site, http://www.knmi.nl/voorl/nader/neerslagkans.htm.

Kodric-Brown, A., & Nicoletto, P. F. (2001). Female choice in the guppy (*Poecilia reticulata*): The interaction between male color and display. *Behavioral Ecology and Sociobiology, 50,* 346–351.

Koehler, J. J. (1996a). On conveying the probative value of DNA evidence: Frequencies, likelihood ratios, and error rates. *University of Colorado Law Review, 67,* 859–886.

———. (1996b). The base rate fallacy reconsidered: Descriptive, normative, and methodological challenges. *Behavioral and Brain Sciences, 19,* 1–53.

Kohn, L. T., Corrigan, J. M., & Donaldson, M. S. (Eds.). (2000). *To err is human: Building a safer health system.* Washington, DC: National Academy Press.

Körding, K. P., & Wolpert, D. M. (2004). Bayesian integration in sensorimotor learning. *Nature, 427,* 244–247.

Koriat, A., Lichtenstein, S., & Fischhoff, B. (1980). Reasons for confidence. *Journal of Experimental Psychology: Human Learning and Memory, 6,* 107–118.

Krauss, S., & Atmaca, S. (2004). Wie man Schülern Einsicht in schwierige stochastische Probleme vermitteln kann. Eine Fallstudie über das "Drei-Türen-Problem" [How to give pupils insight into difficult stochastic problems. A case study on the "Three Door Problem"]. *Unterrichtswissenschaft, 32,* 38–57.

Krauss, S., Martignon, L., & Hoffrage, U. (1999). Simplifying Bayesian inference: The general case. In L. Magnani, N. Nersessian, & P. Thagard (eds.), *Model-based reasoning in scientific discovery* (pp. 165–179). New York: Plenum.

Krauss, S., & Wang, X. T. (2003). The psychology of the Monty Hall problem: Discovering psychological mechanisms for solving a tenacious brain teaser. *Journal of Experimental Psychology: General, 132,* 3–22.

Krebs, J. R., Stephens, D. W., & Sutherland, W. J. (1983). Perspectives in optimal foraging. In A. H. Bush & G. A. Clark (eds.), *Perspectives in ornithology: Essays presented for the centennial of the American Ornithologists' Union* (pp. 165–221). Cambridge: Cambridge University Press.

Kühberger, A. (1998). The influence of framing on risky decisions: A meta-analysis. *Organizational Behavior and Human Decision Processes, 75,* 23–55.

Künzler, R., & Bakker, T. C. M. (2001). Female preferences for single and combined traits in computer animated stickleback males. *Behavioral Ecology, 12,* 681–685.

Kurz, E., & Tweney, R. D. (1997). The heretical psychology of Egon Brunswik. In W. G. Bringmann, H. E. Leuck, R. Miller, & C. E. Early (eds.), *A pictorial history of psychology* (pp. 221–232). Carol Stream, IL: Quintessence Publishing Co.

Labarge, A. S., McCaffrey, R. J., & Brown, T. A. (2003). Neuropsychologists' ability to determine the predictive value of diagnostic tests. *Clinical Neuropsychology, 18,* 165–175.

Laplace, P.-S. (1951). *A philosophical essay on probabilities* (F. W. Truscott & F. L. Emory, trans.). New York: Dover. (Original work published 1814)

Lawler, E. L., Lenstra, J. K., Rinnooy-Kan, A. H. G., & Shmoys, D. B. (Eds.). (1985). *The traveling salesman problem.* New York: Wiley.

Lecoutre, M. P., Poitevineau, J., & Lecoutre, B. (2003). Even statisticians are not immune to misinterpretations of null hypothesis significance tests. *International Journal of Psychology, 38,* 37–45.

Lee, M. D., & Cummins, T. D. R. (2004). Evidence accumulation in decision making: Unifying the "take the best" and "rational" models. *Psychonomic Bulletin and Review, 11,* 343–352.

Lindquist, E. F. (1940). *Statistical analysis in educational research.* Boston: Houghton Mifflin.

Lipkus, I. M., & Hollands, J. G. (1999). The visual communication of risk. *Journal of the National Cancer Institute Monographs, 25,* 149–162.

Loftus, G. R. (1991). On the tyranny of hypothesis testing in the social sciences. *Contemporary Psychology, 36,* 102–104.

———. (1993). Editorial comment. *Memory & Cognition, 21,* 1–3.

Lopes, L. L. (1991). The rhetoric of irrationality. *Theory and Psychology, 1,* 65–82.

———. (1992). Three misleading assumptions in the customary rhetoric of the bias literature. *Theory & Psychology, 2,* 231–236.

López-Rousseau, A. (2005). Avoiding the death risk of avoiding a dread risk: The aftermath of March 11 in Spain. *Psychological Science, 16,* 426–428.

Luce, R. D. (1977). Thurstone's discriminal processes fifty years later. *Psychometrika, 42,* 461–489.

———. (1988). The tools-to-theory hypothesis. Review of G. Gigerenzer and D. J. Murray, "Cognition as intuitive statistics." *Contemporary Psychology, 33,* 582–583.

Luce, R. D., & Green, D. M. (1972). A neural timing theory for response times and the psychophysics of intensity. *Psychological Review, 79,* 14–57.

Lücking, A. (2004). *The development of Bayesian reasoning in children.* Unpublished diploma thesis, Free University, Berlin.

Luria, A. R. (1968). *The mind of a mnemonist.* Cambridge, MA: Harvard University Press.

Luttbeg, B. (1996). A Comparative Bayes tactic for mate assessment and choice. *Behavioral Ecology, 7,* 451–460.

MacKay, D. J. C. (1992). Bayesian interpolation. *Neural Computation, 4,* 415–447.

———. (1995). Probable networks and plausible predictions: A review of practical Bayesian methods for supervised neural networks. *Network: Computation in Neural Systems, 6,* 469–505.

Mallon, E. B., & Franks, N. R. (2000). Ants estimate area using Buffon's needle. *Proceedings of the Royal Society B: Biological Studies, 267,* 765–770.

March, J. G. (1978). Bounded rationality, ambiguity, and the engineering of choice. *Bell Journal of Economics, 9,* 587–608.

Marchetti, K. (1998). The evolution of multiple male traits in the yellow-browed leaf warbler. *Animal Behavior, 55,* 361–376.

Martignon, L., & Hoffrage, U. (1999). Why does one-reason decision making work? A case study in ecological rationality. In G. Gigerenzer, P. M. Todd, & the ABC Research Group, *Simple heuristics that make us smart* (pp. 119–140). New York: Oxford University Press.

Martignon, L., & Hoffrage, U. (2002). Fast, frugal and fit: Lexicographic heuristics for paired comparison. *Theory and Decision, 52,* 29–71.

Martignon, L., & Laskey, K. B. (1999). Bayesian benchmarks for fast and frugal heuristics. In G. Gigerenzer, P. M. Todd, & the ABC Research Group, *Simple heuristics that make us smart* (pp. 169–188). New York: Oxford University Press.

Martignon, L., Vitouch, O., Takezawa, M., & Forster, M. R. (2003). Naive and yet enlightened: From natural frequencies to fast and frugal decision trees. In D. Hardman & L. Macchi (eds.), *Thinking: Psychological perspectives on reasoning, judgment, and decision making* (pp. 189–211). Chichester, UK: Wiley.

Matheson, D. (2006). Bounded rationality, epistemic externalism, and the Enlightenment picture of cognitive virtue. In R. Stainton (ed.), *Contemporary debates in cognitive science* (pp. 134–144). Oxford, UK: Blackwell.

Mazur, D., & Hickam, D. H. (1994). Assumptions patients make when interpreting graphical displays of surgical data. *Theoretical Surgery, 9,* 129–133.

McCloskey, D. N., & Ziliak, S. (1996). The standard error of regression. *Journal of Economic Literature, 34,* 97–114.

McKenzie, C. R. M., & Amin, M. B. (2002). When wrong predictions provide more support than right ones. *Psychonomic Bulletin and Review, 9,* 821–828.

McKenzie, C. R. M., & Nelson, J. D. (2003). What a speaker's choice of frame reveals: Reference points, frame selection, and framing effects. *Psychonomic Bulletin and Review, 10,* 596–602.

McLeod, P., & Dienes, Z. (1996). Do fielders know where to go to catch the ball or only how to get there? *Journal of Experimental Psychology: Human Perception and Performance, 22,* 531–543.

McNamara, J. M., & Houston, A. I. (1985). Optimal foraging and learning. *Journal of Theoretical Biology, 117,* 231–249.

———. (1987). Memory and the efficient use of information. *Journal of Theoretical Biology, 125,* 385–395.

Meehl, P. E. (1978). Theoretical risks and tabular asterisks: Sir Karl, Sir Ronald, and the slow progress of soft psychology. *Journal of Consulting and Clinical Psychology, 46,* 806–834.

Mellers, B., Hertwig, R., & Kahneman, D. (2001). Do frequency representations eliminate conjunction effects? An exercise in adversarial collaboration. *Psychological Science, 12,* 269–275.

Melton, A. W. (1962). Editorial. *Journal of Experimental Psychology, 64,* 553–557.

Menzel, R., & Giurfa, M. (2001). Cognitive architecture of a mini-brain: The honeybee. *Trends in Cognitive Science, 5,* 62–71.

Menzel, R., Greggers, U., & Hammer, M. (1993). Functional organization of appetitive learning and memory in a generalist pollinator, the honey bee. In D. R. Papaj & A. C. Lewis, (eds.), *Insect learning: Ecological and evolutionary perspectives* (pp. 79–125). New York: Chapman & Hall.

Meyers, D. G. (1993). *Social psychology* (4th ed.). New York: McGraw Hill.

Michalewicz, Z., & Fogel, D. (2000). *How to solve it: Modern heuristics.* New York: Springer.

Michotte, A. (1963). *The perception of causality*. London: Methuen. (Original work published 1946)

Miller, G. A. (1956). The magical number seven, plus or minus two: Some limits on our capacity of processing information. *Psychological Review, 63*, 81–97.

Miller, G. A., & Buckhout, R. (1973). *Psychology: The science of mental life*. New York: Harper & Row.

Mitchell, T. M. (1997). *Machine learning*. New York: McGraw-Hill International.

Monahan, J., & Steadman, H. J. (1996). Violent storms and violent people: How meteorology can inform risk communication in mental health law. *American Psychologist, 51*, 931–938.

Morrison, D. E., & Henkel, R. E. (1970). *The significance test controversy*. Chicago: Aldine.

Mugford, S. T., Mallon, E. B., & Franks, N. R. (2001). The accuracy of Buffon's needle: A rule of thumb used by ants to estimate area. *Behavioral Ecology, 12*, 655–658.

Mulaik, S. A., Raju, N. S., & Harshman, R. A. (1997). There is a time and a place for significance testing. In L. L. Harlow, S. A. Mulaik, & J. H. Steiger (eds.), *What if there were no significance tests?* (pp. 65–115). Mahwah, NJ: Erlbaum.

Müller, M., & Wehner, R. (1988). Path integration in desert ants, *Cataglyphis fortis*. *Proceedings of the Academy of Sciences of the United States of America, 85*, 5287–5290.

Murphy, A. H., Lichtenstein, S., Fischhoff, B., & Winkler, R. L. (1980). Misinterpretations of precipitation probability forecasts. *Bulletin of the American Meteorological Society, 61*, 695–701.

Murphy, A. H., & Winkler, R. L. (1971). Forecasters and probability forecasts: Some current problems. *Bulletin of the American Meteorological Society, 52*, 239–247.

Myers, D. G. (2001). Do we fear the right things? American Psychological Society *Observer, December,* 3.

Nagel, T. (1993). Moral luck. In D. Statman (ed.), *Moral luck* (pp. 57–71). Albany: State University of New York Press.

Nakata, K., Ushimaru, A., & Watanabe, T. (2003). Using past experience in web relocation decisions enhances the foraging efficiency of the spider *Cyclosa argenteoalba*. *Journal of Insect Behavior, 16*, 371–380.

National Commission on Terrorist Attacks upon the United States. (2004). *The 9/11 Report*. New York: St. Martin's.

National Research Council. (1989). *Improving risk communication*. Washington, DC: National Academy Press.

National Weather Service Tulsa. (1998). *General forecast terminology and tables*. Retrieved May 5, 2003; from http://www.srh.noaa.gov/tulsa/forecast terms.html#pop/.

Naylor, C. D. (2001). Clinical decisions: From art to science and back again. *The Lancet, 358*, 523–524.

Newell, A., & Simon, H. A. (1972). *Human problem solving*. Englewood Cliffs, NJ: Prentice-Hall.

Newell, B. R., Rakow, T., Weston, N. J., & Shanks, D. R. (2004). Search strategies in decision-making: The success of "success." *Journal of Behavioral Decision Making, 17*, 117–137.

Newell, B. R., & Shanks, D. R. (2003). Take the best or look at the rest? Factors influencing "one-reason" decision-making. *Journal of Experimental Psychology: Learning, Memory, and Cognition, 29,* 53–65.

Newell, B. R., Weston, N., & Shanks, D. R. (2003). Empirical tests of a fast and frugal heuristic: Not everyone "takes-the-best." *Organizational Behavior and Human Decision Processes, 91,* 82–96.

Newport, E. L. (1990). Maturational constraints on language learning. *Cognitive Science, 14,* 11–28.

Newton, I. (1952). *Opticks; or, A treatise of the reflections, refractions, inflections, and colours of light.* New York: Dover. (Original work published 1704)

Neyman, J. (1950). *First course in probability and statistics.* New York: Holt.

————. (1957). Inductive behavior as a basic concept of philosophy of science. *International Statistical Review, 25,* 7–22.

Nickerson, R. S. (2000). Null hypothesis significance testing: A review of an old and continuing controversy. *Psychological Methods, 5,* 241–301.

Nisbett, R. E., & Ross, L. (1980). *Human inference: Strategies and shortcomings of social judgment.* Englewood Cliffs, NJ: Prentice-Hall.

Nosofsky, R. M. (1990). Relations between exemplar-similarity and likelihood models of classification. *Journal of Mathematical Psychology, 34,* 393–418.

Nosofsky, R. M., & Bergert, F. B. (2007). Limitations of exemplar models of multi-attribute probabilistic inference. *Journal of Experimental Psychology: Learning, Memory, and Cognition, 33,* 999–1019.

Nunally, J. C. (1975). *Introduction to statistics for psychology and education.* New York: McGraw-Hill.

Nyström, L., Larsson, L.-G., Wall, S., Rutqvist, L., Andersson, I., & Bjurstam, N., et al. (1996). An overview of the Swedish randomised mammography trials: Total mortality pattern and the representativity of the study cohorts. *Journal of Medical Screening, 3,* 85–87.

Oakes, M. (1986). *Statistical inference: A commentary for the social and behavioral sciences.* New York: Wiley.

Oaksford, M., & Chater, N. (1994). A rational analysis of the selection task as optimal data selection. *Psychological Review, 101,* 608–631.

Oaksford, M., & Chater, N. (2007). *Bayesian rationality: The probabilistic approach to human reasoning.* Oxford: Oxford University Press.

Oppenheimer, D. M. (2003). Not so fast! (and not so frugal!): Rethinking the recognition heuristic. *Cognition, 90,* B1–B9.

Pachur, T., & Biele, G. (2007). Forecasting from ignorance: The use and usefulness of recognition in lay predictions of sports events. *Acta Psychologica, 125,* 99–116.

Pachur, T., Bröder, A., & Marewski, J. N. (in press). The recognition heuristic in memory-based inference: Is recognition a non-compensatory cue? *Journal of Behavioral Decision Making.*

Pachur, T., & Hertwig, R. (2006). On the psychology of the recognition heuristic: Retrieval primacy as a key determinant of its use. *Journal of Experimental Psychology: Learning, Memory, and Cognition, 32,* 983–1002.

Paling, J. (2003). Strategies to help patients understand risks. *British Medical Journal, 327,* 745–748.

Partan, S., & Marler, P. (1999). Communication goes multimodal. *Science, 283,* 1272–1273.

Pascal, B. (1970). Correspondence Pascal-Fermat. In J. Mesnard (ed.), *Oeuvres complètes [Complete works of Pascal]* (vol. 1, pp. 1136–1158). Paris: Desclées de Brouwer. (Original work published 1713)

————. (1962). *Pensées.* Paris: Editions du Seuil. (Original work published 1669)

Patricelli, G. L., Uy, J. A. C., & Borgia, G. (2003). Multiple male traits interact: Attractive bower decorations facilitate attractive behavioural displays in satin bowerbirds. *Proceedings of the Royal Society B: Biological Sciences, 270,* 2389–2395.

Paulos, J. A. (1988). *Innumeracy: Mathematical illiteracy and its consequences.* New York: Hill and Wang.

Payne, J. W., Bettman, J. R., & Johnson, E. J. (1993). *The adaptive decision maker.* Cambridge: Cambridge University Press.

Pearson, E. S. (1939). "Student" as statistician. *Biometrika, 30,* 210–250.

Perlman, M. D., & Wu, L. (1999). The emperor's new tests. *Statistical Science, 14,* 355–381.

Pfeiffer, P. E. (1994). Are we overconfident in the belief that probability forecasters are overconfident? *Organizational Behavior and Human Decision Processes, 58,* 203–213.

Piaget, J., & Inhelder, B. (1975). *The origin of the idea of chance in children.* New York: Norton. (Original work published 1951)

Piattelli-Palmarini, M. (1994). *Inevitable illusions: How mistakes of reason rule our minds.* New York: Wiley.

Pohl, R. F. (2006). Empirical tests of the recognition heuristic. *Journal of Behavioral Decision Making, 19,* 251–271.

Pollard, P., & Richardson, J. T. E. (1987). On the probability of making Type I errors. *Psychological Bulletin, 102,* 159–163.

Polya, G. (1954). *Mathematics and plausible reasoning: Vol. 1. Induction and analogy in mathematics.* Princeton, NJ: Princeton University Press.

Quinlan, J. R. (1993). *C4.5: Programs for machine learning.* Los Altos, CA: Morgan Kaufmann.

Rabin, M. (1998). Psychology and economics. *Journal of Economic Literature, 36,* 11–46.

Raguso, R. A., & Willis, M. A. (2002). Synergy between visual and olfactory cues in nectar feeding by naïve hawkmoths, *Manduca sexta. Animal Behavior, 64,* 685–695.

Real, L. A. (1990). Predator switching and the interpretation of animal choice behavior: The case for constrained optimization. In R. N. Hughes (ed.), *Behavioural mechanisms of food selection* (pp. 1–21). NATO ASI Series, vol. G20. Berlin: Springer.

————. (1991). Animal choice behavior and the evolution of cognitive architecture. *Science, 253,* 980–986.

————. (1992). Information processing and the evolutionary ecology of cognitive architecture. *American Naturalist, 140,* 108–145.

Reddy, R. (1988). Foundations and grand challenges of Artificial Intelligence: AAAI Presidential Address. *AI Magazine, 9,* 9–21.

Reimer, T., & Katsikopoulos, K. (2004). The use of recognition in group decision-making. *Cognitive Science, 28,* 1009–1029.

Reyna, V. F. (1991). Class inclusion, the conjunction fallacy, and other cognitive illusions. *Developmental Review, 11,* 317–336.

Richter, T., & Späth, P. (2006). Recognition is used as one cue among others in judgment and decision making. *Journal of Experimental Psychology: Learning, Memory, and Cognition, 32,* 150–162.

Rieskamp, J., & Hoffrage, U. (1999). When do people use simple heuristics, and how can we tell? In G. Gigerenzer, P. M. Todd, & the ABC Research Group, *Simple heuristics that make us smart* (pp. 141–167). New York: Oxford University Press.

Rieskamp, J., & Otto, P. E. (2006). SSL: A theory of how people learn to select strategies. *Journal of Experimental Psychology: General, 135,* 207–236.

Rips, L. J. (1994). *The psychology of proof: Deductive reasoning in human thinking.* Cambridge, MA: MIT Press.

———. (2002). Circular reasoning. *Cognitive Science, 26,* 767–795.

Roberts, S., & Pashler, H. (2000). How persuasive is a good fit? A comment on theory testing. *Psychological Review, 107,* 358–367.

Römer, H., & Krusch, M. (2000). A gain-control mechanism for processing of chorus sounds in the afferent auditory pathway of the bushcricket *Tettigonia viridissima* (Orthoptera; Tettigoniidae). *Journal of Comparative Physiology, A 186,* 181–191.

Rosander, K., & von Hofsten, C. (2002). Development of gaze tracking of small and large objects. *Experimental Brain Research, 146,* 257–264.

Rosenthal, R., & Rubin, D. R. (1982). Comparing effect sizes of independent studies. *Psychological Bulletin, 92,* 500–504.

Rouanet, H. (1961). Études de décisions expérimentales et calcul de probabilités [Studies of experimental decision making and the probability calculus]. In *Colloques Internationaux du Centre National de la Recherche Scientifique* (pp. 33–43). Paris: Éditions du Centre National de la Recherche Scientifique.

Rowe, C. (1999). Receiver psychology and the evolution of multicomponent signals. *Animal Behavior, 58,* 921–931.

Rowe, C., & Skelhorn, J. (2004). Avian psychology and communication. *Proceedings of the Royal Society B: Biological Sciences, 271,* 1435–1442.

Rucci, A. J., & Tweney, R. D. (1980). Analysis of variance and the "second discipline" of scientific psychology: A historical account. *Psychological Bulletin, 87,* 166–184.

Samuels, R., Stich, S., & Bishop, M. (2004). Ending the rationality wars: How to make disputes about human rationality disappear. In R. Elio (ed.), *Common sense, reasoning, and rationality* (pp. 236–268). New York: Oxford University Press.

Sarfati, D., Howden-Chapman, P., Woodward, A., & Salmond, C. (1998). Does the frame affect the picture? A study into how attitudes to screening for cancer are affected by the way benefits are expressed. *Journal of Medical Screening, 5,* 137–140.

Sargent, T. J. (1993). *Bounded rationality in macroeconomics.* New York: Oxford University Press.

Sato, Y., Saito, Y., & Sakagami, T. (2003). Rules for nest sanitation in a social spider mite, *Schizotetranychus miscanthi* Saito (Acari: Tetranychidae). *Ethology, 109,* 713–724.

Savage, L. J. (1954). *The foundations of statistics.* New York: Wiley.

Saxberg, B. V. H. (1987). Projected free fall trajectories: I. Theory and simulation. *Biological Cybernetics, 56,* 159–175.

Schacter, D. L. (2001). *The seven sins of memory: How the mind forgets and remembers.* New York: Houghton Mifflin.

Schapira, M., Nattinger, A., & McHorney, C. (2001). Frequency or probability? A qualitative study of risk communication formats used in health care. *Medical Decision Making, 21,* 459–467.

Scheibehenne, B. (2008). *The effect of having too much choice.* Unpublished dissertation, Humboldt-Universität, Berlin.

Scheibehenne, B., & Bröder, A. (2007). Can lay people be as accurate as experts in predicting the results of Wimbledon 2005? *International Journal of Forecasting, 23,* 415–426.

Schlottmann, A. (2001). Children's probability intuitions: Understanding the expected value of complex gambles. *Child Development, 72,* 103–122.

Schlottmann, A., & Anderson, N. H. (1994). Children's judgments of expected value. *Developmental Psychology, 30,* 56–66.

Schooler, L. J., & Hertwig, R. (2005). How forgetting aids heuristic inference. *Psychological Review, 112,* 610–628.

Schwartz, B., Ward, A., Monterosso, J., Lyubomirsky, S., White, K., & Lehman, D. R. (2002). Maximizing versus satisficing: Happiness is a matter of choice. *Journal of Personality and Social Psychology, 83,* 1178–1197.

Scott, A. (2002). Identifying and analysing dominant preferences in discrete choice experiments: An application in health care. *Journal of Economic Psychology, 23,* 383–398.

Sedlmeier, P. (1999). *Improving statistical reasoning: Theoretical models and practical applications.* Mahwah, NJ: Erlbaum.

Sedlmeier, P., & Gigerenzer, G. (1989). Do studies of statistical power have an effect on the power of studies? *Psychological Bulletin, 105,* 309–316.

———. (2001). Teaching Bayesian reasoning in less than two hours. *Journal of Experimental Psychology: General, 130,* 380–400.

Sedlmeier, P., Hertwig, R., & Gigerenzer, G. (1998). Are judgments of the positional frequencies of letters systematical biased due to availability? *Journal of Experimental Psychology: Learning, Memory, and Cognition, 24,* 754–770.

Seeley, T. D. (1995). The wisdom of the hive. Cambridge, MA: Harvard University Press.

Selten, R. (1998). Aspiration adaptation theory. *Journal of Mathematical Psychology, 42,* 191–214.

———. (2001). What is bounded rationality? In G. Gigerenzer & R. Selten (eds.), *Bounded rationality: The adaptive toolbox* (pp. 13–36). Cambridge, MA: MIT Press.

Sen, A. (2002). *Rationality and freedom.* Cambridge, MA: Harvard University Press.

Serwe, S., & Frings, C. (2006). Who will win Wimbledon? The recognition heuristic in predicting sports events. *Journal of Behavioral Decision Making, 19,* 321–332.

Shaffer, D. M., Krauchunas, S. M., Eddy, M., & McBeath, M. K. (2004). How dogs navigate to catch Frisbees. *Psychological Science, 15,* 437–441.

Shaffer, D. M., & McBeath, M. K. (2002). Baseball outfielders maintain a linear optical trajectory when tracking uncatchable fly balls. *Journal of Experimental Psychology: Human Perception and Performance, 28,* 335–348.

Shanteau, J. (1992). How much information does an expert use? Is it relevant? *Acta Psychologica, 81,* 75–86.

Shanteau, J., & Thomas, R. P. (2000). Fast and frugal heuristics: What about unfriendly environments? *Behavioral and Brain Sciences, 23,* 762–763.

Shepard, R. N. (1987). Evolution of a mesh between principles of the mind and regularities of the world. In J. Dupré (ed.), *The latest on the best: Essays on evolution and optimality* (pp. 251–275). Cambridge, MA: MIT Press.

Sher, S., & McKenzie, C. R. M. (2006). Information leakage from logically equivalent frames. *Cognition, 101,* 467–494.

Sherden, W. A. (1998). *The fortune sellers: The big business of buying and selling predictions.* New York: Wiley.

Shettleworth, S. J. (1998). *Cognition, evolution, and behavior.* New York: Oxford University Press.

Shiller, R. J. (2000). *Irrational exuberance.* Princeton, NJ: Princeton University Press.

Shine, R., Phillips, B., Waye, H., LeMaster, M., & Mason, R. T. (2003). The lexicon of love: What cues cause size-assortative courtship by male garter snakes? *Behavioral Ecology and Sociobiology, 53,* 234–237.

Shuman, F. G. (1989). History of numerical weather prediction at the National Meteorological Center. *Weather and Forecasting, 4,* 286–296.

Siegler, R. S. (1999). Strategic development. *Trends in Cognitive Science, 3,* 430–435.

———. (2000). The rebirth of children's learning. *Child Development, 71,* 26–35.

Silver, E. A. (1986). Using conceptual and procedural knowledge. In J. Hiebert (ed.), *Conceptual and procedural knowledge: The case of mathematics* (pp. 181–198). Hillsdale, NJ: Erlbaum.

Simão, J., & Todd, P. M. (2002). Modeling mate choice in monogamous mating systems with courtship. *Adaptive Behavior, 10,* 113–136.

Simon, H. A. (1947). *Administrative behavior: A study of decision-making processes in administrative organizations.* New York: Macmillan.

———. (1955). A behavioral model of rational choice. *Quarterly Journal of Economics, 69,* 99–118.

———. (1956). Rational choice and the structure of the environment. *Psychological Review, 63,* 129–138.

———. (1982). *Models of bounded rationality.* Cambridge, MA: MIT Press.

———. (1986). Rationality in psychology and economics. In R. Hogarth & M. Reder (eds.), *Rational choice: The contrast between economics and psychology* (pp. 25–40). Chicago: University of Chicago Press.

———. (1990). Invariants of human behavior. *Annual Review of Psychology, 41,* 1–19.

———. (1992). What is an "explanation" of behavior? *Psychological Science, 3,* 150–161.

Sivak, M., & Flannagan, M. J. (2003). Flying and driving after the September 11 attacks. *American Scientist, 91*, 6–8.

———. (2004). Consequences for road traffic fatalities of the reduction in flying following September 11, 2001. *Transportation Research Part F: Traffic Psychology and Behaviour, 7*, 301–305.

Skinner, B. F. (1972). *Cumulative record.* New York: Appleton-Century-Crofts.

———. (1984). *A matter of consequences.* New York: New York University Press.

Slaytor, E. K., & Ward, J. E. (1998). How risks of breast cancer and benefits of screening are communicated to women: Analysis of 58 pamphlets. *British Medical Journal, 317*, 263–264.

Slegers, D. W., Brake, G. L., & Doherty, M. E. (2000). Probabilistic mental models with continuous predictors. *Organizational Behavior and Human Decision Processes, 81*, 98–114.

Slovic, P. (1987). Perception of risk. *Science, 236*, 280–285.

Slovic, P., Monahan, J., & MacGregor, D. G. (2000). Violence risk assessment and risk communication: The effects of using actual cases, providing instructions, and employing probability versus frequency formats. *Law and Human Behavior, 24*, 271–296.

Snook, B., & Cullen, R. M. (2006). Recognizing National Hockey League greatness with an ignorance-based heuristic. *Canadian journal of experimental psychology, 60*, 33–43.

Starkey, P., & Cooper, R. G. J. (1980). Perception of numbers by human infants. *Science, 210*, 1033–1035.

Stephens, D. W. (2002). Discrimination, discounting and impulsivity: A role for an informational constraint. *Philosophical Transactions of the Royal Society B: Biological Sciences, 357*, 1527–1537.

Stephens, D. W., & Anderson, D. (2001). The adaptive value of preference for immediacy: When shortsighted rules have farsighted consequences. *Behavioral Ecology, 12*, 330–339.

Stern, E., Rode, C., Fang, G., & Zhu, L. (2001). *More than just numbers: Active diagrammatic competencies in Chinese and German secondary school students.* Poster session presented at the Biennial Meeting of the Society for Research in Child Development, Minneapolis, MI.

Stevens, S. S. (Ed.). (1951). *Handbook of experimental psychology.* New York: Wiley.

———. (1960). The predicament in design and significance. *Contemporary Psychology, 9*, 273–276.

Stich, S. P. (1985). Could man be an irrational animal? *Synthese, 64*, 115–135.

Stigler, G. J. (1961). The economics of information. *Journal of Political Economy, 69*, 213–225.

Stigler, S. M. (1999). Statistics on the table: The history of statistical concepts and methods. Cambridge, MA: Harvard University Press.

Sunstein, C. R. (Ed.). (2000). *Behavioral law and economics.* Cambridge: Cambridge University Press.

Sweetser, E. E. (1990). *From etymology to pragmatics: Metaphorical and cultural aspects of semantic structure.* Cambridge: Cambridge University Press.

Swijtink, Z. G. (1987). The objectification of observation: Measurement and statistical methods in the nineteenth century. In L. Krüger, L. Daston, & M. Heidelberger (eds.), *The probabilistic revolution: Vol. 1. Ideas in history* (pp. 261–285). Cambridge, MA: MIT Press.

Tankard, J. W. (1979). The H. G. Wells quote on statistics: A question of accuracy. *Historia Mathematica, 6,* 30–33.

Tanner, W. P., Jr., & Swets, J. A. (1954). A decision-making theory of visual detection. *Psychological Review, 61,* 401–409.

Thomson, J. D. (1996). Trapline foraging by bumblebees: I. Persistence of flight-path geometry. *Behavioral Ecology, 7,* 158–164.

Thornes, J. E. (1996). The quality and accuracy of a sample of public and commercial weather forecasts in the UK. *Meteorological Applications, 3,* 63–74.

Thornes, J. E., & Stephenson, D. B. (2001). How to judge the quality and value of weather forecast products. *Meteorological Applications, 8,* 307–314.

Thurstone, L. L. (1927). A law of comparative judgment. *Psychological Review, 34,* 273–286.

Tinbergen, N. (1958). *Curious naturalists.* London: Country Life.

Todd, P. M., & Miller, G. F. (1999). From pride to prejudice to persuasion: Satisficing in mate search. In G. Gigerenzer, P. M. Todd, & the ABC Research Group, *Simple heuristics that make us smart* (pp. 287–308). New York: Oxford University Press.

Todorov, A. (2002). *Predicting real outcomes: When heuristics are as smart as statistical models.* Unpublished manuscript.

Trivers, R. L. (2002). *Natural selection and social theory: Selected papers of Robert Trivers.* New York: Oxford University Press.

Tukey, J. W. (1969). Analyzing data: Sanctification or detective work? *American Psychologist, 24,* 83–91.

Tversky, A. (1972). Elimination by aspects: A theory of choice. *Psychological Review, 79,* 281–299.

Tversky, A., & Kahneman, D. (1971). Belief in the law of small numbers. *Psychological Bulletin, 76,* 105–110.

———. (1974). Judgment under uncertainty: Heuristics and biases. *Science, 185,* 1124–1131.

———. (1982). Judgments of and by representativeness. In D. Kahneman, P. Slovic, & A. Tversky (eds.), *Judgment under uncertainty: Heuristics and biases* (pp. 84–98). Cambridge: Cambridge University Press.

———. (1983). Extensional versus intuitive reasoning: The conjunction fallacy in probability judgment. *Psychological Review, 90,* 293–315.

———. (1986). Rational choice and the framing of decisions. *Journal of Business, 59,* S251–S278.

U.S. Department of Transportation, Federal Highway Administration. n.d. 1996–1999 data: *Table 1—Estimated individual monthly motor vehicle travel in the United States [2000–2001 data].* http://www.fhwa.dot.gov/ohim/tvtw/02septvt/table1.htm

———. 2000 data: *Table 1—Estimated individual monthly motor vehicle travel in the United States [2000–2001 data].* http://www.fhwa.dot.gov/ohim/tvtw/nov_tvt/table1.htm/.

U. S. Department of Transportation. 2001 data: *Table 1—Estimated individual monthly motor vehicle travel in the United States [2001–2002 data].* http://www.fhwa.dot.gov/ohim/tvtw/02dectvt/table1.htm/.

———. 2002/2003 data: *Table 1—Estimated individual monthly motor vehicle travel in the United States [2002–2003 data].* http://www.fhwa.dot.gov/ohim/tvtw/03dectvt/table1.htm/.

van Alphen, J. J. M., Bernstein, C., & Driessen, G. (2003). Information acquisition and time allocation in insect parasitoids. *Trends in Ecological Evolution, 18,* 81–87.

Volz, K. G., Schooler, L. J., Schubotz, R. I., Raab, M., Gigerenzer, G., & von Cramon, D. Y. (2006). Why you think Milan is larger than Modena: Neural correlates of the recognition heuristic. *Journal of Cognitive Neuroscience, 18,* 1924–1936.

von Helmholtz, H. (1962). *Treatise on psychological optics* (J. P. C. Southall, trans.). New York: Dover. (Original work published 1856–1866)

von Mises, R. (1957). *Probability, statistics, and truth.* London: Allen and Unwin. (Original work published 1928)

Wajnberg, E., Fauvergue, X., & Pons, O. (2000). Patch leaving decision rules and the Marginal Value Theorem: An experimental analysis and a simulation model. *Behavioral Ecology, 11,* 577–586.

Wajnberg, E., Gonsard, P.-A., Tabone, E., Curty, C., Lezcano, N., & Colazza, S. (2003). A comparative analysis of patch-leaving decision rules in a parasitoid family. *Journal of Animal Ecology, 72,* 618–626.

Wald, A. (1947). *Sequential analysis.* New York: Wiley.

Waller, N. G. (2004). The fallacy of the null hypothesis in soft psychology. *Applied and Preventive Psychology, 11,* 83–86.

Wallraff, H. G. (2001). Navigation by homing pigeons: Updated perspective. *Ethology, Ecology, and Evolution, 13,* 1–48.

Wason, P. C. (1966). Reasoning. In B. M. Foss (ed.), *New horizons in psychology* (pp. 135–151). Harmondsworth, UK: Penguin.

Wason, P. C., & Johnson-Laird, P. N. (1972). *Psychology of reasoning: Structure and content.* Cambridge, MA: Harvard University Press.

Wells, G. L., & Windschitl, P. D. (1999). Stimulus sampling and social psychological experimentation. *Personality and Social Psychology Bulletin, 25,* 1115–1125.

Wells, H. G. (1994). *World brain.* London: Cambridge University Press. (Original work published in 1938)

Wells, M. S. (1988). Effects of body size and resource value on fighting behaviour in a jumping spider. *Animal Behavior, 36,* 321–326.

Wiegmann, D. D., Real, L.A., Capone, T. A., & Ellner, S. (1996). Some distinguishing features of models of search behavior and mate choice. *American Naturalist, 147,* 188–204.

Wilke, A., Hutchinson, J. M. C., & Todd, P. M. (2004). Testing simple rules for human foraging in patchy environments. In K. Forbus, D. Gentner, & T. Regier (eds.), *Proceedings of the 26th Annual Conference of the Cognitive Science Society* (p. 1656). Mahwah, NJ: Erlbaum.

Wilkinson, L., & Task Force on Statistical Inference (TFSI). (1999). Statistical methods in psychology journals: Guidelines and explanations. *American Psychologist, 54,* 594–604.

Williams, B. (1981). *Moral luck.* Cambridge: Cambridge University Press.

Wilson, D. K., Purdon, S. E., & Wallston, K. (1988). Compliance to health recommendations: A theoretical overview of message framing. *Health Education Research, 3,* 161–171.

Wiltschko, R., & Wiltschko, W. (2003). Avian navigation: From historical to modern concepts. *Animal Behavior, 65,* 257–272.

Wright, P. (2001). Document-based decision making. In J. F. Rouet, A. Levonen, & A. Biardeau (eds.), *Multimedia learning: Cognitive and instructional issues* (pp. 31–43). Amsterdam: Pergamon.

Wundt, W. (1973). *An introduction to psychology* (R. Pintner, trans.). New York: Arno. (Original work published 1912)

Wynn, K. (1992). Addition and subtraction by human infants. *Nature, 358,* 749–750.

Yee, M., Hauser, J. R., Orlin, J. B., & Dahan, E. (2007). Greedoid-based non-compensatory two-stage consideration-then-choice inference. *Marketing Science, 26,* 532–549.

Zhu, L., & Gigerenzer, G. (2006). Children can solve Bayesian problems: The role of representation in mental computation. *Cognition, 98,* 287–308.

Zuk, M., Ligon, J. D., & Thornhill, R. (1992). Effects of experimental manipulation of male secondary sex characters on female mate preference in red jungle fowl. *Animal Behavior, 44,* 999–1006.

NAME INDEX

GENERAL INDEX

optimizing search, 30–31
oral contraceptives, 199
overconfidence bias, 3, 13–16, 86, 109
overestimation of low risks, 15
overfitting, 10, 40, 53, 84–85, 170
overlapping waves model, 176, 187–190

paired comparison, 45, 111, 115
panic, 17
parameters, adjustable, 40–41, 84–85, 170
Pascal's wager, 138–139, 147, 193
patch-leaving, 51–52, 57–58, 63
paternity suits, 146
perceptual illusion. *See* visual illusions
personal construct theory, 110
perspective, 12, 67, 134
pheromone, 50–51
Philanthus triagulum, 59
physicians, 16–18, 35, 42–44, 73–74, 127–135, 148, 182–183, 198–200
Polistes dominulus, 51
polygamy, 142
polysemy, 71–75
pop-out dots, 66–67
pre-Bayes, 182–187
prediction
    counterintuitive, 45
    ex ante, 84
    out-of-population, 43
    out-of-sample, 43
predictive accuracy, 37, 40–41, 47–49
predictive uncertainty, 10, 42
predictive value, positive, 129–130
preference reversals, 15
preparedness, 93, 97, 112
primula problem, 70, 73
probabilistic mental models theory, 35–36
probabilistic revolution, 193
probability
    calculus of, 11, 20, 193
    classical theory of, 140, 146
    conditional, 16–17, 33, 128–132, 135, 173–179, 181, 183, 188–190, 197–200

inverse, 142–143, 194
posterior, 143, 173, 183, 198
prior, 15, 143–146, 173
single-event, 118, 124–126, 128–129, 132, 135, 195–199
subjective, 141, 144, 196
theory of, 4, 20, 69, 73, 136–141, 146, 150, 172, 192–198
probability, interpretations of, 118–126, 128–129, 132–135, 141, 146, 150
    epistemic, 146
    ontic, 146
    subjective, 141, 144, 196
probability matching, 15, 58
probability of rain, 117–126, 128, 194, 197
problem, ill-defined, 85
problem structure, 9–10, 15
propensities, 141, 150
Prozac, 128–129
p-value, 107, 153–154, 157, 160–165, 168–170
Pyx, trial of the, 105

quality control, 99–100, 105, 113, 156, 165

rationality, 3–11, 18–19, 78–79, 80–91, 139–141
    bounded, 6–7, 50, 80–91, 165
    ecological, 4, 7–10, 16–19, 23–25, 31, 35–38, 44–45, 54, 63, 78, 81, 89–90
    full, 4, 6, 80–82
    internalist conception of, 11
    procedural, 80
    substantial, 80
    unbounded, 3–6, 18, 52
rationality war, 19
reason-based heuristics, 31–37, 41–44, 114–115
reasoning, development of, 172–173, 178–190
reciprocal altruism, theory of, 12
recognition, 24–30, 82, 90–91
recognition heuristic, 24–30, 45, 50, 54
recognition validity (alpha), 25–28

social values, 15
specificity, 128–132, 135
speed of action, 9
statistical power, 106–109, 153, 155,
    164–170
statistical rituals, 149, 166. *See also*
    ritual
statistical thinking, 127, 136–151,
    152–153, 166–171, 192–201
statistical toolbox, 100–103,
    110–116, 153–155, 160
statistics, 17, 69, 99, 104, 108,
    110, 127, 141–150, 152–171,
    193–201
  Bayesian, 15, 152–153
  descriptive, 153, 164–165
  medical, 128
stopping point, optimal, 5–6, 81
stopping rule, 5–6, 30–34, 42–45,
    50, 90, 114–115
  multiple reason, 34
  one-reason, 32–34, 43
St. Petersburg paradox, 139–141
strategies, developmental change in,
    176, 187
strategy-selection theory, 39

take-the-best. *See* heuristic, take-
    the-best
tallying heuristic. *See* heuristic,
    tallying
terrorism, al-Qaeda, 92
terrorist attacks, 92–98. *See also*
    Madrid attacks
Tetris, 20
textbooks, psychology/statistics,
    152–157, 162–163, 171,
threshold, critical, 93
thromboembolism, 199
Thurstone's law of comparative
    judgment, 107–108
trade-off, cost-benefit, 5, 156
traffic rules, 44
transparency, 23, 42, 44, 171

risk communication, 18, 132–133,
    198–200
traveling salesman problem, 20, 56,
    82–83
tree
  classification, 43, 115
  decision, 47–49
  fast-and-frugal, 42–50
Triver's theory of reciprocal
    altruism, 12
truth-table logic, 11–12, 19
types, ideal, 103–104

unconscious behavior, 22–23, 31,
    38, 47–49, 68, 93, 113–114,
    159, 166–167
underconfidence, 14
underestimation of high risks, 15
unit-weight models, 33, 115

validity
  cue, 32–38, 47, 61
  order of, 34, 36, 47, 61
  search by, 32
  unconditional, 33
variability
  interindividual, 180
  random, 66, 108
  unsystematic, 14
variance, 41, 84, 90, 101, 110–112
Venturia canescens, 52
violations of logical reasoning. *See*
    logical reasoning, violations of
visual illusion, 66–71, 74, 78

Wald's sequential tests, 153. *See
    also* sequential decision theory
warfarin, 134
wasp, 51–52, 59
weighted additive rule, 24, 35, 39
win-shift, 58
win-stay, 58

Xanthomyza phrygia, 58

CPSIA information can be obtained at www.ICGtesting.com
Printed in the USA
267708BV00003B/3/P

9 780199 747092